ALSO AVAILABLE FROM HANS BEUMER

----------TRAVEL----------

Swiss Camino – Volume I: North-East Switzerland

Swiss Camino – Volume II: Central Switzerland

Kumano Kodo Pilgrimage

Japan's Travel Culture

20'000 km by Train

----------SELF-HELP----------

Success for Everyone

Happiness for Everyone

Travel Guide to Self-actualization

----------INTERNAL AUDIT----------

The Leadership & Managerial Habits of Highly Effective CAEs

The 7 Leadership Habits of Highly Effective CAEs

The 7 Managerial Habits of Highly Effective CAEs

The Internal Audit Handbook

Audit Function Strategy

Audit Engagement Strategy

Audit Risk Management

Visit www.hansbeumer.com

Swiss Camino – Volume I: North-East Switzerland

GENERAL INTRODUCTION
Organizational Tips, Religious Context, Church Terminology, Hiking Routes, Raising Expectations

KONSTANZ TO EINSIEDELN

Stage K1:	Konstanz to Märstetten	16 km
Stage K2:	Märstetten to Fischingen	35 km
Stage K3:	Fischingen to Rapperswil	33 km
Stage 4:	Rapperswil to Einsiedeln	18 km

RORSCHACH TO EINSIEDELN

Stage R1a:	Rorschach to St. Gallen	18 km
Stage R1b:	St. Gallen to Herisau	11 km
Stage R2:	Herisau to Wattwil	26 km
	via Rapperswil:	
Stage R3:	Wattwil to Rapperswil	29 km
Stage 4:	Rapperswil to Einsiedeln	18 km
	via Siebnen:	
Stage S1:	Wattwil to Siebnen	31 km
Stage S2:	Siebnen to Einsiedeln	19 km

Available as
- Hiking edition: ISBN 978-3-906861-32-6
- Luxury edition: ISBN 978-3-906861-33-3
- eBook edition: ISBN 978-3-906861-34-0

Swiss Camino – Volume II: Central Switzerland

EINSIEDELN TO FRIBOURG via Alpine Lakes

Stage 5:	Einsiedeln to Ingenbohl	27 km
Stage 6:	Ingenbohl to Stans	26 km
Stage 7:	Stans to Sachseln	22 km
Stage 8:	Sachseln to Brienzwiler	26 km
Stage 9:	Brienzwiler to Interlaken	27 km
Stage 10:	Interlaken to Spiez	19 km
Stage 11:	Spiez to Wattenwil	26 km
Stage 12:	Wattenwil to Schwarzenburg	24 km
Stage 13:	Schwarzenburg to Fribourg	27 km

ALTERNATIVE VIA LUZERN/BERN

Stage L1:	Ingenbohl to Werthenstein	24 km
Stage L2:	Werthenstein to Huttwil	31 km
Stage L3:	Huttwil to Burgdorf	25 km
Stage L4:	Burgdorf to Bern	31 km
Stage L5:	Bern to Schwarzenburg	36 km

Available as
- Hiking edition: ISBN 978-3-906861-35-7
- Luxury edition: ISBN 978-3-906861-36-4
- eBook edition: ISBN 978-3-906861-37-1

SWISS CAMINO

Volume III: South-West Switzerland

300 Churches
800 km Hiking
1'000 yrs History
on
the Way of St. James
through Switzerland

HANS BEUMER

HB Publications
Unterägeri, Switzerland
www.hansbeumer.com

First edition published in September 2019

This book is available as:

- Hiking edition (B/W):	ISBN 978-3-906861-38-8
- Luxury edition (Color):	ISBN 978-3-906861-39-5
- eBook edition (EPUB):	ISBN 978-3-906861-40-1

Printed and distributed by Lulu Press, Inc.

CONTENTS

MOUDON TO GENEVA/FRENCH BORDER 115

APPENDICES 241

Foreword

Liber Sancti Jacobi Helvetia

The first Way of St. James Pilgrim's Handbook was handwritten around 1130. The Latin manuscript was called the 'Liber Sancti Jacobi' (also Codex Callixtus – attributed to Pope Callixtus II) and consisted of five parts. Two parts related to stories, miracles, and legends of St. James. The fifth part described four French Ways to the Pyrenees and Santiago de Compostela. These route descriptions included all important churches the pilgrim was to visit along the way.

Nearly 900 years after the Liber Sancti Jacobi for France, my book describes the Way of Saint James for Switzerland in a comparable manner. The 'Swiss Camino' is the definitive guide for the 21st century pilgrim on the Swiss routes. Hence its Latin title: *Liber Sancti Jacobi Helvetia.*

Three Volumes

The Swiss Camino pilgrim's guide is split into three volumes:

Volume I consists of two main sections:

1. A general introduction to the 18- to 21-day pilgrimage on the Way of St. James through Switzerland, including:
   - Organizational tips for a successful pilgrimage at a low cost in this high-cost country.
   - Religious context of St. James, Roman catacomb relics, saints, monastic Orders, and the Swiss religious Reformation in the 1520s-30s.
   - Church terminology, designations, architecture, interiors, and monastic Order terminology.
   - Route decisions, route possibilities, stages, and route signaling.
   - Raising expectations of the routes, churches, monasteries, and points of interest.
2. A complete coverage of the pilgrimage routes with details of the trails, churches, saints, catacomb relics, monasteries, castles, cities, and other points of interest in German-speaking North-East Switzerland:
   - From Konstanz to Einsiedeln, via Rapperswil (101 km in 4 stages); and
   - From Rorschach to Einsiedeln, via Rapperswil (101 km in 4 or 5 stages) and via Siebnen (105 km in 4 or 5 stages).

Volume II provides a complete coverage of the pilgrimage routes with details of the trails, churches, saints, catacomb relics, monasteries, castles, cities, and other points of interest in German-speaking Central Switzerland:

- From Einsiedeln to Fribourg, via Alpine Lakes (224 km in 9 stages); and
- From Einsiedeln to Fribourg, via Luzern/Bern (200 km in 7 stages).

Volume III (this book) provides a complete coverage of the pilgrimage routes with details of the trails, churches, saints, catacomb relics, monasteries, castles, chateaus, cities, and other points of interest in French-speaking South-West Switzerland:

- From Fribourg to Moudon, via Romont (47 km in 2 stages) and via Payerne (54 km in 2 stages);
  and onwards
- From Moudon to Geneva, and French border (123 km in 5 stages).

The 54-page General Introduction to the Swiss Way of St. James of Volume I is not copied in the other two volumes. This prevents a repetition of many pages, even though its content equally applies to Volumes II and III. Therefore, for the General Introduction to the Swiss Camino please refer to Volume I.

This foreword to Volume III is kept short. Please see Volume I for the extensive introductory foreword.

Thank you for using this book as your guide on the Swiss Way of St. James.

Bon Camino!
drs. Hans Beumer
September 2019

SOUTH-WEST SWITZERLAND

TO THE CALVINIST REFORMATION HOTSPOT

Overview of Routes

The Way of St. James in South-West Switzerland

South-West Switzerland routes

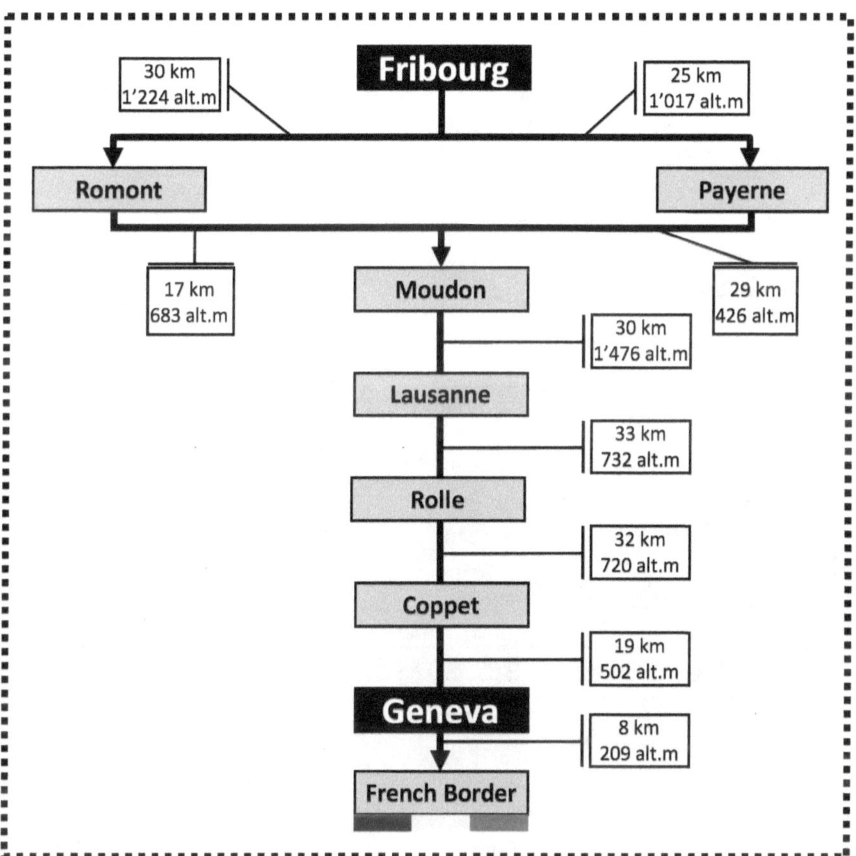

Route choices

For the choice of the route via Romont or Payerne, consider the following for your decision:

- Romont is a unique small medieval town built on top of a hill, surrounded by agricultural fields. The town has a beautiful 800-year-old church, a medieval castle, and remnants of medieval city fortifications. Unique in Switzerland is the stained-glass museum, where you get insight in the art and craft of making stained-glass church windows (of which you see many hundreds along the Swiss Way of St. James). The town is a historical pilgrimage station on the way to Santiago de Compostela and has a pilgrim inn in a Cistercian convent.

- Payerne is a larger and livelier town in the Broye River valley, which is well-known for its 1'050-year-old former Cluniac Abbey. The Cluniac church is a magnificent example of 10th century Cluniac architecture, but is undergoing a four-year renovation project that will be completed in May 2020. From then the monumental church will be open again. The attached museum provides great insight in the history of the former Cluniac Abbey and its church. Payerne has no pilgrim inn.

- The Payerne route to Moudon is 7 km longer but has 464 (24 percent) fewer altitude meters. This route closely follows the Broye River valley for a large part, which is very relaxed and easy to hike (without any hills).

My recommendation: choose the route via Romont.

Route stats

The two possible routes (with overlapping stages 16 to 20) compare as follows.

	#	From	To	Km	Alt. m	Churches
1	14	Fribourg	Romont	30	1'224	16
2	15	Romont	Moudon	17	683	6
3	16	Moudon	Lausanne	30	1'476	6
4	17	Lausanne	Rolle	33	732	10
5	18	Rolle	Coppet	32	720	9
6	19	Coppet	Geneva	19	502	9
7	20	Geneva	French Border	8	209	4
	From Fribourg to Geneva/French Border, via Romont			**170**	**5'546**	**60**
1	P1	Fribourg	Payerne	25	1'017	11
2	P2	Payerne	Moudon	29	426	9
3	16	Moudon	Lausanne	30	1'476	6
4	17	Lausanne	Rolle	33	732	10
5	18	Rolle	Coppet	32	720	9
6	19	Coppet	Geneva	19	502	9
7	20	Geneva	French Border	8	209	4
	From Fribourg to Geneva/French Border, via Payerne			**177**	**5'082**	**58**

Route summaries

From Fribourg to Moudon, via Romont

Stage 14 (Fribourg to Romont) guides you across the highland plateau of the Glâne District, south of the city of Fribourg, to Romont. The highland plateau is named after the Glâne River that flows from Romont to Fribourg. Stage 14 starts in the city center of Fribourg and follows a route through the city and its southern suburbs for the first 5 km. The route enters the Glâne District highland plateau and stays on that plateau until Romont. Despite being on the plateau, there are many short and gradual ascents and descents accumulating to 1'224 altitude meters. Most of the route is on quiet country roads along agricultural fields; it goes through patches of forest only a few times. The route is in catholic Canton Fribourg and passes by 16 churches/chapels and five points of interest. The medieval city of Romont is the highlight of the day, having a Savoy castle, a unique stained-glass museum, 13th century city fortifications, and a church with significant catholic art.

Stage 15 (Romont to Moudon) guides you from the Glâne District highland plateau to the Broye River valley and Moudon. The route is short and mostly downhill or flat. It should take less than 5 hours (easy pace) to hike from Romont to Moudon and visit the four churches along the way. In case you have not been able to visit the stained-glass museum in Romont at the end of stage 14, you should have enough time to do so before starting your pilgrimage of this stage 15. When you spent the night in Romont you can have a relaxed beginning of the day, visit the museum, and then a late morning start of stage 15. Use this short stage for a resting morning or afternoon. The next three stages towards Geneva are long and offer little time for rest. At km 6 you leave catholic Canton Fribourg and enter protestant Canton Vaud. Agricultural fields dominate the landscape. In km 12-16 you hike next to the Broye River. A visit to Moudon's 700-year-old church and historic upper city end stage 15.

From Fribourg to Moudon, via Payerne

Stage P1 (Fribourg to Payerne) guides you from the Fribourg highland plateau over forested hills and along the Arbogne River in a long descent to the Broye River valley and Payerne. Stage P1 follows the same route as stage 14 (from Fribourg to Romont) for the first 4 km, while passing by four churches in the city of Fribourg. From Villar-sur-Glâne (where the routes split) a major part of the hiking is through forests, following the historical road between Fribourg and Payerne. At km 10 the highest point of the day is reached at 722 meters. The Way of St. James closely follows the Arbogne River valley for about 7 km. After reaching the Broye River valley the route turns south. In this valley the town Corcelles is part of the northern agglomeration of Payerne; the last 3.5 km are hiked in an urban environment. At km 20 the route changes from catholic Canton Fribourg to protestant Canton Vaud. Eleven churches and six points of interest are passed, the highlight being the 1'050-year-old former Cluniac monastery church in Payerne at the end of stage P1. It is Switzerland's largest and best-maintained Cluniac Romanesque church. The church is undergoing a four-year renovation project and is accessible again from May 2020.

Stage P2 (Payerne to Moudon) guides you from Payerne through the Broye River valley in a southern direction to Moudon. The signposted route is next to the Broye River from the start until the end of stage P2. Hiking along the river is relaxed and easy, in absence of any hills or mountains, through beautiful nature with agricultural landscapes. The signposted route nr. 4 does not deviate from the embankment next to the river. To visit the churches along the route you need to briefly leave the signposted route in Granges, Henniez, and Lucens. The route in protestant Canton Vaud passes by nine churches and five points of interest. The route converges with stage 15 (Romont to Moudon) in Curtilles after nearly 23 out of the 29 km. Most of the remaining 6 km are also alongside the Broye River until reaching Moudon. A visit to Moudon's 700-year-old church and historic upper city end stage P2.

From Moudon to Geneva/French Border

Stage 16 (Moudon to Lausanne) guides you from the Broye River valley over the Jorat mountain to the Lake Geneva basin. The route covers a distance of little over 30 km in a southern direction, closely following main road nr. 1 that connects Moudon to Lausanne. After leaving Moudon you only pass by small villages until reaching Lausanne's northern agglomerations. Most of the day is spent in the relative remoteness of agricultural fields and forests. The remainder of the Swiss Way of St. James from Lausanne to Geneva is along densely populated areas, so that stage 16 is the last long stretch in the quietness of nature. Agricultural fields provide wide views over the rolling foothills and the Alps at the eastern horizon. In the forests of the Jorat mountain the route reaches the highest point of the day (876 meters) at km 19. This location marks the watershed between the Rhine (north) and Rhone (south) rivers, and from there the rest of the way is basically downhill to Lausanne. The route is in protestant Canton Vaud and passes by six churches and three points of interest. The highlight of the day is the reformed Cathedral of Lausanne, the largest Gothic church in Switzerland. This cathedral and two castles are remnants of the nearly 1'000-year-rule of the Bishopric Kingdom of Lausanne.

Stage 17 (Lausanne to Rolle) guides you along the western shore of Lake Geneva. It is the first of three stages along the lake. The route descends over about 4 km through the agglomerations of Lausanne to the shore of Lake Geneva. For the remaining 29 km the route stays directly along, or in close vicinity of, the shore. Hiking is easy; it is all flat, except for a few low hills in the second half of the stage. You hike past small yacht ports, small beaches and swimming areas, vineyards, medieval churches, historic cities, and fortified castles. The lakeside route provides nice views and with clear weather you can see the Mont Blanc. This large variation of scenery makes it one of the most pleasant stages of the Swiss Way of St. James. Like a string of pearls, the medieval towns follow each other along the shoreline. The longest stretch in nature (3.5 km) is through the forested Aubonne River delta, a nature protected area. The route is still in protestant Canton Vaud and passes by 10 churches, three former monasteries, and seven points of interest.

Stage 18 (Rolle to Coppet) guides you along the western shore of Lake Geneva. Compared to stage 17, though, the route is not directly along the shore of the lake anymore. Instead, it trails 1 to 2 km from the shoreline most of the time; the route briefly touches the shoreline three times only. Being away from the shoreline has the advantage of great views, hiking along vineyards that line down the hills, and passing by beautiful chateaus that were built on the hilltops overlooking Lake Geneva. Stage 18 has the highest number of points of interest of all stages because of the chateaus built in the 17th and 18th centuries. Like a string of pearls, the chateaus follow quickly after each other between the vineyards. Stage 18 from Rolle to Coppet is one of the most beautiful stages of the Swiss Way of St. James, hiking past vineyards from Chateau to Chateau. The signposted route passes by the train station of Nyon without entering into town. Because Nyon has a 750-year-old castle, a 900-year-old church, and 2'000-year-old Roman ruins, it is worthwhile to make a 1.5 km detour into the city. The route is still in protestant Canton Vaud and passes by nine churches, two former monasteries, and 10 points of interest.

Stage 19 (Coppet to Geneva) guides you along Lake Geneva and across the Rhone River to the historic upper city of Geneva. From km 1 to 13 the route is on a plateau about 1 km west of road nr. 1 and the lake's shore. On the plateau the route passes by a few small vineyards and some parks, but most of the time it is on tarmac streets through the northern agglomerations of the city of Geneva. These agglomerations such as Genthod, Bellevue, Chambésy, and Pregny are not the usual residential areas: they are the Beverly Hills of Geneva. You walk past mansions hidden behind high hedges or iron entrance gates, chateaus owned by the same wealthy families for centuries, foreign embassies, and head offices of international organizations and luxury brand companies. The route descends from the plateau to the Lake Geneva shore over 1 km. The last 5 km are through the streets of the city of Geneva. With only 19.3 km, stage 19 is relatively short; for a good reason. Geneva is a 2'000-year-old city that was under the rule of the Bishopric Kingdom of Geneva for 1'000 years, until the Reformation in 1536. The City played a leading role during the Reformation: the reformed St. Peter Cathedral and the nearby International Reformation Museum demonstrate Jean Calvin's reformative influence on churches and society. Together with a 3'000-square-meter Archaeological Museum underneath the reformed St. Peter Cathedral, these points of interest require enough time to take in their significance. Most of the route is in protestant Canton Geneva and passes by nine churches and eight points of interest.

Stage 20 (Geneva to French border) guides you from the upper city of Geneva to the French border, where the Swiss Way of St. James ends (and the pilgrimage continues on French routes). It takes 5 out of the 8 km to get out of the city and its southern agglomeration Carouge. The last 3 km are on tarmac roads along agricultural fields and several small villages. The route leads south, straight to the Swiss-French border. The short route is in protestant Canton Geneva and passes by four churches and one former monastery.

Route Map and Profile

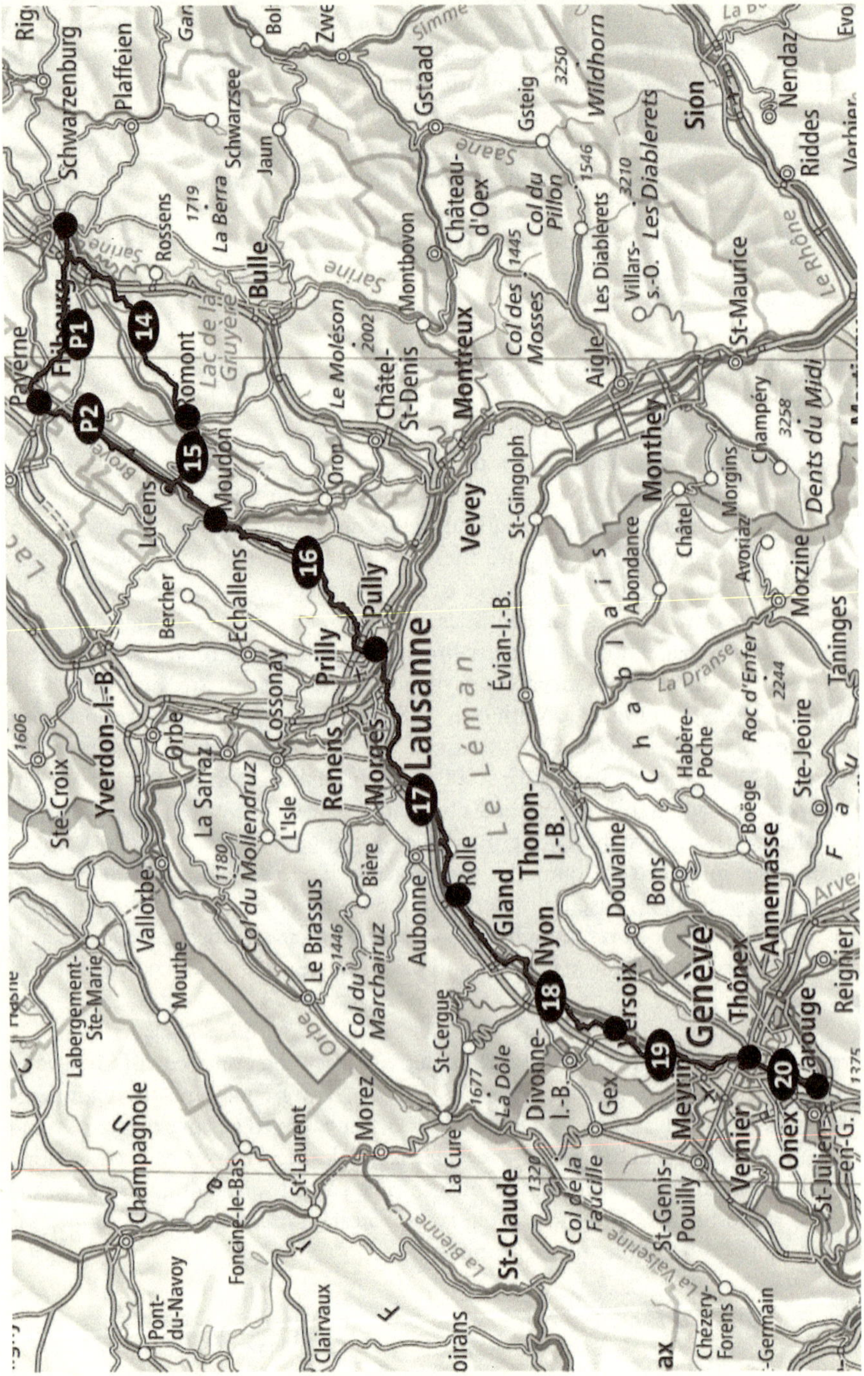
P1
P2
14
15
16
17
18
19
20
Schwarzenburg
Plaffeien
Fribourg
Payerne
Rossens
La Berra
1719
Schwarzsee
Jaun
Bulle
Lac de la Gruyère
Romont
Moudon
Lucens
Bercher
Echallens
Oron
Le Moléson
2002
Châtel-St-Denis
Montbovon
Château-d'Oex
Gstaad
Gsteig
3250
Wildhorn
Col du Pillon
1546
Col des Mosses
1445
Les Diablerets
3210
Les Diablerets
Villars-s.-O.
Sion
Nendaz
Riddes
Montreux
Vevey
Aigle
St-Maurice
Monthey
Champéry
3258
Dents du Midi
Morgins
Châtel
St-Gingolph
Pully
Lausanne
Prilly
Renens
Morges
Cossonay
Yverdon-l.-B.
Ste-Croix
1606
Orbe
La Sarraz
Col du Mollendruz
1180
L'Isle
Bière
Aubonne
Rolle
Gland
Nyon
Le Léman
Évian-l.-B.
Thonon-l.-B.
Abondance
Avoriaz
Morzine
Habère-Poche
Roc d'Enfer
2244
Boëge
Ste-Jeoire
Taninges
Douvaine
Bons
Annemasse
Genève
Thônex
Carouge
Reignier
Onex
Vernier
Meyrin
St-Julien-en-G.
Versoix
Gex
Divonne-l.-B.
La Dôle
1677
St-Cergue
La Cure
Morez
Col du Marchairuz
1446
Le Brassus
Vallorbe
Labergement-Ste-Marie
Mouthe
Champagnole
Foncine-le-Bas
St-Laurent
Pont-du-Navoy
Clairvaux
St-Claude
Col de la Faucille
1320
St-Genis-Pouilly
Chézery-Forens
La Valserine
La Bienne
Orbe
Broye
Sarine
Simme
Saane
Le Rhône
La Dranse
Arve

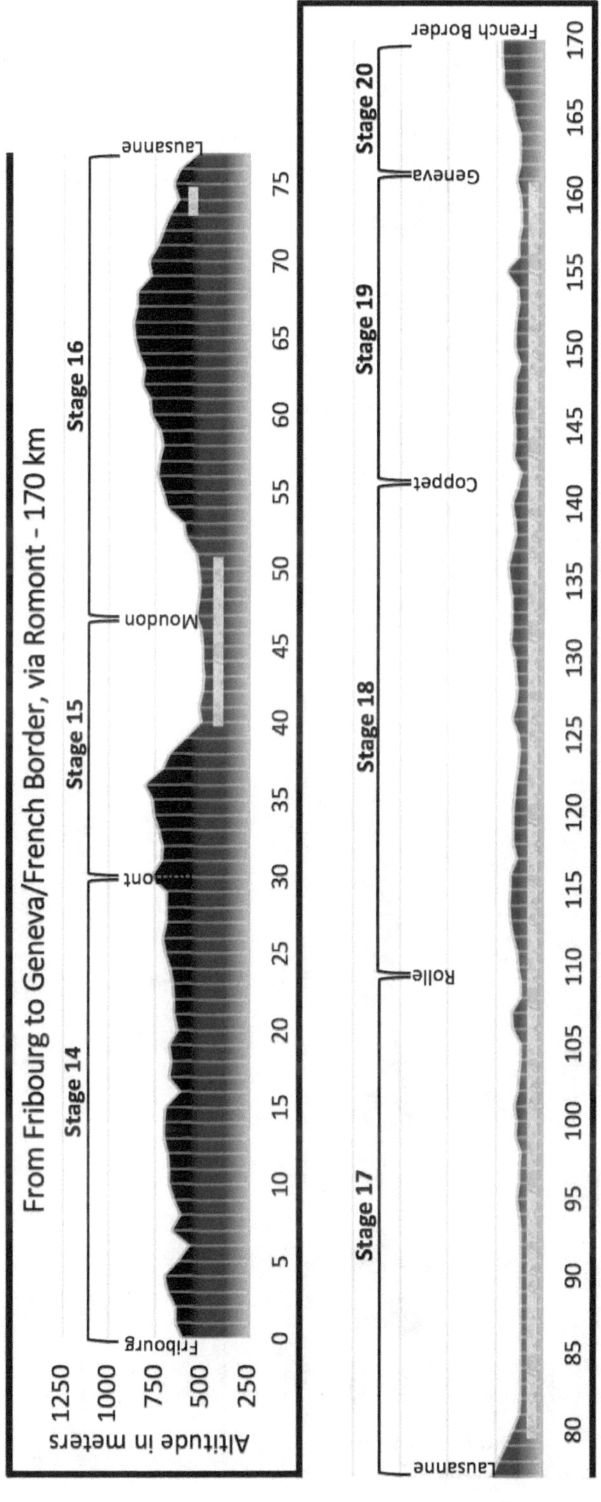
From Fribourg to Geneva/French Border, via Romont - 170 km
Altitude in meters
1250
1000
750
500
250
Stage 14
Stage 15
Stage 16
Stage 17
Stage 18
Stage 19
Stage 20
Fribourg
Moudon
Lausanne
Rolle
Coppet
Geneva
French Border
0
5
10
15
20
25
30
35
40
45
50
55
60
65
70
75
80
85
90
95
100
105
110
115
120
125
130
135
140
145
150
155
160
165
170

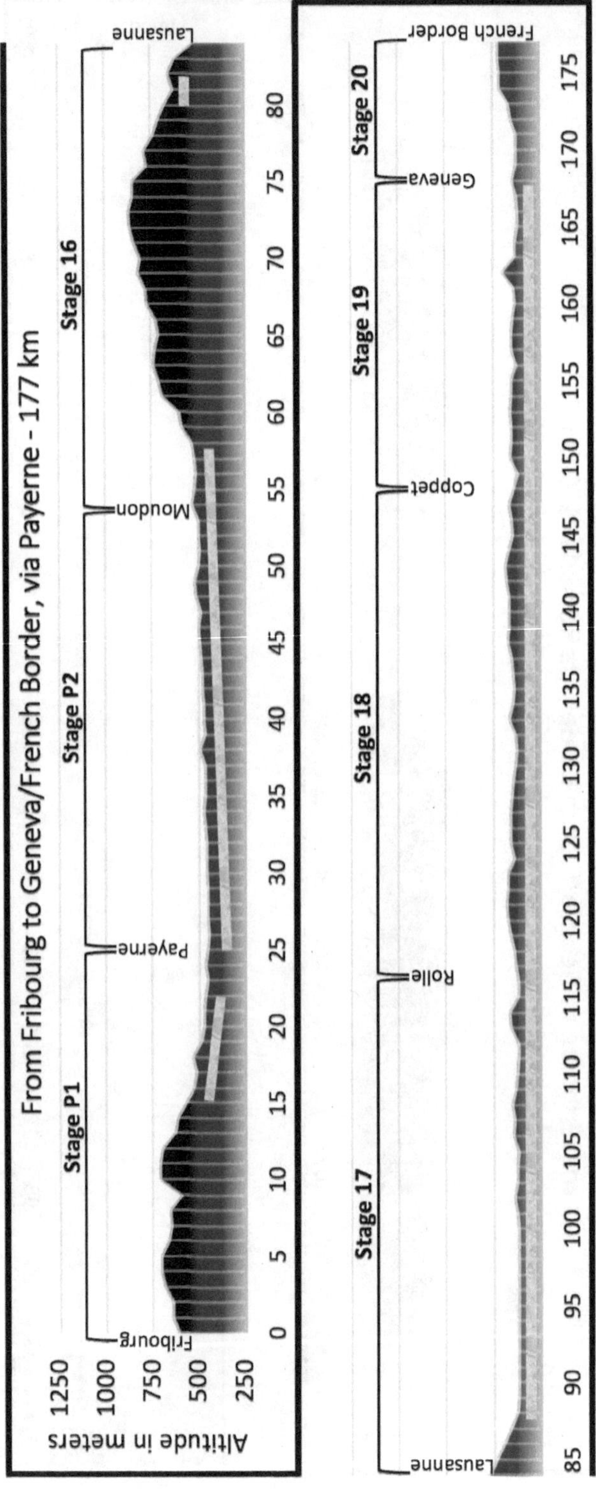
From Fribourg to Geneva/French Border, via Payerne - 177 km
Altitude in meters
1250
1000
750
500
250
Stage P1
Stage P2
Stage 16
Fribourg
Payerne
Moudon
Lausanne
0
5
10
15
20
25
30
35
40
45
50
55
60
65
70
75
80
Stage 17
Stage 18
Stage 19
Stage 20
Lausanne
Rolle
Coppet
Geneva
French Border
85
90
95
100
105
110
115
120
125
130
135
140
145
150
155
160
165
170
175

Overview of Cantons

Understanding the relevant history of the Cantons

In South-West Switzerland you will be hiking through the following Cantons:

- Via Romont: Fribourg, Vaud, and Geneva
- Via Payerne: Fribourg, Vaud, and Geneva

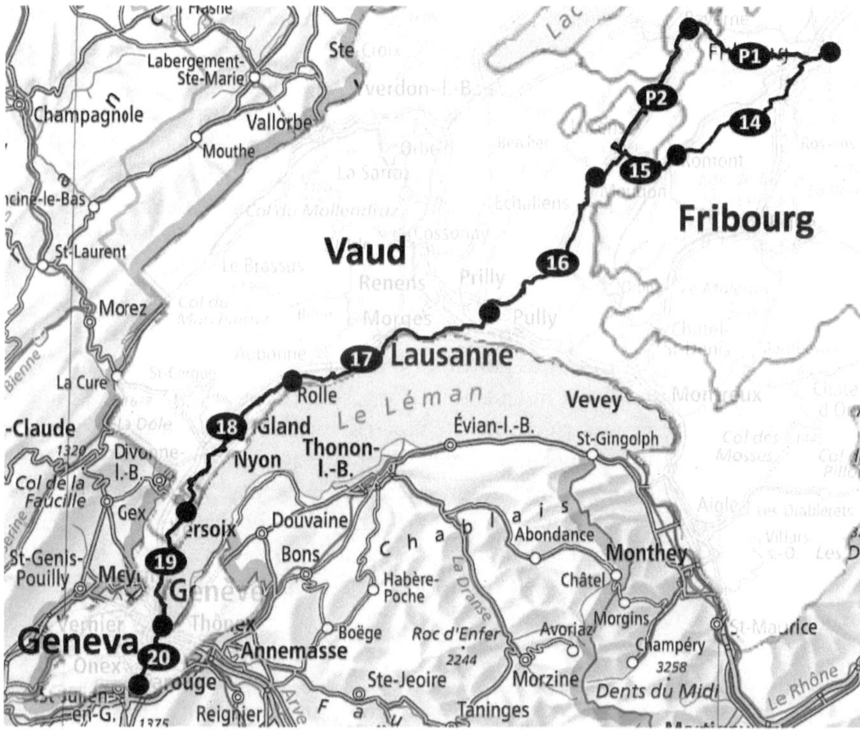

The following sections provide an overview of the above-mentioned Cantons, highlighting their religious history. Read the background information provided below, whenever you enter a new Canton. This will provide the appropriate social, cultural, and religious context of the churches, monasteries, and points of interest.

In the chapters of the individual stages you will find a reference to the Canton and changes from one Canton to the other. As you come across such references, you can flip back to these pages.

Canton Fribourg

Stage 14 and part of stages 15 and P1 are in catholic Canton Fribourg.

In Canton Fribourg the car license plates start with FR. The Canton has two official languages: German and French. Swiss-German is spoken in the region northeast of Fribourg, called the Sense District (between the Sense and Sarine rivers), where the Canton borders German-speaking Cantons (greeting with *Grüessich*). Swiss-French is spoken in the much larger region southwest of Fribourg, where the Canton borders French-speaking Cantons (greeting with *Bonjour*). The City of Fribourg itself officially has two languages, though most of its population speaks French (but will also understand German). In the city most signs and information are both in French and German. The historical explanation for the two languages in the city and Canton is that the areas were divided between French-speaking rulers and German-speaking rulers. In medieval times the Kingdom of Burgundy/Duchy of Savoy (French) occupied the southwestern area (west of the Sarine River) that nowadays makes up the French-speaking part of Switzerland. At the same time the House of Habsburg (German) occupied the northeastern area (east of the Sarine River) that nowadays makes up the German-speaking part of Switzerland.

The Canton was formed in 1481 (the year it joined the Swiss Confederation), after it became independent from the House of Savoy in 1477. From 1478 until 1798 the City of Fribourg was an independent City-State (Republic) and the political powerhouse of the region, ruled by a few patrician families. With military force they expanded their landownership to what became Canton Fribourg, named after its capital city, Fribourg (Freiburg in German, meaning 'Free Castle'). The black/white coat-of-arms dates from 1478 and was the banner of the City-Republic of Fribourg, from the time it became independent from the House of Savoy. The Canton has about 315'000 inhabitants (4 percent) and covers about 4 percent of Switzerland's land area.

At the time of the religious Reformation in the 1520s-30s, Canton Fribourg, being conservative catholic, strongly rejected the Protestantism coming from Bern. In 1524 Canton Fribourg imposed Catholicism on its population and subsequently persecuted and exiled those who had converted to Protestantism. When Canton Bern used military force to expand Protestantism to the lands of Vaud in 1536, Canton Fribourg did the same to establish Catholicism in the regions south of its city (thereby expanding its Canton). The Canton's opposition against the Reformation frequently resulted in military conflicts in the border regions with Canton Bern. The City of Fribourg became a major force in the Counter-Reformation; it was a catholic island surrounded by protestant Cantons (Bern and Vaud). As part of the Counter-Reformation many monastic Orders settled in the city of Fribourg and the Bishopric of Lausanne relocated to the city too.

The Canton's strive for independence from the protestant Cantons of the Swiss Confederation culminated in the formation of an alliance with six other catholic Cantons (*Sonderbund*) in 1845. This caused a civil war (***Sonderbund*** **War**) based on a religious dispute. The *Sonderbund* wanted to defend their catholic autonomy against a centralization of authority by the liberal Swiss Confederation, mainly consisting of protestant progressive Cantons led by Bern. Fifteen Confederate Cantons put together an army and defeated the *Sonderbund* alliance in 1847 (in a battle with only very few casualties). Up to that time Switzerland as a country consisted of loosely organized and independent Cantons. The victory resulted in the Confederates solidifying their power through a new Federal Constitution in 1848, limiting the autonomy of the Cantons and bringing them under one modern roof; the Swiss Federal State was born.

At the formation of the Swiss Confederation freedom of religion for the whole of Switzerland was declared in the country's constitution. Still, Canton Fribourg remained conservative catholic: you will come across many catholic chapels and churches, but hardly any protestant churches on its territory.

During the (late) middle ages **Swiss Mercenaries** were well-known and had a good reputation on the battlefield; they were feared and had an excellent track-record of victories. Usually they were hired as a contingent of highly skilled soldiers, who came battle-ready with their armory of long spears, pikes, and halberds. Foreign armies could simply contract them from Cantonal governments, who trained these professional soldiers. It is estimated that between one and two million of such Swiss mercenaries fought in foreign battles in the 15th to 18th centuries. Most of these men escaped poverty at home for a well-paid job as a hired soldier. Such mercenary contingents fought all over the continent, mainly for the armies of the French and Spanish Kings.

The last remaining mercenaries are the **Swiss Guard at the Vatican**; after the new Federal constitution of 1848, all mercenary activities were prohibited except for the Swiss Guards hired by the Pope. The Vatican has already been contracting these Swiss mercenaries for the protection of the Pope since 1506 – for more than 500 years. Nowadays the Swiss Guard consists of 135 foot-soldiers, still in their traditional outfits with halberd (as well as small modern weapons). They are the sole (hired) military of the Vatican State. Only unmarried Swiss catholic men between 19 and 30 years, who trained in the Swiss army, can qualify for service in the Pontifical Swiss Guard.

Canton Vaud

Stages 15 and P1 are partially and stages P2, 16, 17, and 18 are completely in protestant Canton Vaud.

In Canton Vaud the car license plates start with VD. The people speak Swiss-French and greet with *Bonjour*. The name Vaud was derived from the German word 'Wald', which means forest ('Wald' became

'Waadt' and in French pronunciation Vaud). The white/green coat-of-arms was designed in 1803, when the lands of Vaud became a Canton. The white/green came from the banner that the lands of Vaud used in the 1790s in their battles against Canton Bern and symbolized their strive for independence from oppression (inspired by the French revolution of that period). '*Liberté et Patrie*' is French for 'Freedom and Fatherland', representing their independence (after more than 260 years of oppression by the Bernese). It is the only Swiss Cantonal coat-of-arms that contains a phrase. The Canton has about 790'000 inhabitants (9 percent) and covers about 8 percent of Switzerland's land area. It is third (after Zurich and Bern) in terms of size of the population of the 26 Cantons. The biggest city and capital of the Canton is Lausanne.

At the time of the religious Reformation in the 1520s-30s, most of the lands of Vaud were under the rule of the catholic House of Savoy and the Bishopric Kingdom of Lausanne. In 1536 Bern sought to expand its southern territories and invaded the lands of Vaud, driving out the House of Savoy and exiling the Bishops of Lausanne. This ended a nearly 1'000-year Bishopric rule over the City of Lausanne and its extensive territories around it. The Bernese occupied the lands of Vaud, seized the wealth of the Bishopric Kingdom, and installed their own regional Governor against the will of the local authorities, population, and nobility. Bern enforced the Reformation and all catholic worship was legally forbidden in the lands of Vaud. Nearly all catholic religious icons (statues, altars, paintings, frescos, crucifixes, and so forth) in many churches were destroyed. All monasteries were secularized and their buildings either demolished or utilized for a different purpose. All churches and chapels that were not needed as a parish church were demolished or received a different purpose. For 260 years only protestant worship was allowed (Catholics were pursued, imprisoned, or fined when practicing their worship).

From 1536 there were regular revolts against the Bernese occupation. These peaked in 1798 when, inspired by the French Revolution, Vaud expelled the Bernese Governor and declared their own Republic. When Napoleon invaded Switzerland in the same year, the lands of Vaud were maintained as an independent region within the Helvetic Republic (1798-1803). At the dissolution of the Helvetic Republic in 1803, the lands of Vaud formally became an independent Canton in the reinstated Swiss Confederation.

The new Canton established a law that declared freedom of religion in 1810. Catholic services were held again and new catholic churches were built after 274 years of suppression by the Bernese. Still, the churches you will pass by in Canton Vaud are few and mostly reformed: they are mainly the former parish churches from before 1536 (all others having been demolished or reutilized) and a few catholic churches built after 1810.

Canton Geneva

Stages 19 and 20 are in protestant Canton Geneva.

In Canton Geneva the car license plates start with GE. The people speak Swiss-French and greet with *Bonjour.* The Canton was formed in 1815 and was named after its capital city, Geneva. The yellow/red coat-of-arms with the half-eagle and one key has been in use since the 15th century as banner of the City of Geneva. The half-eagle symbolizes its medieval status as an independent City-State (Republic or free imperial city). The key of St. Peter symbolizes the Bishopric seat. Upon the establishment of Canton Geneva in 1815, the City's flag was chosen as the coat-of-arms of the Canton. The Canton has about 495'000 inhabitants (6 percent) and covers about 0.7 percent of Switzerland's land area. The Canton is the fifth-smallest in terms of land area, but the sixth-largest in terms of size of the population of the 26 Cantons.

The history of Canton Geneva is basically the history of the City of Geneva. From the 4th century the Bishopric Kingdom ruled the city. The bishops came from the ruling families of the region (e.g. Grandson, Savoy) and used their connections to bring wealth, power, and prestige to Geneva. By 1275 the Bishopric Kingdom encompassed 387 parishes and extensive lands in the region. Their Kingdom ended because of the Reformation in 1535. The City of Geneva converted to Protestantism and formed a protective alliance with the protestant City-Republic of Bern. The Reformation had a particularly big impact on Geneva and its churches because of Jean Calvin. He personally implemented the reforms in Geneva and its cathedral in 1536-64. All catholic worship was legally forbidden in the lands of Geneva from 1536. Protestantism was enforced, resulting in the destruction of nearly all catholic religious icons (statues, altars, paintings, frescos, crucifixes, and so forth) in many churches. All monasteries were secularized and their buildings either demolished or utilized for a different purpose. For 260 years only protestant worship was allowed (Catholics were pursued, imprisoned, or fined when practicing their worship). At the time of the Reformation in 1536, the City of Geneva changed from Bishopric Kingdom to independent City-State. The City was an independent Republic until 1798, when the French occupied Switzerland and established the Helvetic Republic (1798-1803).

However, Geneva was not part of this Helvetic Republic: from 1798 until 1813 Geneva was the capital of a French province. Napoleon's troops left Geneva in 1813, after which the City became an independent Republic again. Two years later (1815) the re-established City-Republic of Geneva rejoined the Swiss Confederation as 22nd Canton. After the establishment of the Swiss Confederation of 1848 freedom of religion was declared in the constitution and Canton Geneva allowed catholic services and the construction of new catholic churches after 312 years of suppression.

A second period of difficulties for the Catholics in Canton Geneva soon arose during the '***Kulturkampf***' ('Culture Fight'). This was a political fight between the

State and catholic religious institutions, which led to a significant reduction of the catholic religious influence on politics, policies, and practices of the public institutions, such as government. This Kulturkampf started in Germany and spread over most European countries, including Switzerland, in the second half of the 19th century. It had a particularly strong impact on the Catholics in Canton Geneva, where Government forced the closure of many catholic organizations and churches in 1875-1907. During 32 years catholic worship was suppressed again. As a result, the catholic churches fell into disrepair and had to be renovated before they could be used again from 1910 onwards. Most of the churches you will visit in Canton Geneva are protestant; a few catholic churches were built after 1848.

FRIBOURG TO MOUDON: VIA ROMONT

Stage 14: Fribourg to Romont 30 km

The Way to the 750-year-old Pilgrim Station

Route stats

	Distance in km	*Time in hrs:min*
Signposted route nr. 4	28.3	5:50
Churches/chapels	1.7	2:10
Points of interest		1:00
Rest/lunch		1:00
Stage 14	30.0	10:00

In case you hike this stage as a daytrip, you need to add 600 meters in Fribourg and 600 meters in Romont (from and to the train stations).

Ascent/descent/total	+696 / -528 / 1'224 altitude meters
Lowest/highest altitude	569 / 781 meters
Pathway/condition	easy / moderate
Churches/chapels	Fribourg (4), Villars-sur-Glâne (2), Muéses, Posieux, Ecuvillens, Posat, Autigny, Chavannes-sous-Orsonnens, Romont (4)
Monasteries	Ursuline Convent Fribourg, Former Norbertine Convent Posat, Cistercian Convent Romont, Former Capuchin Monastery Romont
Points of interest	St. James Cross, Healing Spring, Castle of Romont, Stained-Glass Museum, Medieval City Fortifications

Route summary

Stage 14 continues in catholic **Canton Fribourg.** From Fribourg until Geneva/French border (stages 14 to 20) you are in the French-speaking part of Switzerland (Romandie).

Stage 14 guides you across the highland plateau of the Glâne District to the city of Romont.

Road nr. 155 connects Fribourg to Romont. The Way of St. James follows the same direction as road nr. 155, most of the time trailing about 2 km southeast of this road. The route passes through an area that is called the Glâne District. It is a highland plateau named after the Glâne River that flows through it. When you look at the profile map you see three main inclinations in the profile (at km 6, 16, and 20). Each of these are caused by a descent into the Glâne River valley, a crossing of the river, and an ascent back to the highland plateau. The remainder of the time the route is on the plateau, until you ascend the hill on which the city of Romont is built (at km 29).

Stage 14 starts in the city center of Fribourg and takes 5 km before you leave the city and its southern agglomerations behind you. The route enters the Glâne District highland plateau and stays on the plateau until Romont. Despite being on the plateau, there are many short and gradual ascents and descents accumulating to 1'224 altitude meters. Most of the route is on quiet country roads along agricultural fields. The route goes through patches of forest only a few times. This is mostly the case when crossing the Glâne River valley.

Stage 14 is a long day with 16 churches/chapels and five points of interest along the way. The medieval city of Romont is the highlight of the day, with a Savoy castle, a unique stained-glass museum, 13th century city fortifications, and a church with significant catholic art. The stained-glass museum closes at 18:00 (April until October). You can either plan to arrive before it closes or visit the museum the next morning.

Getting to the starting point

Today's starting point in Fribourg is at the Ursuline Convent Church, directly on the signposted route nr. 4.

In case you hike stage 14 as a daytrip, you need to walk 600 meters from the train station to the church. From the train station turn left towards the old city and follow the *Avenue de la Gare*, straight across the roundabout, through the pedestrian street of *Rue de Romont*, across the square *Place Georges Python*, and into the pedestrian street of *Rue de Lausanne*, where you arrive at the church (house nr. 92, on the right). The route goes back to the train station exactly the same way you came. While hiking these 600 meters you pass by the Ursuline convent church and the reformed church. In case you have already visited these two churches, you could also save the 600 meters to and 600 meters from these churches, and just start at the train station.

Route Map and Profile

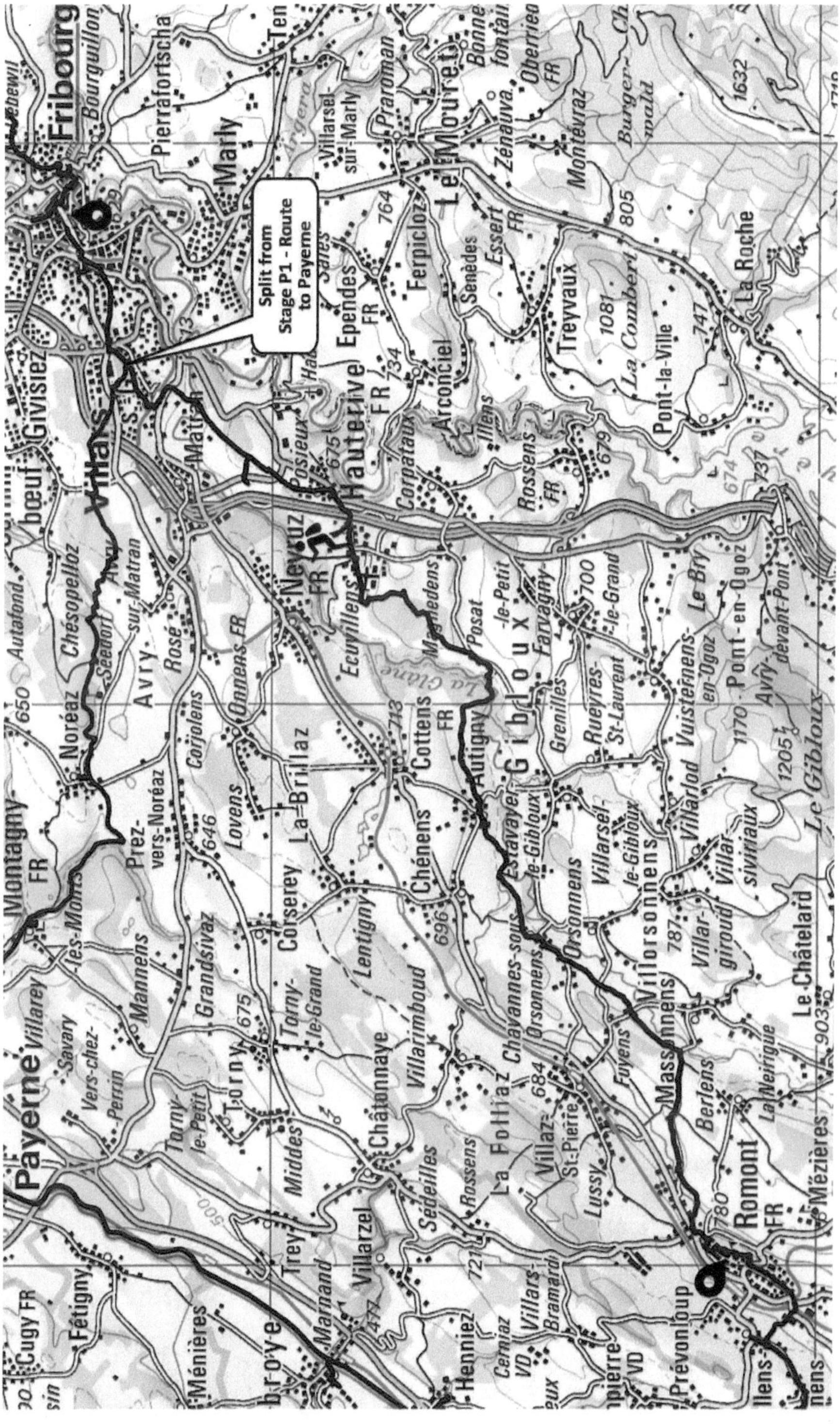
Split from Stage P1 - Route to Payerne
Fribourg
Bourguillon
Pierrafortscha
Marly
Villarsel-sur-Marly
Praroman
Le Mouret
Bonnefontaine
Zénauva
Oberried FR
Montévraz
Givisiez
Villars-s-Gl.
Matran
Posieux
Hauterive FR
Ependes FR
Ferpicloz
Arconciel
Senèdes
Essert FR
Treyvaux
La Combert
Pont-la-Ville
La Roche
Corpataux
Rossens FR
Neyruz FR
Ecuvillens
Magnedens
Posat
Farvagny-le-Petit
Farvagny-le-Grand
Gibloux
Le Bry
Vuisternens-en-Ogoz
Pont-en-Ogoz
Avry-devant-Pont
Le Gibloux
Autigny
Cottens FR
Chénens
Estavayer-le-Gibloux
Grenilles
Rueyres-St-Laurent
Villarlod
Villarsel-le-Gibloux
Orsonnens
Villorsonnens
Villargiroud
Villarsiviriaux
Le Châtelard
Chavannes-sous-Orsonnens
Massonnens
Fuyens
Berlens
La Neirigue
Romont FR
Mézières
Lussy
Villaz-St-Pierre
La Folliaz
Rossens
Sédeilles
Villarimboud
Châtonnaye
Lentigny
La Brillaz
Lovens
Onnens FR
Corserey
Torny-le-Grand
Torny
Torny-le-Petit
Middes
Grandsivaz
Mannens
Prez-vers-Noréaz
Corjolens
Noréaz
Avry-sur-Matran
Rosé
Chésopelloz
Seedorf
Autafond
Montagny FR
Montagny-les-Monts
Villarey
Payerne
Savary
Vers-chez-Perrin
Cugy FR
Fétigny
Ménières
Broye
Marnand
Trey
Villarzel
Henniez
Cerniaz VD
Villars-Bramard
Prévonloup
Chapelle VD

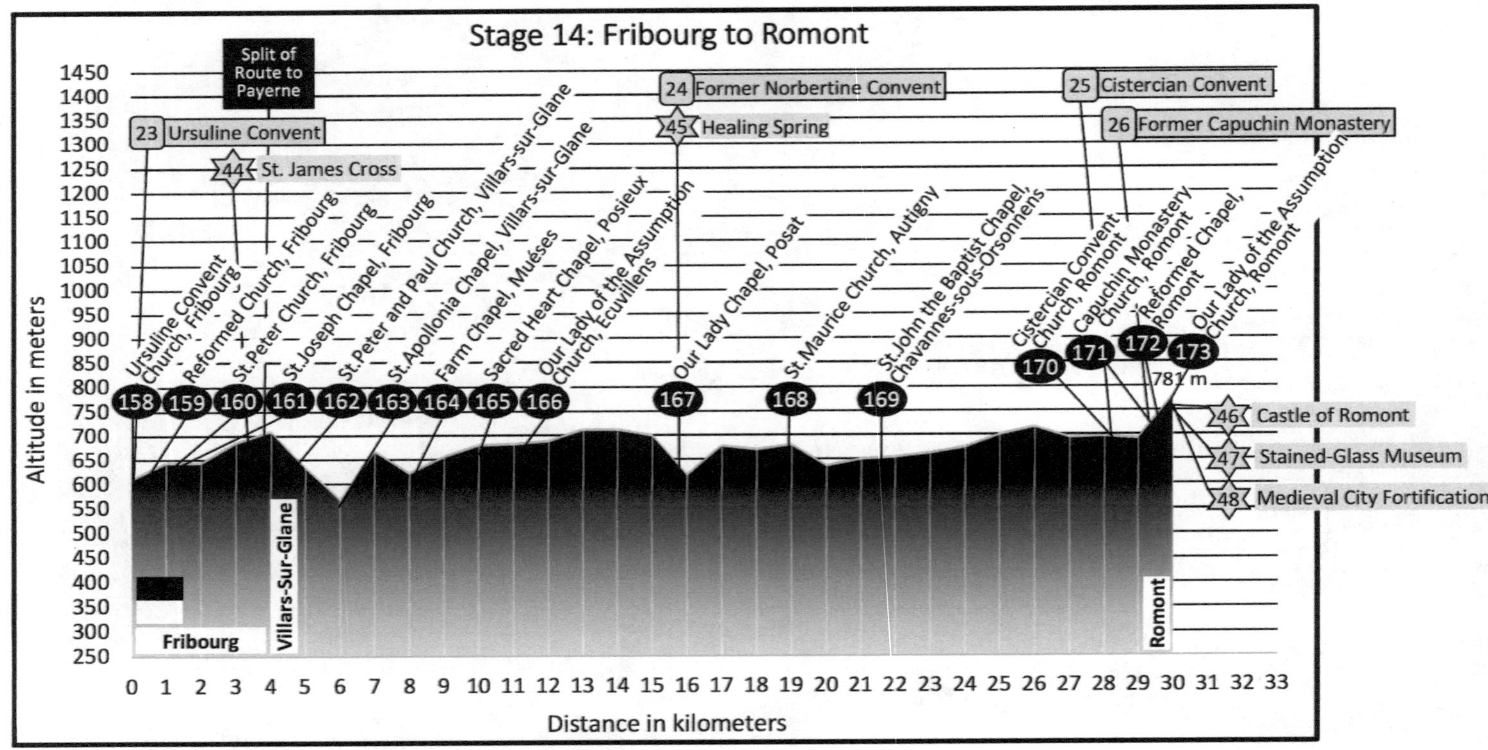
Stage 14: Fribourg to Romont
Altitude in meters
1450
1400
1350
1300
1250
1200
1150
1100
1050
1000
950
900
850
800
750
700
650
600
550
500
450
400
350
300
250
Distance in kilometers
0 1 2 3 4 5 6 7 8 9 10 11 12 13 14 15 16 17 18 19 20 21 22 23 24 25 26 27 28 29 30 31 32 33
Split of Route to Payerne
23 Ursuline Convent
24 Former Norbertine Convent
25 Cistercian Convent
26 Former Capuchin Monastery
44 St. James Cross
45 Healing Spring
46 Castle of Romont
47 Stained-Glass Museum
48 Medieval City Fortifications
158 Ursuline Convent Church, Fribourg
159 Reformed Church, Fribourg
160 St.Peter Church, Fribourg
161 St.Joseph Chapel, Fribourg
162 St.Peter and Paul Church, Villars-sur-Glane
163 St.Apollonia Chapel, Villars-sur-Glane
164 Farm Chapel, Muèses
165 Sacred Heart Chapel, Posieux
166 Our Lady of the Assumption Church, Ecuvillens
167 Our Lady Chapel, Posat
168 St.Maurice Church, Autigny
169 St.John the Baptist Chapel, Chavannes-sous-Orsonnens
170 Cistercian Convent Church, Romont
171 Capuchin Monastery Church, Romont
172 Reformed Chapel, Romont
173 Our Lady of the Assumption Church, Romont
781 m
Fribourg
Villars-Sur-Glane
Romont

Hiking the Route

From the outside the Ursuline convent church looks inconspicuous; it is fully integrated in the row of houses along the shopping and restaurant street *Rue de Lausanne*. Its stained-glass windows are high up, there is no bell tower (only a short steeple on the roof), and it does not seem to have a door; if you are not looking for it, you will probably miss it. The white building to the right of the sandstone-colored church is the convent. You are looking at the narrow northern side of the convent's building, with its long-stretched southern side behind it. The entrance door to the white building also provides access to the church.

Ursuline Convent Church, Fribourg (Eglise des Ursulines) **158**

- Rue de Lausanne 92, 1700 Fribourg
- St. Ursula
- The church was built as part of the convent in 1653-54. It served as church for the nuns and their girls' school.
- You cannot access the nave of the church; an iron gate keeps the access restricted to the front portal. The wall fresco at the chancel depicts St. Ursula and her virgin maids coming off the ship. Other than that, the small church has an austere and simple interior without any coloring on the walls.

Ursuline Convent, Fribourg (Couvent des Ursulines) **23**

- Rue de Lausanne 92, 1700 Fribourg

Ursuline Order

The convent was established in 1634, with the purpose of educating young girls. They were part of the second wave of catholic monastic Orders, established during the Counter-Reformation, and were the female counterpart of the Jesuit Collegium. The Ursulines instituted higher-level education for girls, whereas the Visitation Sisters (see monastery nr. 20 in stage 13, Volume II) provided the lower-level education for girls in Fribourg. (The Jesuits managed the higher-level education for boys; the Capuchins provided the lower-level education for boys – see stage 13, Volume II.)

Similar to the Visitation Sisters (1635), several nuns of the French Ursuline Order settled in Fribourg (1634) to seek refuge from the Thirty Years' War (fought between catholic Habsburg countries and opposing protestant States in Central Europe in 1618-48). They opened a school and attracted several hundreds of female students, of which many stayed at the boarding facilities of the convent.

In 1798 the convent and school were occupied by French troops, who plundered and burned down their buildings. The nuns found refuge at the Convent of the Cistercians of Maigrauge, on the other side of the Sarine River.

The sisters returned in 1804, and rebuilt their convent and school. After Fribourg had lost the Sonderbund War, the convent and its school were closed (1848) and their assets seized. The 44 sisters were allowed to stay, but were not allowed to teach. After an interruption of 11 years the sisters were allowed to return to teaching and reopened their school (1859). The school flourished at the beginning of the 20th century, when they expanded their college into several faculties (business, teacher training, nursing, languages).

High age, lack of novices, and a reducing number of sisters forced them to scale down in the second half of the 20th century. Part of their buildings were sold and the schools relocated to other locations in Fribourg. Only the convent's Spiritual Center remained at the present location.

From the convent's church continue up the hill in the direction of the train station. Across the *Place Georges Python* and through the pedestrian street of the *Rue de Romont* with its daily morning market, the route leads you to the reformed Church of Fribourg, standing slightly elevated on your right (at km 0.3).

Reformed Church, Fribourg (Eglise Reformée) 159

- Rue du Temple 1, 1700 Fribourg
- The church was built in 1875, and renovated several times since. It was the first reformed church in the catholic stronghold of Fribourg, since protestant services were allowed to be held from 1836. It is the only protestant church in the city of Fribourg and the Glâne District (south of town).
- Typical for protestant churches, its interior decorations are limited (no altars, no statues, no crucifixes). The stained glass windows have bright colors in a modern design and do not depict any religious symbols or scenes. The doors are often closed; they are mainly open during services.

From the church cross the roundabout and continue up the hill through the *Avenue de la Gare* until you get to the train station. Follow the direction of the nr. 4 sign to a tunnel underneath the railway tracks, which is also used by public transportation. On your right is the underground bus station where large buses drive in and out, emitting black clouds of exhaust fumes that stay trapped between the concrete walls and ceiling. Better walk quickly. The route turns left and ascends out of the underpass into the fresh air beside the railway tracks (on your left). At the first crossing the signposted route continues straight, but it is worthwhile to make a 350-meter detour to the next church. Turn right into the *Avenue Beauregard* (road nr. 181) and then the first street right into the *Avenue Jean-Gambach*. Up the hill on your right you arrive at the St. Peter Church (at km 1.0).

St. Peter Church, Fribourg (Eglise St-Pierre) 160

- Avenue Jean-Gambach 4, 1700 Fribourg
- St. Peter, St. Nicholas of Flüe, St. Thérèse of Lisieux, Four Evangelists
- The catholic church was built in 1924. It has a long and high nave, a deep and rectangular chancel, no transept, and three side-chapels. The church was renovated in 1970-71, when the chancel was rearranged in accordance with the second Vatican Council. Further renovations were undertaken in 2003 and 2018.
- The reason for making the detour from the signposted route nr. 4 is the interior decorations: mosaics, frescos, and stained-glass created over a period of 25 years. The mosaics were created by the famous Italian artist Severini and are the most unique Art-Deco and Cubism (mosaic) ornaments along the Swiss Way of St.

James and throughout the whole of Switzerland. You find these exceptional decorations in the chancel, the three left side-chapels, and on the right wall.

The giant mosaic at the back wall of the chancel has a size of 7 by 10.5 meters and depicts Jesus handing over a key to St. Peter, surrounded by the religious symbols of the Four Evangelists. The mosaic tiles were made in Rome by Mattia, and Severini made them into these works of art in 1950-51.

The mosaic decoration at the Sacred Heart side-chapel is the most artistic and colorful one in the church and in Switzerland, recognized for its religious Art-Deco far beyond the borders of Switzerland. The mosaic was created by four artists, including Cingria and Berchem, in 1932-33. Look at how the gold and red colored beams of light radiate away from Jesus' heart.

The mosaic decorations of the crucifixion way stations were completed by Severini in 1957. They appear in reverse order from the main entrance (during the last renovation they reversed the order – they were reinstalled from the side entrance).

The stained-glass windows are in Art Nouveau style and were installed in 1941-45. They beautifully reflect the light in blueish and reddish colors.

Have a closer look at the three side-chapels: the chapel of St. Nicholas of Flüe with the meditation wheel depicted in the stained-glass window; the Sacred Heart chapel with the unique mosaic and a metal Pietà; and the St. Thérèse of Lisieux chapel (remember her from stage 6 in Emmetten?).

Underneath the chancel of the church is the St. Joseph Chapel. To go there, take a right exit and the stairs down underneath the bell tower. The entrance of the chapel is marked by black and white marble around the frame of the doors.

St. Joseph Chapel, Fribourg (Chapelle Saint-Joseph) **161**

- Avenue Jean-Gambach 4, 1700 Fribourg
- St. Joseph
- The chapel was built as part of the church in 1924.
- Its modern interior dates mostly from 1959. The chapel's small windows have colorful stained-glass that were created by the famous regional artist Yoki. They represent scenes from the life of St. Joseph. The chapel is used for services during the week.

From the chapel walk back to the signposted route nr. 4 the same way you came. Continue along the busy road of the *Avenue du Midi* along the train tracks in a southern direction. The route turns right into the *Route de la Vignettaz*, forks left into the *Route de la Gruyère*, and continues straight on the *Route du Grand Pré*. You walk through residential areas with four-story apartment buildings surrounded by gardens. The route continues to ascend gradually and passes by a grassland hill, after which it passes through residential areas with low apartment blocks. The route turns right and left, and is back on road nr. 181. At a double roundabout the route stays on the left. In front you see the Shopping Center Fribourg-Sud. The route turns south and enters the forest behind (south of) the shopping center.

At the entrance of the forest (*Bois de Belle Croix*) is the **St. James Cross**. A brown information sign explains its history.

Since the 13th century this location has been an important passage for pilgrims along the Way of St. James. To serve the pilgrims, the Cistercian Convent of Maigrauge in Fribourg (still existing today in the Neuveville part of Fribourg; not along the route) built a small chapel dedicated to St. James around the year 1470. During the 18th century the number of pilgrims reduced and the convent neglected the chapel, so that it fell into ruins. It was demolished in 1771. Two years later, in 1773, a memorial stone cross (made from stones of this area) was erected on the fundaments of the former chapel, and received the name St. James Cross. During the Sonderbund War in 1847 the cross stood in the middle of a battlefield. In 1866 the cross was vandalized and demolished. The pieces were gathered and the cross was reassembled at another location by a private person. In 1953 the cross was moved to yet another location, before it was returned to its historical location in 1981.

The route enters the forest in a westward direction and passes by contemporary indicators of the Way of St. James. A small statue representing the Virgin Mary with baby Jesus is in a small encasing fixed to a tree with scallops hanging under it. After a gradual ascent you reach a high point of 712 meters in the forest, where the Way of St. James splits. One green/blue nr. 4 sign directs straight, whereas another one directs to the right. The one directing straight continues to Romont and then Moudon. The one forking to the right is an alternative route via Payerne to Moudon. See stages P1 and P2 on pages 77 to 114 for the description of the alternative route via Payerne. In this stage 14 you continue to Romont.

Split of Route to Payerne

Continue straight on the gravel path. The route descends and leaves the forest 600 meters later. You walk along the edge of the forest through a southwestern suburb of Fribourg, with villas and swimming pools in their gardens. In front of you, further down the hill, you can already see the steeple of the next church. At the end of the *Chemin des Rochettes* you arrive at the St. Peter and Paul Church at km 4.7. You need to walk around the cemetery to the left to reach the front entrance.

162 St. Peter and Paul Church, Villars-sur-Glâne (Eglise St-Pierre et Paul)

- Route de l'Eglise 2, 1752 Villars-sur-Glâne
- St. Peter and Paul
- On a small table left of the glass entrance portal
- The present church was built in 1915-16, and is the fourth church on this site. The first mention of a church in Villars-sur-Glâne dates from 1156. This first church had Romanesque features, which were remodeled in 1450 and 1786. Not much was documented about the first three churches. At the beginning of the 20th century the church was dilapidated and had become too small for the growing parish of Villars-sur-Glâne. The third church was demolished and the

present one was built in 1915-16. Only the three bells (dated 1350, 1609, and 1840) are from the predecessor churches; the bell dating from 1350 may be one of the oldest in Canton Fribourg. The church was built in a neo-Romanesque style in the footprint of a Latin cross. Even the bell tower was remodeled in an old style, with a fire-watch platform below the steeple.

The stained-glass windows (1916) break the sunlight into a spectrum of colors. Notice how various saints are depicted in the glass. The interior does not have the usual three altars; it was kept very simple.

From the church the route continues down the hill towards the train tracks and passes underneath the small train station of Villars-sur-Glâne to the southern side of the tracks. The route shortly follows an eastern direction on road nr. 155, passes by a road cross, crosses a roundabout, and turns right along a narrow patch of forest. Following a small stream, the Way of St. James descends on a narrow trail through a small patch of forest and crosses a small road to an old arched bridge.

The present stone **Glâne Bridge** (*Pont de la Glâne*) was built in the 16th or 17th century. A first wooden bridge at this location already existed before 1243, which was replaced by a stone bridge around 1509. This was one of the first bridges crossing the Glâne River, making it an important passage along the Way of St. James since medieval times.

The small St. Apollonia Chapel is on the other side of the cobbled stone bridge (at km 6.0).

163 St. Apollonia Chapel, Villars-sur-Glâne (Chapelle de Sainte-Apolline)

Route de Sainte-Apolline 18, 1752 Villars-sur-Glâne

St. Apollonia

The chapel was first mentioned in 1147. The present building was reconstructed after a fire in 1566, and was renovated several times since, last in 1994 (look at the dates written underneath the overhanging front roof).

The wooden altar and its paintings date from the renovations in 1690. Excavations discovered many decayed teeth around the chapel, as St. Apollonia is the patroness Saint of dentists and tooth problems.

The route continues on the southern bank of the Glâne River and climbs out of the valley. On half grass/half gravel-rock trails the route crosses through meadows and along the edge of a patch of forest. You pass by a large sand pit on your left, but you cannot see it; it is hidden behind the trees. When you look back you see the steeple of the St. Peter and Paul church at the horizon. After crossing a farm road and another meadow, the trail follows a sunken lane through a small forest.

The **Sunken Lane** (also called Holloway) indicates the heavy use during the middle ages. The sunken lanes were created by erosion of the soft and humid forest underground, caused by the traffic of carriages, carts, and horses over many centuries. At the time of heavy use, the sunken lanes had more or less straight walls on the left and right side (U-shape). Because these sunken lanes were dirt roads, they made traveling difficult during rainy periods. The development of bigger and heavier carriages made traveling these soft roads increasingly problematic. Wooden boards were used to stabilize the road, when stones or gravel were not available. After the route was abandoned for newer, faster roads that could carry heavy carriages (such as the mail coach), the sidewalls collapsed and the path got a V-shape. Erosion and vegetation growing on the sides finally reduced the path to a hollow footpath.

At the end of the forest the route sign directs straight ahead. However, at this location a 500-meter detour is needed to reach the next chapel. Turn right on the concrete farm road and walk down the hill. After crossing a road, you reach the Chapel of Muéses at km 8.0.

Farm Chapel, Les Muéses (Chapelle Muéses) 164

Route des Muéses 45, 1725 Posieux

St. Peter, St. Barbara, Our Lady

The chapel was built as a commemorative chapel (like most farm chapels) in 1672. It is located between a small cluster of barns and opposite a long-stretched farmhouse.

The small chapel has an unusual history. The lands of Muéses belonged to the Abbey of Hauterive (about 2 km southeast of the chapel), which leased out the domain during the middle ages. The Manli family leased the lands during the 16th-17th centuries, and built a chapel next to their farmhouse. The name (Peter Manli) and date (1673, in Roman numbers) are inscribed at the bottom of the altar. The chapel was built to commemorate the safe return of a Peter Manli, who was a Swiss mercenary in service of the Spanish army. (See page 23 for the general description of the history of Swiss mercenaries.)

The wooden door of the chapel is behind a metal gate. When you open the door, a rope hangs in front of you; it is there to toll the little bell in the short steeple on its roof. Just give it a couple of pulls (the old neighbor might come out to check what is happening). The ceiling is vaulted and large slabs of stone are on the floor; very similar to what you saw at the old Romanesque churches. Faded frescos decorate the walls. Two small pews are left and right of the small nave. The altar paintings depict St. Peter, St. Barbara, and Our Liberating Lady.

From the chapel walk back the same 500 meters up the hill to the signposted route nr. 4. Turn right and continue on the grass trail in a southern direction. Because of the elevation you have wide views over agricultural fields in all directions. The Alps fill the southeastern horizon. The trail changes from grass to concrete farm road and after a short left and right (follow the yellow arrow painted on the ground) continues south towards the town Posieux. A gravel path leads up a hill, after which you reach a tarmac street (*Route de Matran*).

You pass by apple trees and a life-size wood-carved statue representing a walking pilgrim (notice the resemblance of this statue with the one in Brienz – see stage 9, Volume II). Paintings on a rock depict the blue sign of the scallop and a pilgrim. Clearly the house owner wishes the passing pilgrims on the Way of St. James a good journey. At the carpark of the house the owner offers the pilgrims a place to rest and refreshments.

Continuing on the *Route de Matran* you see the next chapel on your right. It is on a small hill and has an unusual shape. The grounds outside the chapel look neglected. The steps leading up are crooked, and weed and grass grow on the pavement around the building. The two metal doors and their stained-glass windows are weathered; rust, peeled off paint, and dirty windows give the entrance a dilapidated appearance. The door is held closed by a small chain, apparently for a long time already. A note asks you to keep the doors closed to avoid birds from flying in. Fortunately, the interior does not reflect the state of the exterior of the Sacred Heart Chapel of Posieux (at km 10.0).

165 Sacred Heart Chapel, Posieux (Chapelle du Sacré-Coeur)

- Route de Matran 29, 1725 Posieux
- St. Nicholas of Flüe

The chapel was built as a memorial at the highest point of the village in 1911-24. The decision to build a memorial chapel was already made in 1884; it took almost 40 years for the chapel to be built and consecrated.

The chapel commemorates the resistance of local conservative Catholics who wanted to keep their catholic traditions from being curtailed by a radical-liberal Fribourg government. The Swiss Federal Constitution of 1848 caused a leniency in protestant progressiveness (after the Catholics lost the Sonderbund War in 1847). In 1852 around 15'000 people gathered around the hill (nowadays called 'the Assembly of Posieux'). They publicly protested the reformative authorities of Fribourg. The assembly started the decline of this radical-liberal regime, which was replaced by a conservative catholic government in 1856.

The memorial chapel has several special features: it has the footprint of a Greek cross, with the tower in the middle of the transept; the ceiling beneath the tower is square and has special woodwork; the chancel has a large fresco depicting the uprising; the southern apse has large frescos depicting St. Nicholas of Flüe at the assembly of the Treaty of Stans in 1481 (remember from church nr. 102 in Sachseln, Volume II, this is fictional: he never was at that assembly – it was priest Heimo am Grund who sped from Stans to Brother Klaus in Flüeli-Ranft to obtain his counsel); the northern apse with a statue representing Jesus as the Sacred Heart (in contradiction to the remainder of the chapel, this statue is colorless).

As a nice touch, the chapel specifically welcomes pilgrims on their way to Santiago de Compostela. Leaflets with pilgrim prayers in several languages can be bought for a minor donation.

About 2.2 km east of the chapel, in a meander of the Sarine River (a beautiful but isolated location), lies the large and well-known **Cistercian Monastery of Hauterive**. The abbey was founded in 1138, closed in 1527 (Reformation), reopened, closed in 1848 (Sonderbund War), and reopened again in 1939. The abbey has an interesting history and church, provides guided tours, and can accommodate three pilgrims in their guesthouse (*www.abbaye-hauterive.ch*). Given the significant detour from the signposted route (4.4 km plus time to spend at the abbey) in an already long and busy stage 14, it is not included in this book.

From the chapel continue south along the *Route de Matran*. At the T-crossing turn right on road nr. 12 (*Route de Fribourg*). You pass by an old wooden house with small windows and the municipal office. At a split of the road take the road on the right that goes underneath Highway A12. The route goes up a hill and a little later you arrive at the Our Lady of the Assumption Church of Ecuvillens at km 11.1.

166 **Our Lady of the Assumption Church, Ecuvillens** (Eglise Notre-Dame de l'Assomption)

- Route de Posieux 1, 1730 Ecuvillens
- Our Lady
- The catholic church was first mentioned in official documents as a Romanesque church dedicated to Our Lady in 1138. Not much was documented about this first church. The church building was dilapidated by the end of the 18th century, and reconstructed and expanded in 1809-11. By 1912 the church had become too small and was expanded again: the tower was heightened; the old east-aligned chancel demolished and rebuilt with a northern alignment; and the nave was lengthened and realigned to the new position of the chancel.
- The interior is simple with limited decorations. Other than the crucifixion way stations and a few statues, there are no altars or other opulent decorations.

From the church follow the route along the *Route du Village* in a westward direction. The route forks to the left and goes along the northern side of the runway of **Ecuvillens' regional airport** (built in 1949). A gravel road curves around the western end of the runway and goes up the hill along the edge of a forest. When you look back you have a good view over the small airport (mostly used for sports flying) and its runway. The route turns right into the forest, where it makes a left and right to come out on its western side. On a small tarmac road, the route goes down the hill to the village Posat. You follow a road called *Route Saint-Jacques* (St. James Way), commemorating the many pilgrims that passed here for centuries. At the end of the village the route turns right, and you arrive at the Our Lady Chapel of Posat at km 15.8.

Our Lady Chapel, Posat (Chapelle de Notre-Dame Posat) 167

- Chemin de la Glâne 8, 1726 Posat
- Our Lady
- In front of the left side-altar

The chapel was first built as part of a small Norbertine Convent (see below) around 1140. To finance the establishment of the Jesuit Collegium St. Michael in Fribourg, the convent was closed and the chapel became the property of the Jesuits in 1580 (see stage 13, Volume II). The Jesuits neglected the chapel and the building was in near ruins, before it was reconstructed and expanded by the Jesuits in 1675. They dedicated the chapel to Our Lady.

In 1701 the walls and ceiling were elaborately decorated with frescos. Fifteen frescos of the Mysteries of the Holy Rosary were painted: 10 in the nave and five in the chancel, of which the altar painting of the Visitation is the 5th (a pregnant Mary visiting a pregnant Elisabeth; for details about the Visitation, see stage 13, Volume II). These rosary frescos made the chapel a regional pilgrimage destination dedicated to the Virgin Mary.

The Mysteries of the Holy Rosary form a collection of prayers (15) on the main events in the life, death, and resurrection of Jesus. They were an old prayer ritual that was standardized by Pope Pius V in veneration of the Virgin Mary in 1569. These 15 meditations were divided in three categories: Joyful Mysteries, Sorrowful Mysteries, and Glorious Mysteries. In 2002 Pope John Paul II added five additional prayers, under a fourth category of Luminous Mysteries.

Unfortunately, the ceiling and all walls, including the 14 rosary frescos, were whitewashed in the 19th century. Interior renovations and fresco restorations were undertaken in 2003-04, when all ceiling, wall, and window frescos were recovered, except for the rosaries. These remained empty, as you see them today.

Another artistic decoration is the tabernacle at the high-altar, with a statue representing the Virgin Mary and baby Jesus. Have a closer look through the iron gate (rood screen) that separates the chancel from the nave. It is a beautifully carved and gold painted 18th century piece of art, given to the Jesuits by the French Court of King Louis XV.

24 Former Norbertine Convent, Posat (Couvent de St-Norbert)

Chemin de la Glâne 8, 1726 Posat

Norbertine Order

The former Norbertine convent was established by the Norbertine Monastery of Marsens (about 10 km south of Posat) around 1140, after a local landowner had donated the lands in Posat to the monastery. The monastery established a farm, built the chapel, and relocated nuns from their convent in Marsens to work on the farm. Not much is known of the convent in Posat. From 1420 the monastery leased the farm and lands to other farmers, as a result of which most (if not all) nuns left.

To finance the new Collegium St. Michael in Fribourg, Pope Gregor XIII closed the Norbertine monastery of Marsens and transferred its assets (lands, vineyards, and forests, including the convent in Posat) to the Jesuits in Fribourg in 1580 (see stage 13, Volume II). What was left of the convent was closed, and the Jesuits let the convent and chapel fall into ruins. About 100 years later the chapel was rebuilt, but the convent was not. The inn called La Croix d'Or (the Golden Cross) that is at the beginning of the street was built on the ruins of this convent.

Left (west) of the chapel, you see a small spring.

The **Healing Spring** is in a recess in a small side-chapel. Fresh drinking water flows from the small spring. In the middle ages it was believed that the water had healing power (particularly for the eyes) and many pilgrims drank the water (and washed their eyes) to become or stay healthy. You can do the same.

Behind the chapel the route follows a narrow zigzagging trail that descends steeply into the valley of the Glâne River. You cross the river on a narrow wooden footbridge. On the other side the trail zigzags through the forest out of the river valley. The trail widens, becomes a gravel forest road, and leaves the forest. The route turns in a westward direction and follows a more or less straight country road between agricultural fields.

From the highland plateau you have wide views over the fields and can already see the steeple of the next church in Autigny. You pass by farms and some houses, among others the typical wooden Bernese houses with the small windows and protruding front roof. On a tarmac pavement you follow the road into the town. At km 19.0 you arrive at the St. Maurice Church of Autigny.

St. Maurice Church, Autigny (Eglise St-Maurice) **168**

- Route de Chénens 1, 1742 Autigny
- St. Maurice, St. Mary, St. James the Greater
- On a table right of the main entrance
- The church was first mentioned in 1228. This first church was destroyed in the village fire of 1545. It was rebuilt in 1555, and after it was nearly in ruins, rebuilt again in a neoclassical style in 1830-31. The front porch was added during the renovations in 1980-86.
- The arched wall between the chancel and nave has an unusual petrol color. The stained-glass windows of the chancel are dedicated to the Virgin Mary. They are beautiful; made in an Art Nouveau style by Cingria in 1934. One window in the nave has a stained-glass medallion depicting St. James with a pilgrim stick and a scallop. Equally artful is the marble high-altar with gold finish and the painting depicting St. Maurice, dating from 1831. Fourteen stations depict the crucifixion way of Christ.

The route continues south of the church and follows a road forking to the left (*Ruelle de la Forge*). Between grasslands the road curves down the hill to the Glâne River valley. On your right you pass by a wooden stable, keeping cows with bells that sound like a carillon. The route turns left and on a small road bridge crosses the Glâne River.

After some houses the road gradually ascends a hill. When you look ahead you see the treetops of a patch of forest form a tunnel. The road leads straight to Chavannes-sous-Orsonnens. After a left turn you arrive at the St. John the Baptist Chapel at km 21.7.

169 St. John the Baptist Chapel, Chavannes-sous-Orsonnens (Chapelle St-Jean-Baptiste)

- Chemin de la Chapelle 8, 1694 Chavannes-sous-Orsonnens
- St. John the Baptist, St. Andrew, St. James the Lesser
- Attached to the wooden post of the staircase, left of the entrance
- The chapel was built in the 16th century, enlarged in 1769, and renovated in 1950.
- For such a small chapel it is richly decorated with marble side-altars and two wall frescos, depicting St. Andrew and St. James the Lesser. Because of the low ceiling of the chancel, there is no high-altar structure.

From the chapel the route continues south on the *Route des Granges* and forks to the left onto a concrete country road. The road is sloping up ever so slightly and you can see far ahead. The landscape is beautiful: small towns on top of the hills, with their church towers trying to draw your attention. Up ahead in the distance you see a church on a hilltop. It is the church of the town Massonnens. Though it seems like the route is going there, it is not. The hill lies on the other side of the Neirigue River, which the route does not cross.

For 3 km the route follows a slowly curving country road parallel to the curving Neirigue River. Not that you can see the river; it is on your left (east) behind the tree line that follows the bank of the river. Along the way you pass by three metal road crosses. Another church tower on a hilltop appears in front of you in the distance. This is the church of Berlens. Again, it seems like the route is going there; but, also in this case, it is not.

After the 3 km the route makes a sharp right (west), away from the Neirigue River (which you never saw). On a tarmac road the route gradually descends. A white gravel path along the road, next to cornfields, is for the pedestrians; but there is no traffic on this country road and it is safe to walk on the street. You pass by a white city sign of Romont, but the town is nowhere to be seen as a patch of forest blocks that view. After curving around the forest, the view of Romont appears.

The town is built on a hill, with a church tower and several medieval watchtowers sticking out over the roofs of the other buildings. It is still 4 km to Romont, but even from a distance the town on the hill looks impressive. This must have been even more so for medieval pilgrims approaching the town.

The fortified town Romont is at an elevation of around 770 meters, towering nearly 100 meters above the agricultural landscapes in the region. As the tarmac road continues down the hill, the view disappears. The route forks left onto a gravel/grass tractor path behind a farm. You pass by several meadows with horses (instead of the usual cows). In the 19th century Romont was the main center for horse trading in French-speaking Switzerland, which is why you still see the horse farms around here. On your right, partly behind trees, you see thirteen large green-colored oil silos.

The tarmac country road between meadows and corn fields approaches the hill of Romont, until the route makes a sudden right. On a gravel farm road the path curves to the right (north), around a line of trees. You may not have noticed it, but you crossed the Glâne River, which is reduced to a very small stream (more like a ditch) at this location. Behind the trees you arrive at the Cistercian Convent Church of Romont at km 28.6.

170 Cistercian Convent Church, Romont (Eglise de Couvent Cistercienne)

- Route de Fribourg 2, 1680 Romont
- On a shelf in a recess, left of the entrance
- The church was built over a period of 80 years, from 1268 until 1346, as part of the Cistercian convent (see below). The long construction period was caused by the difficulties in generating enough own funding as a result of their physical labor, though local benefactors provided some financial support.

  The church and convent fell into disrepair repeatedly. In 1726 a fire destroyed much of the convent and church. Its reconstruction took six years until 1732. By 1873 the buildings were almost in ruins again; a remodeling shortened the church by about two-thirds, while the freed-up space was used to expand the dorm, library, and other areas. A complete renovation was undertaken in 1990-96, restoring the church to its original full length. The short steeple on the roof dates from 1993.
- The original choir stalls, dating from 1618, were placed in front of the chancel during the renovations in 1990-96. The stained-glass windows, created by British artist Brian Clarke, were renewed in a modern appearance consistent with Cistercian tradition in 1996. Remnants of frescos decorate the walls and arch to the chancel. They were either whitewashed or faded away over the centuries, and could only be partly recovered during the renovations in the 1990s.

  The nuns did not have money to acquire luscious interior decorations; the interior of the church is simple and austere, without the usual marble high- and side-altars.

Cistercian Convent of the Daughters of God, Romont (Abbaye Cistercienne de la Fille-Dieu) 25

Route de Fribourg 2, 1680 Romont

Cistercian Order, Trappist Order

The French name of the convent 'la Fille-Dieu' translates as 'the Daughters of God'. The convent was established by three religious women from the region in 1268. The three religious women started their community under the Cistercian and Benedict Rule. It was not until 1346 that their church was consecrated and the religious women were incorporated into the Cistercian Order (formally establishing their convent).

Following the Cistercian interpretation of the Rule of St. Benedict, they had to live from physical labor. Their income was generated by working on the lands that they had received as a donation at the inception of their community. Lack of money shaped the history of their convent; life was hard at the small convent (with up to 20 sisters) as a result of the minimum income that could be generated from their physical labor. Because of their minimal income it took nearly 80 years for the church to be completed in 1346. Their convent has the same building and reconstruction history as the church described above.

The convent prospered in the 14th century, went through hard economic times in the 15th century, and stabilized in the 16th and 17th centuries. The wall surrounding the property was built in 1613. In the 18th century a fire destroyed much of the convent. Reconstruction significantly changed the layout of the convent and church.

Like most other Swiss monasteries and convents, during the time of the Helvetic Republic (1798-1803) it was closed. During the 19th century the buildings gradually dilapidated again, and significant renovations were undertaken in 1872-73.

Since 1906 nuns of the Order of the Trappists have been managing the convent. Renovations in 1990-96, for its 650-year celebration, restored much of the original appearance.

The convent is well-known for the four types of mustard they sell in their shop, made by the 15 nuns still living there today. The nuns also bake the Hosts for the surrounding parishes.

The route leaves the convent on its former driveway, passes by a stone road cross, and arrives at main road nr. 155. You already crossed this road in Villars-sur-Glâne, at the beginning of the stage. The route turns left, crosses the roundabout, and follows a curving road (*Chemin du Brit*) up the hill to the medieval town. In town you see a church on your right. At km 29.6 you arrive at the Church of the former Capuchin Monastery of Romont.

171 **Capuchin Monastery Church, Romont** (Eglise des Capucins)

- Grand-Rue 48, 1680 Romont
- St. Francis of Assisi, St. Anthony of Padua, St. Donatus
- The (same) pilgrim stamp can be obtained at five places in Romont: at this church (on a table behind the last left pew); at the Our Lady of the Assumption Church (see below); at the Tourist Office; at the stained-glass museum; and at the Hotel du Lion d'Or.
- The church was built with the donations and volunteer work of local laborers in 1745-46. It took 20 years for the friars to collect enough donations to be able to finance the construction of their church. Consistent with their vows to poverty, the church has an austere interior without the opulence displayed by some of the other Orders. Notice the absence of a transept and side-chapels, and the low steeple on the roof above the chancel.
- The frescos depict Franciscan Saints. The stained-glass windows date from 1882. In the style of the other Capuchin churches along the Swiss Way of St. James, they have three equally large dark-wooden altars with large paintings. The left side-altar depicts St. Francis of Assisi, the high-altar depicts the transfiguration of Jesus (where He becomes radiant in glory on a mountain), and the right side-altar depicts St. Anthony of Padua.

  The Order abandoned the monastery and church in 1979; nowadays the church is mostly used for concerts and cultural events.
- Have a closer look at the vitrine below the high-altar. Behind the elaborate wood carvings lies a beautifully decorated skeleton. Notice the precious stones and pearls sewed on the ribs, and the skull with its teeth. It is a catacomb saint dedicated to Saint Donatus. People came to pray at his relics for protection against bad weather and eye diseases.

Former Capuchin Monastery, Romont (Couvent de Capucins) 26

Grand-Rue 48, 1680 Romont

Minim Order, Capuchin Order

The mendicant Order of Minims established a monastery in Romont as part of the Counter-Reformation in 1620. They were the first ones that were within the city walls (all other Orders were outside the walls). In 1725 the Minim Order fell out of the Lausanne Bishop's grace and was expelled from Romont.

In 1727 the Capuchin Order moved into their monastery, after the Bishop of Lausanne had approved their arrival in Romont, and had given them the task to set up a Collegium. They were the only monastery within the city walls that existed for a long period of time, because they maintained a Latin school.

Like most other Swiss monasteries, during the time of the Helvetic Republic (1798-1803) it was closed. The Capuchins led the Latin boarding school until 1859, after which it changed to a secondary school with boarding facilities. The City took over the school in 1974. They relocated it to the southern part of Romont, outside the city walls at the foot of the hill, and closed the dormitories.

Five years later (1979) the Order closed their monastery. Lack of novices, over-ageing of the remaining monks, and failing monastic tasks in the city of Romont led to its closure. Their buildings were given a different use, while the church became a place for cultural events.

From the church walk down the *Rue des Moines* (east). On the left (northeast) corner of the street you pass by a residence that houses the town's only protestant chapel. You can recognize the house by the short steeple with bell on its roof. Right of the house, down a few steps in the garden, a big white sign directs to the entrance of the chapel. A few more steps down and you arrive at the reformed Chapel of Romont (at km 29.7).

172 **Reformed Chapel, Romont** (Chapelle Le bon Berger)

Rue des Moines 70, 1680 Romont

The chapel housed within the parish office from the beginning of the 19th century, when the protestant parish settled in Romont. The building was owned by the Cistercian Convent of the Fille-Dieu from 1539 and was reconstructed in the 18th century. The chapel is named 'the good Shepherd'.

From the outside you cannot see that there is a chapel; it is a normal room that was turned into a place of worship. The chapel has a modern interior with a small organ in the corner. You cannot access the chapel outside service hours.

Romont was an important station for travelers, pilgrims, and traders between Lausanne and Fribourg, and therefore occupied many inns (24 in 1775). The hotel Saint-Georges was already open for business from the 16th century. From 1275 the town already had a small hospital for pilgrims, which also housed a pilgrim inn. The reason for the many inns was that each monastic Order maintained its own inn to accommodate the pilgrims that belonged to their Order. The Benedictines, Augustinians, Cistercians, Dominicans, Franciscans, and Norbertines all maintained an inn. As part of the Counter-Reformation several convents maintained a presence for a relatively short time between 1591 and 1664. The Order of St. Clare, the Ursulines, and the Order of Annunciation came and went. The only convent that is still present is the Cistercian convent of the Daughters of God at the foot of the hill (established in 1268).

Beware that after the Capuchin church the next few Way of St. James signposts briefly change to the blue square signs with the yellow *Chemin de St-Jacques* text (like in Fribourg). In the *Rue des Montes* the route takes a narrow alley (*Ruelle Saint-Jacques*) on the right (the blue sign is fixed on the wall). After 30 meters you arrive at the square of St. James (*Place Saint-Jacques*), with the post office and a car parking. The square is named after a former inn called St-Jacques (St. James), to commemorate the many pilgrims that have visited Romont since the 13th century. Nowadays the post office houses in the building of the former inn. The next blue sign is on the concrete wall of the bus stop. In a niche below the sign is a small statue representing St. James.

The route continues up the hill in the *Rue des Béguines*. You walk on a street along the backside of the next church. After a left turn you arrive at the front door of the Our Lady of the Assumption Church of Romont at km 30.0.

Our Lady of the Assumption Church, Romont (Eglise Notre-Dame de l'Assomption) 173

- Rue de l'Eglise 81, 1680 Romont
- Our Lady
- On the shelves with the information brochures, in a niche left of the entrance in the nave. The stamp is the same as for the Capuchin church.
- The church was built over a period of 31 years, from 1240 until 1271. It was the first church in Romont.

The church was nearly destroyed by a village fire in 1434, caused by plundering Bernese troops during the Burgundy War; only the right side of the nave was still standing. The church was rebuilt in a flamboyant Gothic style and enlarged 22 years later (1456) on the same site. As you can see, the church has a lower front portal attached to the nave. This front portal was added in the 14th century, and rebuilt after the fire of 1434.

Since 1515 the church has been called a Collegiate church due to its size, though it never housed a Collegiate.

During the Reformation and the Bernese invasion of the lands of Vaud (of which Romont was part), the catholic House of Savoy abandoned the town Romont. The City turned to Fribourg for protection (against the Bernese invaders) to remain catholic and became part of catholic Canton Fribourg; this prevented the destruction of the church's treasures.

In 1970 the parish council started a step-by-step renovation project to restore the church to its original state.

The Gothic interior is one of the most beautiful along the Way of St. James through Switzerland. Admire the stained-glass windows from the 19th century and Art Nouveau from the early 20th century.

The artistically wood-carved choir stalls, depicting the Apostles and Prophets, date from 1464. The side-chapel in the front portal contains a sculpture representing the Virgin Mary and baby Jesus from the end of the 13th century.

The frescos in the front portal and several of the stained-glass windows were made by Cingria (1938) and Yoki (1968), who also worked on the artistic interior decorations of other churches in the region.

Many pieces of medieval religious art can be seen in the church. Take your time to admire them. The automatically playing church music and Gregorian chanting create a special atmosphere.

The Our Lady of the Assumption Church is the last church of stage 14. There is, however, more to see: the Romont castle, the stained-glass museum, and the medieval city fortifications. About 100 meters south of the church you arrive at the castle's entrance.

The town Romont (its name derived from the Latin name of 'round mount') was founded after the Lord of Billens sold a forested hill to Duke Peter II of Savoy in 1240. He established the town as a strategic stronghold on the northern parts of his lands. He built the fortified **Castle of Romont** in 1240-60, while the church was constructed at the same time (1240-1271). Fortified city walls and four towers made up the outer defenses of the city. The castle served as a final defense in case the city walls would be breached. It was built in the typical Savoy square shape with a 38-meter-high living tower (called dungeon).

The purpose of the castle was to expand the influence of the House of Savoy to the north and to control the trade route between Fribourg and Lausanne. During the 13th to 16th centuries it was an important basis for military campaigns to expand and defend the territory of the House of Savoy. Together with Lausanne, Romont became one of the most important and largest cities in the region (nowadays it has around 5'300 inhabitants).

When the Bernese troops conquered the House of Savoy in the lands of Vaud in 1536 (as part of the expansion of their Reformation), the Savoy abandoned the city of Romont. The City turned to Fribourg for protection (against the Bernese invaders) to remain catholic, and became part of Canton Fribourg.

By 1579 the castle was in disrepair and in ruins. It was rebuilt by Fribourg in 1591, which housed their Sheriff (with administrative and judicial functions) at the castle until the French invasion in 1798. Between 1843 and 1865 five fires destroyed much of the medieval city of Romont. Most of the Gothic buildings were replaced by more modern architecture during those times.

The castle had a moat, of which only the southern section is left; nowadays used as a driveway to the back of the building. The wooden drawbridge over the moat was replaced by a stone bridge.

Immediately behind the striped doors, on the left, you see a large wooden 4.5-meter-diameter wheel dating from the 18th century. Prisoners used to walk inside the wheel to operate a lifting mechanism for the buckets in the well. The well, from the 16th century, is 40 meters deep. Along the left wall is an elevated walkway. When you go up the steep stone steps you have a nice view over the town Romont. Several more steps lead up to a door in the tower. However, this door is locked; you cannot get into the tower.

The right side of the compound also had a fortified wall with an elevated walkway, until the Sheriffs of Fribourg built their residences there in 1591 (when the castle was rebuilt). These buildings have been housing the regional governmental offices from 1848. A giant tree provides shade in the courtyard.

47

The **Stained-Glass Museum** was co-founded by the artist Yoki and has been housing in the castle since 1981. It is called the Vitromuseum, the Swiss Museum of Stained Glass and Glass Arts. The museum has a unique collection of stained-glass, exhibiting their development from the middle ages, the Renaissance, and Art Nouveau, to contemporary creations. Next to the museum is the Vitrocenter, which researches the history, conservation, and technology of stained-glass and glass painting.

The museum displays permanent and temporary exhibitions. You can admire the work of famous artists (including Yoki, Cingria, Giacometti, Chagall, and Linda McCartney) as well as a medieval stained-glass window from the Cathedral of Chartres (France). The museum claims to have the world's largest and most refined collection in terms of quality, quantity, and variety, with a selection of 300 works on permanent display. As it is housed in the old castle buildings, you also get to see the castle's interior space.

Given the many stained-glass windows that you are seeing along the Swiss Way of St. James, it is a must to visit this museum. It will significantly expand your knowledge and understanding of stained-glass windows, and the making thereof.

The museum is closed on Mondays. On the other six days of the week it is open 10:00-13:00 and 14:00-18:00, from April until October (in winter it closes at 17:00). A ticket costs CHF 12.

It is possible you may not make it before closing time. After all, stage 14 is 30 km and passes by 16 churches and chapels, some with very interesting histories, unique artwork, and spiritual atmospheres inviting for sightseeing, prayers, and reflection. But it is no problem at all if you do not make it before closing time. The next stage 15 is very short, only 17 km and six churches, which will not take you more than five hours. This should give you ample time to rest and visit the museum the next morning when it opens at 10:00. A late morning start of stage 15 will still leave enough time for a relaxing hike that day.

At the Tourist Information Office, opposite the entrance of the castle, you can obtain a brochure of a 1hr:30min sightseeing tour around the historic city of Romont (if you are on time; alternatively, you can download it prior to your trip from their website, *www.romontregion.ch*).

The sightseeing tour passes by the castle, two churches, the watchtowers, fortified walls, and some other historical places and buildings. Since you already visited the two churches and the castle, the required time is probably around 20 minutes.

The **medieval City Fortifications** used to have four towers, but three city-gate towers were demolished to make room for urbanization in 1842-54. They were restored in accordance with their original plans during the 20th century.

The tower south of the castle is called the Boyer Tower and is still the original one. This tower was initially built as part of the city's fortification (1250-60), but was turned into a residential tower that had its own fortified walls around it. At its base the walls are 3.10-meter thick; its height is 38 meters. Its name Boyer is derived from the person who bought the tower in the 19th century, with the plan to disassemble it and use its bricks for another construction. The City prevented this by buying the tower from this person; the name remained. At the foot of the tower is a children's playground. Continue the historical tour to visit the fortifications and the other three towers.

From the ending point

The Our Lady Church/Castle of Romont is the ending point of stage 14, directly on the signposted route nr. 4.
In case you are a day-hiker, you need to walk 600 meters (downhill) to the train station (to the west).

In case you are a thru-hiker and spend the night in Romont, there are several accommodations including a pilgrim inn. Low priced pilgrim accommodations can be found at the Cistercian Convent (see monastery nr. 25; tel. 026 651 90 10; office@fille-dieu.ch; www.fille-dieu.ch) and at private residences. There are two hotels in Romont. Check out www.jakobsweg.ch or www.viajacobi4.ch for the accommodation possibilities.

You can also visit the Tourist Information Office (Rue du Château 112, 1680 Romont; tel. 026 651 90 55; www.romontregion.ch; info@romontregion.ch) and have them help you with the accommodations. However, they are only open from Monday until Friday between 10:00-12:00 and 14:00-16:00. It is therefore likely that you arrive when they are closed. If so, you can also go to the ticket counter of the Vitromuseum, which functions as a back-up.

The next Stage

Stage 15 guides you from the Glâne District highland plateau to the Broye River valley and Moudon. The route is short and mostly downhill or flat. Read the next chapter to find out what that entails.

Stage 15: Romont to Moudon 17 km

The Way to the Broye River Valley

Route stats

	Distance in km	Time in hrs:min
Signposted route nr. 4	14.9	3:00
Churches/chapels	1.7	1:00
Points of interest		0:30
Rest/lunch		0:30
Stage 15	16.6	5:00

In case you hike this stage as a daytrip, you need to add 600 meters in Romont and 400 meters in Moudon (from and to the train stations).

Ascent/descent/total	+221 / -462 / 683 altitude meters
Lowest/highest altitude	496 / 811 meters
Pathway/condition	easy / easy
Churches/chapels	Billens, Hennens, Lovatens, Curtilles, Moudon (2)
Monasteries	none
Points of interest	Former Castle of Billens, Former Castle of the Bishopric Kingdom of Lausanne Curtilles, Historic Upper City Moudon

Route summary

Stage 15 continues in catholic **Canton Fribourg** and enters protestant **Canton Vaud** at km 6.0. The following stages 16, 17, and 18 are all in protestant Canton Vaud.

Stage 15 guides you from the Glâne District highland plateau to the Broye River valley and Moudon.

The stage is short and mostly downhill or flat. In case you were not able to visit the stained-glass museum in Romont at the end of stage 14, you should have enough time to do so before starting your pilgrimage of stage 15. When you spent the night in Romont you can have a relaxed beginning of the day, visit the museum, and then a late morning start of stage 15. Alternatively, an early start in Romont will give you a free afternoon in Moudon. Use this short stage for resting in the morning or afternoon. The following three stages towards Geneva are long and offer little time for rest.

Stage 15 starts with a descent from the hill of Romont in a southward direction. The route stays on the Glâne District highland plateau and gradually ascends to the highest point of the day of 811 meters at km 6. This hilltop provides panoramic views towards the east (back) to Romont and the Alps, and towards the west (front) to Lucens and the Jura mountain range. The hilltop marks the change from Canton Fribourg to Canton Vaud. The route descends steeply to the Broye River valley over 4 km. Agricultural fields dominate the landscape. Upon reaching the valley at km 10, the route converges with the Way of St. James coming from Payerne. The last 7 km the route is in the valley, of which 4 km on the embankment next to the Broye River.

Getting to the starting point

Today's starting point in Romont is at the Our Lady of the Assumption Church (*Eglise Notre-Dame de l'Assomption*), directly on the signposted route nr. 4. In case you hike stage 15 as a daytrip, you need to walk 600 meters (uphill) from the Romont train station to the church. Turn left from the station and then right into the *Avenue Gérard Clerc*. At the *Grand-Rue* take another right to follow a small footpath to the front of the church.

Route Map and Profile

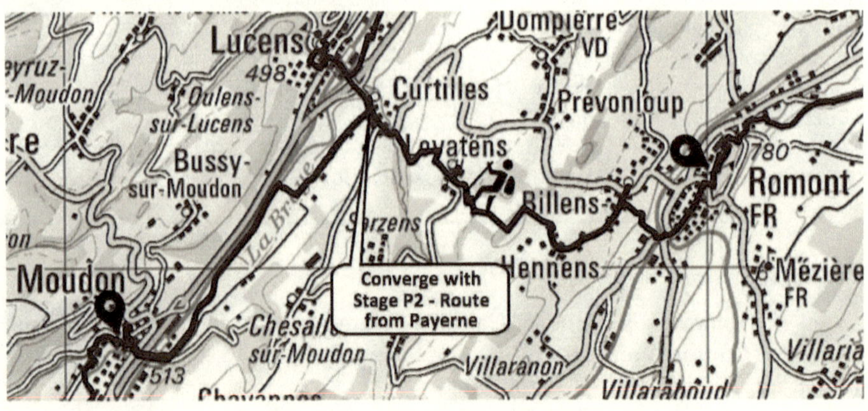

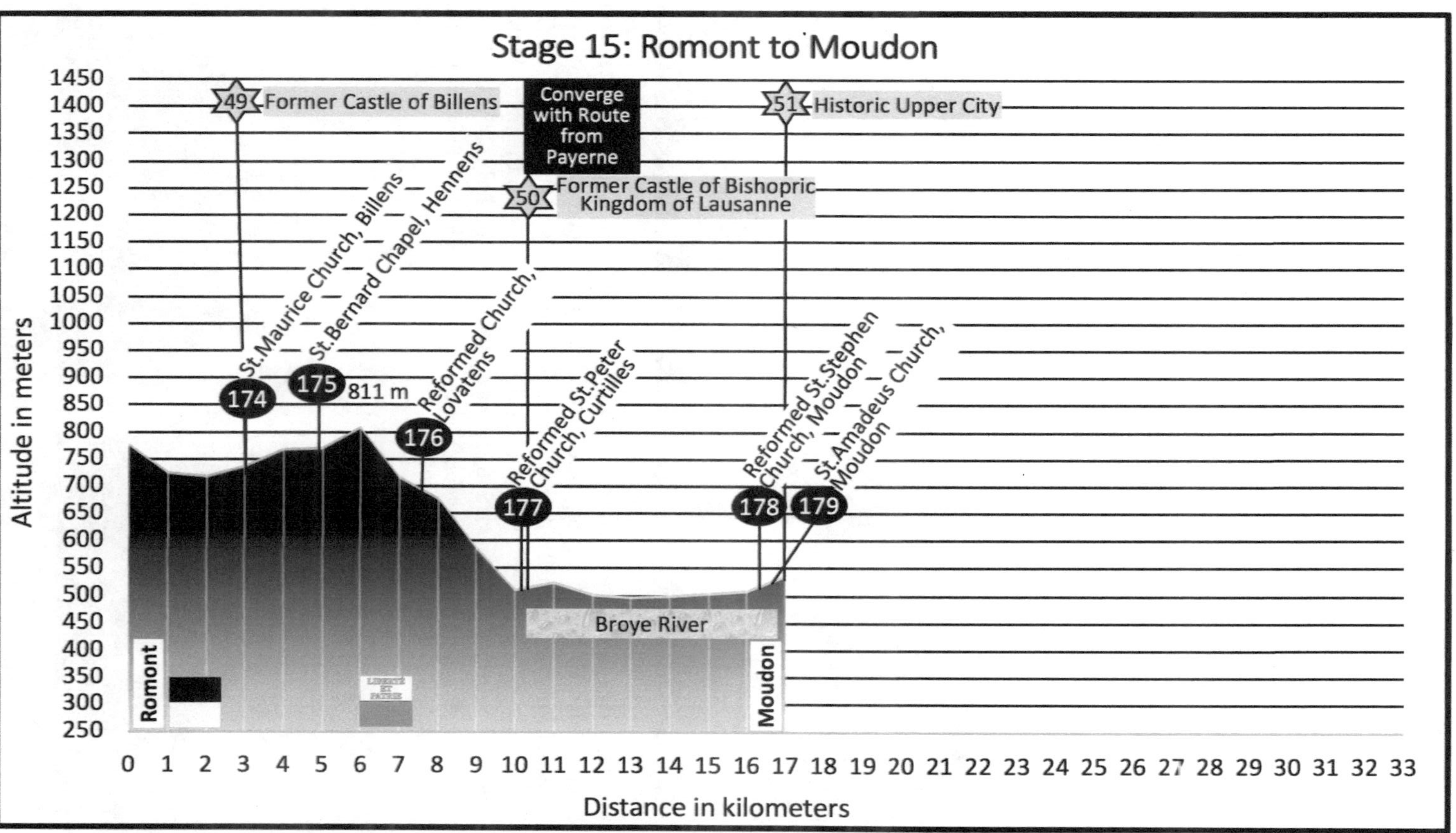
Stage 15: Romont to Moudon
49 Former Castle of Billens
Converge with Route from Payerne
50 Former Castle of Bishopric Kingdom of Lausanne
51 Historic Upper City
174 St.Maurice Church, Billens
175 St.Bernard Chapel, Hennens
811 m
176 Reformed Church, Lovatens
177 Reformed St.Peter Church, Curtilles
178 Reformed St.Stephen Church, Moudon
179 St.Amadeus Church, Moudon
Romont
Broye River
Moudon
Altitude in meters
1450 1400 1350 1300 1250 1200 1150 1100 1050 1000 950 900 850 800 750 700 650 600 550 500 450 400 350 300 250
Distance in kilometers
0 1 2 3 4 5 6 7 8 9 10 11 12 13 14 15 16 17 18 19 20 21 22 23 24 25 26 27 28 29 30 31 32 33

Hiking the Route

From the church follow the signposted route downhill to the south (*Rue du Château*). You pass by the Boyer Tower and the cemetery, and after 500 meters the route makes a sharp right following the *Chemin de la Côte* street. At the roundabout you are at the foot of the hill. The signpost nr. 4 directs to the left and, after a few meters along road nr. 156, forks to the right and continues through a residential area (*Route d'Arruffens*). The route crosses another roundabout and goes over the railway tracks. To the south you see a large Nespresso factory; one of their three Swiss production facilities. In a westward direction the Way of St. James turns onto a gravel road between two large warehouses at an industrial site. The gravel road turns right, passes through a small patch of forest, and crosses a small stream (*La Glaney*). On your left you see a small area, like a garden, cordoned off by conifers. It looks like a handmade shrine for the Virgin Mary (*Notre-Dame*). According to some signs the garden-like chapel seems to already have been there since 1971.

The path curves to the west and continues across fields to the village Billens. You are surrounded by gently sloping landscapes with agricultural fields, dotted with patches of forest and small villages. Through a sunken lane you arrive at a T-crossing. The signpost directs left, but the church of Billens is to the right. At this location you need to briefly deviate from the signposted route and follow the *Route d'Hennens* to the right for 260 meters. You cross road nr. 156 and arrive at the St. Maurice Church of Billens (at km 3.0).

St. Maurice Church, Billens (Eglise St-Maurice) 174

Route de l'Eglise 4, 1681 Billens-Hennens

St. Maurice

The church must have already existed in the 13th century or earlier; the first time it was mentioned in documents was in 1228. Not much is known of its early history. The church was expanded in 1659. At the beginning of the 19th century the church fell into disrepair and was demolished in 1826. It took five years to reconstruct it (1827-31), during which time the services were held in the small St. Bernard chapel in Hennens (see below). Since 1831 multiple renovations were undertaken; the latest interior renovation was completed in 2018.

The two baroque side-altars (1843) and the high-altar (1846) form a unity with the same design, marble, and style of paintings. The high-altar painting depicts St. Maurice in military outfit. Nothing from before 1826 is present at the church.

The Lords of Billens owned extensive lands in the region from the 12th to 15th centuries and sold the forested hill in the east to the House of Savoy, who founded the town Romont. The Lords of Billens were vassals of the Bishop of Lausanne, and later of the House of Savoy. The Lords had their **Castle of Billens** in town, but it was destroyed in battles after 1718. A new castle was built north of the town, which became the property of Canton Fribourg in 1864. The Canton turned it into a hospital, which it still is today.

From the St. Maurice church walk back the same 260 meters to the signposted route and continue straight (south) on the *Route d'Hennens.* You need to walk on the tarmac road, but there is little traffic. You pass by a road cross between two young trees and have good views of the Alps towards the east. The road gradually ascends and curves to the right (west) between the few houses that make up the settlement Hennens. The St. Bernard Chapel is left of the road (at km 4.9).

St. Bernard Chapel, Hennens (Chapelle St-Bernard) 175

Route de la Chapelle 15, 1681 Billens-Hennens

St. Bernard

The chapel was built based on donations by a local landowner of Hennens in 1653 (inscription above the door). Look at its location in the courtyard of the farm; this is another farm chapel. The small chapel was renovated in 1870 and several times during the 20th century.

The interior is tidy and neat, and two carpets give it a warm appearance. The altar painting depicts St. Bernard.

Continuing westward you pass by a road cross between old trees, after which the trail becomes steeper. A concrete farm road crosses through agricultural fields up a hill. The route makes a sharp left and continues south on a grass trail. At km 6.0 you reach the highest point of stage 15 at 811 meters. It is a hilltop with a cellular tower, surrounded by agricultural fields. The hilltop provides great views. To the east you see the medieval town Romont on a hill; behind it the jagged peaks of the Alps.

To the west you see the town Lucens in a valley, with the medieval Castle of Lucens (*Château de Lucens*) and its round tower and white mansion, and at the horizon the forested Jura mountain range (stretching from north to south along the Swiss/French border, with altitudes up to 1'600 meters).

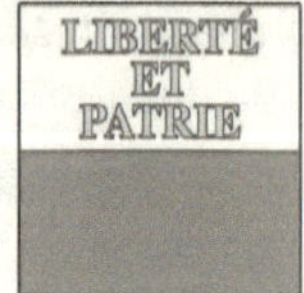

At the location of the cellular tower you cross from Canton Fribourg into **Canton Vaud**, where nearly all churches are protestant. The route turns right (west) and steeply descends on a concrete farm road. Over 1.3 km the route descends into Lovatens. The panorama in front of you (Lucens and the Jura mountains) continues to dominate the views.

On the outskirts of Lovatens you pass by a free-standing dead tree and see a small steepled bell tower. When you get to the main street (*Route de la Forneyre*), you notice that it is not a church; it is the town hall. At this location the signposted route continues straight (west).

If you want to visit the church in Lovatens you need to briefly leave the signposted route. Turn right (north) on the town's road and follow the *Route de la Forneyre* for 190 meters, until you arrive at the reformed Church of Lovatens (at km 7.5).

Reformed Church, Lovatens (Eglise Reformée) **176**

Route de la Forneyre 9, 1682 Lovatens

St. Sylvester

Lovatens did not have a church during the middle ages, because of the small size of the village and its close vicinity to the church of Curtilles (see below). A first chapel, dedicated to St. Sylvester, stood on the eastern side of the village. It was first mentioned in 1429, but was demolished to make room for a school in 1840.

Between 1840 and 1914 the Protestants had to attend services at the church in Curtilles. From 1914 periodic services were held in the local school.

The present protestant church was built in 1960-61, about 120 years after the previous chapel was demolished.

Typical for a protestant church, the interior decorations are limited. The light wooden interior gives it a warm atmosphere. The rows of windows to the left and right, behind the wooden lamellae, let in the light. The high ceiling creates space. The doors of the church are only open during services.

From the church walk back the same 190 meters to the signposted route and turn right (west). Over 1.7 km the route descends steeply on concrete farm roads between agricultural fields and along the edge of a patch of forest.

The town Lucens and its castle come closer, and you get a better view of the valley they are in. The route zigzags down the hill and follows the edge of a forest, until you reach road nr. 156 again. The road (*Route de Romont*) curves to the right and gradually descends into Curtilles. After 600 meters the nr. 4 signpost directs to the left (south), into the *Chemin de Prévondens*.

Converge with Route from Payerne

The alternative Way of St. James route from Payerne converges with stage 15 of the route that you are currently on. At this location of convergence, however, do not yet follow the route left (south). Curtilles has an 11th century church that is worth a visit, with a small detour away from the signposted route of stage 15. Go straight (west) for 190 meters (direction Lucens) and you arrive at the reformed St. Peter Church of Curtilles (at km 10.1). A St. James scallop is hanging on the wooden front door.

Reformed St. Peter Church, Curtilles (Eglise St-Pierre) 177

Route de Lucens 24, 1521 Curtilles

St. Peter

Reformed churches usually do not have a name reference to a catholic Saint, but because of the long history of this church, its former name of St. Peter has been maintained. It is believed that the first church, dedicated to St. Peter, was built in connection with a Castle of the Bishopric Kingdom of Lausanne (see below) around 1050. The Bishops' castle, church, and the whole village were destroyed by a great fire in 1230.

After the fire the church was immediately rebuilt in 1231. Its chancel was demolished and completely reconstructed in 1510, while the nave from 1231 was extended in 1525.

As Bernese troops occupied the lands of Vaud during the Reformation in 1536, all catholic statues, altars, and paintings were removed and the walls were whitewashed (covering all frescos).

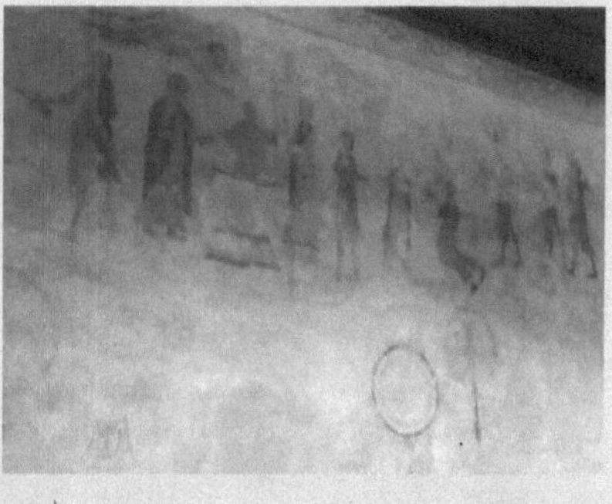

The wall frescos could partly be restored during renovations in 1919. The scenes are rather difficult to make out. These frescos date from around 1360 (the nave being older than the chancel). The church has an unusual arcaded bell tower over the entrance. The two bells date from 1568 and 12th-14th century; the latter is believed to be one of the oldest in Canton Vaud. The stained-glass windows date from 1491 and 1517.

A pilgrim guestbook (but no stamp) lies on a table behind the last pew on the right. In case the church is closed (which should not be the case), a key can be obtained at the Café Fédéral, situated at the corner of the route convergence.

The **former Castle of the Bishopric Kingdom of Lausanne** in Curtilles was the summer residence of the Bishops of Lausanne (which is about 30 km south of Curtilles) already since the 10th century. The castle was destroyed by a great fire in 1230. The Bishops' castle of Curtilles was never rebuilt (and nothings remains of it nowadays), because the Bishops transferred their summer residence to their summer Castle of Lucens, on the other side of the Broye valley in 1230 (see point of interest nr. P-7 of stage P2, on page 110).

From the church walk back the same 190 meters to the signposted route nr. 4 at the corner of the *Chemin de Prévondens*. Turn right (south) and follow the street for 1.8 km. Though you are already in the Broye River valley, the road ascends a little and then descends parallel to the Broye River. You walk on a tarmac country road, but there is hardly any traffic. Along the way you get a better (though still distant) view of the former Bishop's Castle of Lucens.

After 1.8 km you arrive at a T-crossing where you turn right (west). For 300 meters a concrete road leads you to the Broye River. The route continues left (south) on a gravel path on the low embankment next to the river for 3.2 km. Trees align the path. On the other side of the river train tracks and road nr. 1 connect to Moudon.

Hiking is easy; the path is straight and flat, and in the shade of the trees. You pass by the industrial area of Moudon and reach the road bridge over the river, making a right turn into the *Route de Siviriez*. You enter the town Moudon and 400 meters later cross the railway tracks (the train station is on the right). After passing underneath the elevated road nr. 1, you arrive at the reformed St. Stephen Church of Moudon (at km 16.2).

Reformed St. Stephen Church, Moudon (Eglise St-Etienne) 178

Place Saint-Etienne, 1510 Moudon

St. Stephen

At the pilgrim side-chapel, together with a guestbook. A list of pilgrim accommodations may help with finding the right place to spend the night.

The church was first mentioned in official documents in 1134. The interior still looks the same as it did at the end of the 13th century: a Gothic church with a high vaulted ceiling, undecorated pillars and arches, and two side-naves. It has the appearance of a small cathedral.

The church was built as part of the fortified walls around the historic city between 1281 and 1330. The thick-walled bell tower used to be a fortified watchtower (probably built around 1190), functioning as a city-gate and as protection for the medieval town that was built on the hill behind it. The gate in the base of the tower is open for pedestrians and the gun loopholes are still visible. The tower was heightened and its bell-housing was built around 1435. The nave was heightened, new choir stalls were placed (1502), and frescos were painted between 1495 and 1511.

Many treasures were destroyed when the interior was transformed to protestant worship during the Reformation in 1536. All catholic statues, 18 side-altars, and paintings were removed, and the walls were whitewashed (covering all frescos). The organ of 1764 is the oldest in Canton Vaud (after organs were destroyed and forbidden from 1536). Many renovations were undertaken during the 19th and 20th centuries.

Most of the stained-glass windows date from the 1950s, the oldest one from 1927. Take in the many scenes depicted in the glass. The tall and colorful windows of the chancel were made by Charles Clément and date from 1951-53.

Have a closer look at the choir stalls. Not only are they more than 500 years old, but each of the 24 stalls has a woodcarving of an apostle or prophet. Can you find the carving depicting St. James the Greater?

Since 2009 the church has a side-chapel dedicated to the Way of St. James pilgrims (*la Chapelle des pèlerins du chemin de St-Jacques*). A walking cane and stone scallop beside a 3-meter partitioning of vertical timbers indicate the location (left of entrance). Behind the partitioning 10 wooden chairs around a small altar invite for prayers and reflection.

There is a second church to visit in Moudon. This is the town's catholic church which is, however, not on the signposted route. It requires a detour to the north of about 400 meters. From the St. Stephen church walk north and turn left into the *Rue du Poyet*, turn right and then left again into the *Rue Saint-Bernard*, and after the restaurant Le Marronnnier turn diagonally right and walk up the hill along the *Route de Gréchon*. On your right is the catholic St. Amadeus Church (at km 16.6).

179 St. Amadeus Church, Moudon (Eglise St-Amédée)

- Avenue de Bussy 1, 1510 Moudon
- St. Amadeus
- After the Reformation of 1536 the first catholic services were held in a private residence in Moudon in 1886. Until 1895 the Catholics of Moudon were part of the parish of Promasens (Canton Fribourg, about 10 km southeast of Moudon). The Catholics built their own church in 1889-90, which was renovated in 1965.
- The church has an austere interior.

It is easiest to walk back to St. Stephen church and continue from there. Moudon may be a small town (nowadays around 6'000 inhabitants), but it has a long history. Moudon already was a settlement at the time of the Romans. Since the earliest of days, the town was at crossroads of trade and travel routes from Italy to Burgundy (east to west) and from Geneva to Bern (south to north). On the Way of St. James, you will be hiking on the old routes south, from Moudon to Geneva, in stages 16 to 19.

The **Historic Upper City of Moudon** was built on the hill between the Broye and Mérine rivers, protected against flooding and with two natural barriers against invaders. A first church was built in the upper town during the first centuries; any remains are long gone.

A castle was built in the historic town and the city expanded beyond the small hill around 1127. The St. Stephen church stands on the site of a watchtower and wall fortifications. For several centuries Moudon developed as a regional stronghold with a castle and houses in the fortified upper town; the city was the regional capital of the lands of Vaud. Before 1228 the Order of the Knights of St John established their hospice (to care for the poor, ill, and pilgrims), and after 1231 the monks of the Great St. Bernard hospice followed.

The city's decline set in during the 15th century, when the territorial turmoil among the Savoy, Burgundy, and Swiss Confederation increased; during the Burgundy Wars (1474-77) the town was plundered and damaged several times. Until 1536 the town was under the rule of the House of Savoy, after which it came under the government of Bern and was forced to accept the Reformation. Bern took away most privileges and shifted the center of power to Lucens, where their Sheriff (with administrative and judicial functions) resided at the former Castle of the Bishopric Kingdom of Lausanne.

During the 16th and 17th centuries the castle, church, and houses in the upper town fell into disrepair: the nave of the 11th century Our Lady Church was demolished and turned into a cemetery; its bell tower was demolished to make room for a street; the old buildings were replaced by new patrician mansions (*Châteaux*) with gardens. Finally, the remaining old fortifications and city-gates were demolished making room for urbanization in 1830-50.

Nowadays the historic upper town is made up of 16th/17th century mansions and buildings; unfortunately, the medieval buildings have completely vanished – save for the St. Stephen church and its fortified tower at the foot of the hill. The historic upper town has been designated Swiss Cultural Heritage since 1945. A signposted circular tour allows you to discover 26 historical buildings, with information panels offering brief explanations.

The Tourist Information Office near the old town (Grand-Rue 27; www.moudon-tourisme.ch), 250 meters west of the St. Stephen church, also provides the pilgrim stamp (the same as in the St. Stephen church). Tourist Information offers a pilgrim snack pack that includes a drink and a snack, which can be obtained free of charge at the *Kiosque du Pont, Place de d'Hôtel-de-Ville 2*, 150 meters west of the St. Stephen church at the bridge over the Broye River.

From the ending point

The St. Stephen Church is the ending point of stage 15 (directly on the signposted route nr. 4), after having returned from the St. Amadeus church or from the Historic Upper City tour.

In case you are a day-hiker, you need to walk 400 meters to the Moudon train station.

In case you are a thru-hiker and spend the night in Moudon, there are enough accommodation possibilities, though no pilgrim inn. Comparable low-priced alternatives and hotels are available. Check out www.jakobsweg.ch or www.viajacobi4.ch for the accommodation possibilities. The Tourist Information Office (Moudon Région Tourisme; Grand-Rue 27, 1510 Moudon; tel. 021 905 88 66; www.moudon-tourisme.ch; office.tourisme@moudon.ch), 250 meters west of the St. Stephen church, can also assist with finding the appropriate accommodations.

The next Stage

Stage 16 guides you from the Broye River valley over the Jorat mountain to the Lake Geneva basin. Read the chapter of stage 16 (starting on page 117) to find out what that entails.

FRIBOURG TO MOUDON: VIA PAYERNE

Stage P1: Fribourg to Payerne 25 km

The Way to the 1'050-year-old Cluniac Monastery

Route stats

	Distance in km	*Time in hrs:min*
Signposted route nr. 4	22.6	4:40
Churches/chapels	2.7	2:10
Points of interest		0.50
Rest/lunch		1:00
Stage P1	25.3	8:40

In case you hike this stage as a daytrip, you need to add 600 meters in Fribourg and 300 meters in Payerne (from and to the train stations).

Ascent/descent/total	+430/ -587 / 1'017 altitude meters
Lowest/highest altitude	449 / 722 meters
Pathway/condition	easy / moderate
Churches/chapels	Fribourg (4), Noréaz, Montagny, Tours, Corcelles-près-Payerne, Payerne (3)
Monasteries	Ursuline Convent Fribourg, Former Cluniac Monastery Payerne
Points of interest	St. James Cross, Site of Neolithic Pile Houses, Site of Roman Aqueduct, Ruins Castle of Montagny, Medieval City Fortifications, Cluniac Abbey Church Museum

Route summary

Stage P1 continues in catholic **Canton Fribourg** and enters protestant **Canton Vaud** at km 20. The following stages P2, 16, 17, and 18 are all in protestant Canton Vaud. From Fribourg until Geneva/French border (stages P1, P2, and 16 to 20) you are in the French-speaking part of Switzerland (Romandie).

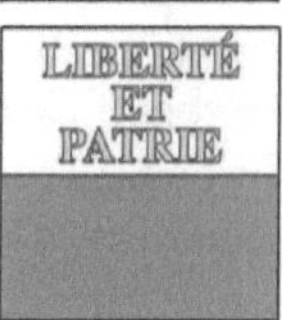

Stage P1 guides you from the Fribourg highland plateau over forested hills and along the Arbogne River in a long descent to the Broye River valley and Payerne.

The first 4 km stage P1 follows the same route as stage 14 (from Fribourg to Romont), while passing by four churches in the city of Fribourg. From Villar-sur-Glâne (where the routes split) a major part of the hiking is through forests, following the historical road between Fribourg and Payerne. From km 4 to 9 the route descends to the Sonnaz River valley, from where it climbs out on a steep forest trail over 1 km. At km 10 it reaches the highest point of the day at 722 meters. From there the route gradually descends towards the Broye River valley. After Noréaz the route turns back into a forest. The Way of St. James closely follows the Arbogne River for about 7 km, of which 2.5 km through the Berley forest. After reaching the Broye River valley, the route turns south. In the valley the town Corcelles is the northern agglomeration of Payerne, and the last 3.5 km are hiked in an urban environment.

At km 20 the route changes from catholic Canton Fribourg to protestant Canton Vaud. Eleven churches and six points of interest are passed by, the highlight being the 1'050-year-old former Cluniac monastery church in Payerne at the end of stage P1. It is Switzerland's largest and best maintained Cluniac Romanesque church. The church is undergoing a four-year renovation project and is accessible again from May 2020.

Getting to the starting point

Today's starting point in Fribourg is at the Ursuline Convent Church, directly on the signposted route nr. 4.

In case you hike stage 14 as a daytrip, you need to walk 600 meters from the train station to the church. From the train station turn left towards the old city and follow the *Avenue de la Gare*, straight across the roundabout, through the pedestrian street of *Rue de Romont*, across the square *Place Georges Python*, and into the pedestrian street of *Rue de Lausanne*, where you arrive at the church (house nr. 92, on the right). The route goes back to the train station exactly the same way you came. While hiking these 600 meters you pass by the Ursuline convent church and the reformed church. In case you have already visited these two churches, you could also save the 600 meters to and 600 meters from these churches, and just start at the train station.

Alternative: making Villars-sur-Glâne the starting point of a day-hike

In case you are a day-hiker and pilgrimage stage P1 as a daytrip, you can also consider to start at the route-split in the forest of Villars-sur-Glâne. In this case you skip the first 4 km through Fribourg. The easiest way to get there is to take bus nr. 11 (direction *Rosé, Gare*) from bus-platform 11 at the bus station of Fribourg. This bus leaves every 3 and 33 minutes past the hour and takes 6 minutes to the *Villars-sur-Glâne, Belle Croix* bus stop. This 6th bus stop is in front of the Fribourg-South Shopping Center (*Centre Fribourg-Sud*). From the bus stop walk east along the *Route de Moncor* to the double roundabout (with the shopping center on your right). At the roundabouts keep right and walk along the *Route de Cormanon* to the entrance of the forest with the St. James Cross (about 400 meters from the bus stop). Enter the forest and after 250 meters you arrive at the route split of stage P1.

Route Map and Profile

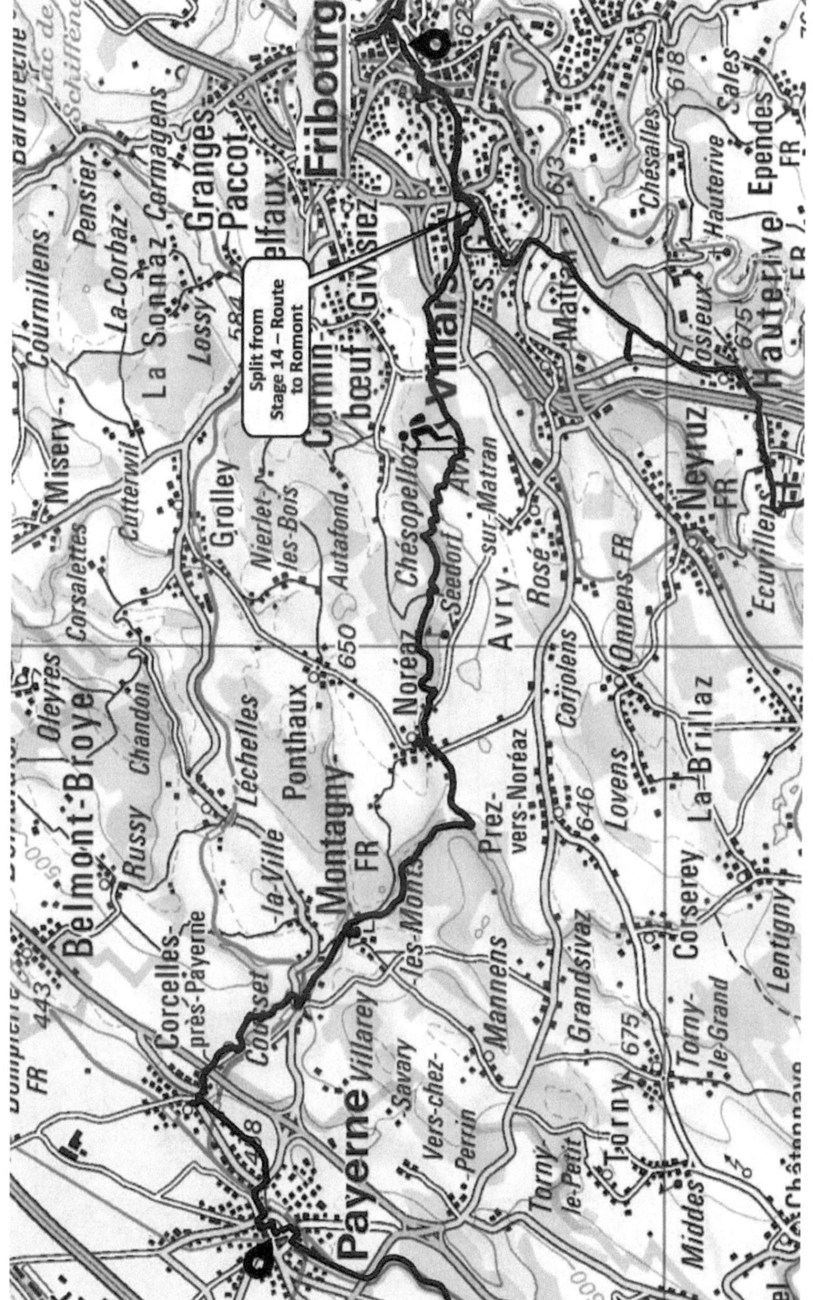

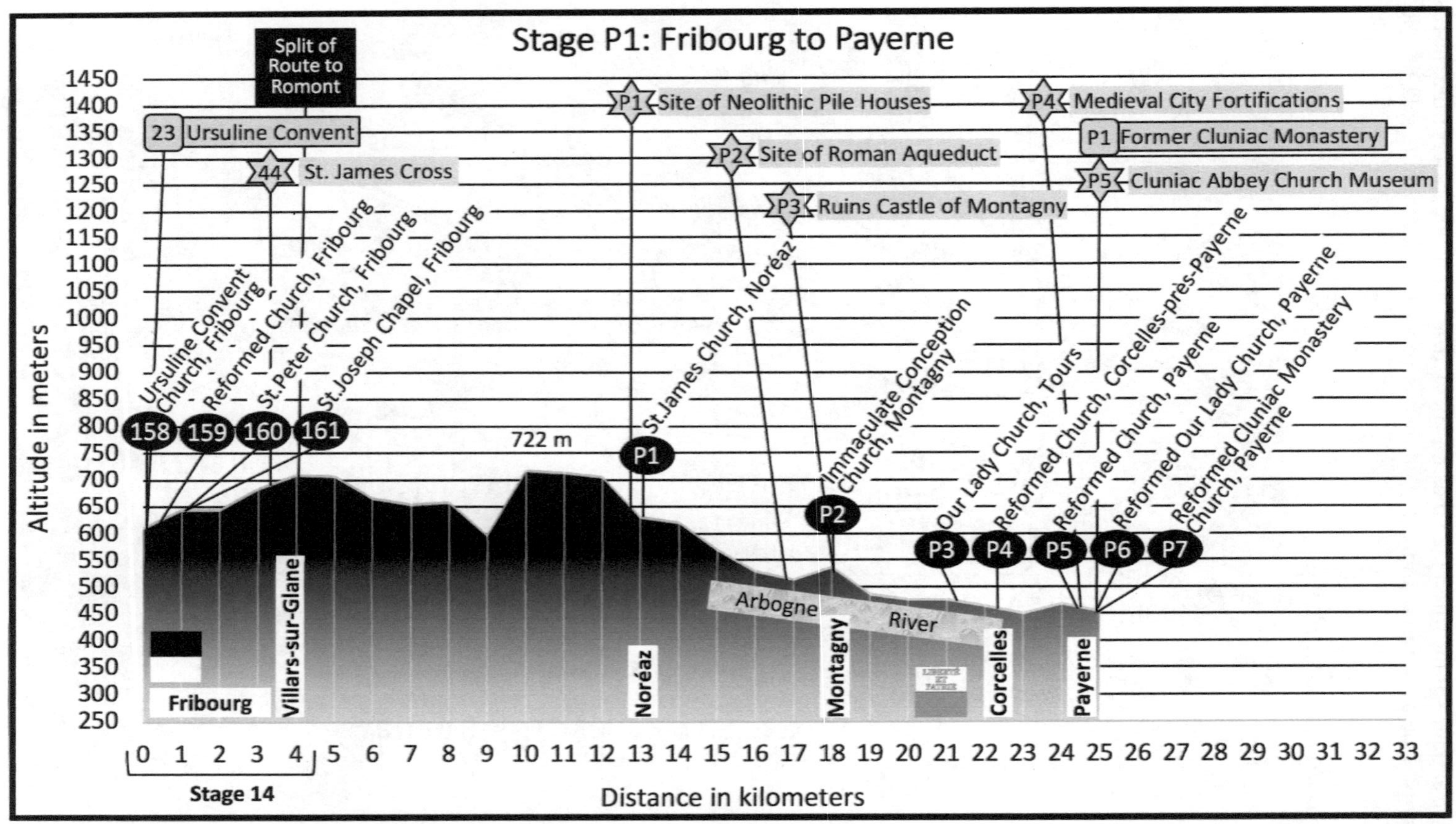
Stage P1: Fribourg to Payerne
Split of Route to Romont
23 Ursuline Convent
44 St. James Cross
P1 Site of Neolithic Pile Houses
P2 Site of Roman Aqueduct
P3 Ruins Castle of Montagny
P4 Medieval City Fortifications
P1 Former Cluniac Monastery
P5 Cluniac Abbey Church Museum
Altitude in meters
1450
1400
1350
1300
1250
1200
1150
1100
1050
1000
950
900
850
800
750
700
650
600
550
500
450
400
350
300
250
Ursuline Convent Church, Fribourg
Reformed Church, Fribourg
St.Peter Church, Fribourg
St.Joseph Chapel, Fribourg
158
159
160
161
722 m
St.James Church, Noréaz
P1
Immaculate Conception Church, Montagny
P2
Our Lady Church, Tours
Reformed Church, Corcelles-près-Payerne
Reformed Church, Payerne
Reformed Our Lady Church, Payerne
Reformed Cluniac Monastery Church, Payerne
P3
P4
P5
P6
P7
Arbogne River
Fribourg
Villars-sur-Glane
Noréaz
Montagny
Corcelles
Payerne
0 1 2 3 4 5 6 7 8 9 10 11 12 13 14 15 16 17 18 19 20 21 22 23 24 25 26 27 28 29 30 31 32 33
Stage 14
Distance in kilometers

Hiking the Route from Fribourg to Villars-sur-Glâne (km 0-4)

The 3.6 km route from Fribourg to Villars-sur-Glâne overlaps with the beginning of stage 14 (Fribourg to Romont). For the detailed description of the route, churches, and points of interest, please read pages 33 to 37 of stage 14.

The route enters the forest in a westward direction and passes by contemporary indicators of the Way of St. James. A small statue representing the Virgin Mary with baby Jesus is in a small encasing fixed to a tree with scallops hanging under it. After a gradual ascent you reach a high point of 712 meters in the forest, where the Way of St. James splits, 3.6 km from the start in Fribourg.

The split occurs at a forest called ***Bois de Belle Croix*** (Forest of the Beautiful Cross), which refers to the St. James Cross that you passed at the entrance of the forest. The forest lies in a western suburb of Fribourg called Villars-sur-Glâne.

One green/blue nr. 4 sign directs straight, whereas another one directs to the right. The one directing straight continues to Romont (stages 14). The one forking to the right is the alternative route via Payerne to Moudon. In this stage P1 you continue to Payerne.

Hiking the Route from Villars-sur-Glâne to Payerne (km 4-25)

At the route split take the gravel path on the right, slightly going up the hill. You pass by a playground with a small fountain and exit the forest on the northern side, west of the Fribourg-South Shopping Center. At the roundabout the route turns left on the *Route de Moncor* and behind the Tamoil gas station goes into the *Bois de Moncor* forest.

The gradually descending route trails through the forest on a broad concrete road for 1.2 km. About halfway you cross over Highway A12. For 900 meters the route follows a tarmac road between agricultural fields, through a small settlement called *Village Suisse* (Swiss village), and turns into the next forest (*Bois de Verdilloud*). The route follows a broad gravel path.

The path narrows to a small forest trail as it descends towards a stream valley. A fallen pine tree blocks the way and you must find a way around it. After 1.7 km the route exits the *Bois de Verdilloud* and briefly continues on a grass trail through an agricultural field. On a narrow forest trail through the next small patch of forest, the route descends more steeply to the Sonnaz stream valley.

You pass by a small statue representing Mary in a housing nailed to a tree. A dried bouquet of flowers is hanging below it. Temporary steps help with the descent towards the small stream. You cross the stream on a small bridge made of eroded wooden boards.

The route continues through the forest and steeply ascends out of the valley (at an area south of *Montossy*) over 600 meters. At the start of this ascent the forest trail is blocked by several uprooted trees. Because of the inclination of the hill there is no way around them: you need to climb over and between branches of several fallen trees that lie at a steep gradient down the slope of the hill. Based on the markings made by previous hikers they seem to have been lying there for a long time. It is difficult to pass them, and even dangerous when the trees are wet and the earth muddy and slippery. Be careful.

Steps of short round wooden beams (to keep the path from eroding during rain) lead steeply up to the edge of the forest. After grassland the route turns back into a forest on a narrow dirt trail through low overhanging bushes. This area was completely deforested several years ago. Nowadays the trees and bushes are still young (low) and only slowly reclaiming their territory from the earth to the sky.

After the steep climb on the narrow trail, the route arrives at a broad gravel road in the Piamont forest (*Forêt du Piamont*) and follows the nr. 4 sign in a western direction (left). Here you reach the highest point of the day at 722 meters. After 400 meters you pass by a hut with a BBQ place.

The route stays in the forest for the next 3 km, of which the first 2 km are more or less flat. Hiking is easy on broad gravel paths, with only a few short sections on forest dirt trails. At this location a large part of the forest is also recovering from deforestation; trees and ground vegetation are still low, providing no shade.

The last kilometer in the forest descends on a tarmac road. As the tree line opens up you can see the town Noréaz in the distance. The white church tower with its steeple serves as a beacon. At the horizon you see the Jura mountain range.

P-1

When you look southeast you see a small lake, called *Lac de Seedorf* (Lake of the village at the lake). In 2009 archaeological excavations discovered that the area had a small village built on poles at the western side of the lake, dating back to around 3850 BC. This **site of Neolithic Pile Houses** received the UNESCO World Heritage designation. The municipality did not erect any commemorative structure to highlight this area to visitors; there is nothing to see. The site remains hidden below the grasslands (the lake was higher 6'000 years ago). Most hikers pass by without being aware of these unique findings.

Northeast of the lake, at the foot of the forested hill that you crossed over, is the **Chateau of Seedorf** that originates from the 12th century (the chateau is not visible from the signposted route nr. 4).

After 500 meters through the outskirts of Noréaz you arrive at a road crossing. The nr. 4 signpost directs to the left. A short detour up the hill to the right is needed to visit the catholic St. James Church at km 13.0.

P-1 St. James Church, Noréaz (Eglise Saint-Jacques)

Route de l'Eglise, 1757 Noréaz

St. James the Greater

A small chapel dedicated to St. James the Greater stood on the site of the tall stone cross at the entrance of the cemetery since 1635. It served pilgrims on the Way of St. James from Fribourg to Payerne. The coat-of-arms of the municipality includes three scallops and St. James is the patron Saint of Noréaz.

It took the small community 35 years (from 1922) to organize the financing of the new church (through donations, lotteries, fairs, legacies, and so forth). The church was built in 1957-58.

The only relic left of the old chapel is a wooden crucifix, which is located in a small chapel in the base of the bell tower (not accessible).

The stained-glass windows and fresco (that include depictions of St. James) at the back wall of the chancel were made by the famous artist Yoki (painter and stained-glass maker from Romont). These artworks date from 1966.

At the front facade of the church, above the entrance portal, you see 'the anchor of hope' that was also designed by Yoki.

From the church walk the same 200 meters down the hill to go back to the road crossing with the route nr. 4 sign. The route continues on a gradually descending tarmac road in a southwestern direction and passes by several farms. Tarmac becomes gravel, which becomes a stony dirt path descending to the Arbogne River valley.

Walking on the trail becomes uncomfortable because of the loose rocks and uneven earth. The beautiful scenery while descending toward the valley, along meadows and tree lines, makes up for the difficult underground.

The last few meters towards the Arbogne River are on a concrete path into the forest (right of the fenced yard of a building called Moulin-de-Préz). For the next 7.3 km the Way of St. James closely follows the river, until reaching Corcelles-près-Payerne.

The first 2 km are through the Berley forest, where the gradually descending route regularly switches between the left and right side of the river. The path is broad and the gravel underground is easy to walk on. It is the historical road between Fribourg and Payerne. Large parts of the Berley forest were deforested in the recent past. Most of the trees are still young and not so high. The forest opens and a meadow provides a long-stretched open space.

P-2

You pass by an orange information sign mentioning the site of a **Roman Aqueduct** from the end of 1st century.

During the first centuries AD the Broye River valley was occupied by the Romans, who established a large town in Avenches inhabiting 20'000 people (about 12 km northeast of Payerne; then called Aventicum). At that time Aventicum was the capital of Roman Switzerland.

The Romans were great engineers and built multiple water pipelines (encased in stone tunnels with a height of 70-80 centimeters) that provided the Roman city with fresh water for their consumption, fountains, baths, and craftsmen. The aqueduct running through the Berley forest received its water from the source at Moulin-de-Préz (the building where you entered the forest).

Remains of this aqueduct, with an original length of about 15 km, were discovered in 1844. Look at the grounds behind and around the orange information sign: can you discover these remains?

The route stays on the edge of the forest along the long-stretched meadow and gradually ascends. On a hill in front of you, you see the ruins of a medieval castle tower. On your right you pass by a sawmill with the strong scent of freshly cut wood. For many centuries the mill used the waterpower of the river to run its saws. Piles of timber lie on iron rails along the road.

The signposted route nr. 4 passes by the elevated castle ruins without directing towards them. The small hill to the left not only contains these ruins, but also a church (which is not visible from the road). At this location you need to briefly leave the signposted route to go to the Immaculate Conception Church of Montagny. Take the road on your left up the hill and you arrive at the church at km 17.7.

Immaculate Conception Church, Montagny (Eglise de l'Immaculée Conception) **P-2**

Route du Pavement 1, 1774 Montagny

St. Mary, Four Evangelists

The catholic church was built in two different centuries, more than 400 years apart. The chancel dates from the 12th century and used to be the castle's chapel. This chapel, dedicated to the Virgin Mary, was a subsidiary chapel of the Church of Tours (see below). It was burned down by Fribourg troops in 1447, restored in 1449, and reconstructed in 1589. The nave was attached to the old chancel in 1760 and renovated in 1926.

Notice the architectural differences between the chancel and the nave: the nave is light and modern, the chancel is Gothic and dark; the nave has small tiles on the floor, the chancel big sandstones; the nave has a curved wooden ceiling, the chancel is vaulted and decorated with frescos.

The oldest frescos in the chancel and the stone statue representing the Virgin Mary (left side-altar) date from the 15th-16th centuries. The Four Evangelists are depicted on the ceiling of the chancel, while frescos of several Saints decorate its walls.

Behind the church, on a small hill, are the ruins of the Castle of Montagny.

P-3

The **Castle of Montagny** was first built as a small square residential tower by the Lords of Montagny around 1107-46 (under protection of the House of Zähringen). The castle was used to control important roads through part of the Broye River valley and the main trade and travel route from Fribourg to Payerne. After the Zähringen family lineage died out in 1218, the Lords of Montagny became subjected to the House of Savoy, when the region became part of the Savoy lands of Vaud in 1265.

Under the House of Savoy, the fortified castle and village were expanded in 1269-1309 and formed a regional stronghold. The village (Montagny-la-Ville, to the north) used to be of considerable size during the 13th and 14th centuries. From 1335 until 1478 the City of Fribourg regularly tried to conquer the area of Montagny and its castle from the House of Savoy (since they controlled the trade routes to the Broye valley). In 1447 they burned down the village and church, and occupied the castle. The Bernese conquered the area a year later, and forced Fribourg to pay damages and rebuild the church, village, and castle. When the Fribourg troops returned from the Battle of Morat (1476), they plundered the town and castle again, and set them on fire.

In 1478 Fribourg purchased the area and housed a regional governor at the castle. The castle was destroyed by a fire in 1504. It was rebuilt by 1510, and the castle was the residence of regional governors of Fribourg, until the French invasion in 1798. The castle, already in poor condition, was abandoned and the building fell into ruins after the French occupancy ended several years later. Its stones were used for construction in the village and hardly anything was left by 1820. The castle used to have a moat, drawbridge, and fortified walls, of which nothing is left.

Nowadays only two ruins can be seen: the remains of the round watchtower (on the small hill) and the remains of part of the wall (at the foot of the small hill). These remains were renovated and a spiral metal staircase was setup inside the tower in 1996. Already during the middle ages, the access door to the watchtower was at an elevated position of nine meters, only accessible by a retractable ladder.

The outer staircase leads to the small opening in the thick wall (its access gate in the wall is not always open). From the viewing platform at the top of the inner staircase (30 meters high) you have a wonderful view over the Arbogne River valley (from where you came) in the east and the Jura mountain range in the west.

The former courtyard area is nowadays used for picnics and BBQing. On top of the wall at the base of the tower is a modern artwork of the long necks of a two-headed metal dragon.

From the castle's ruins walk back down the hill to the signposted route nr. 4. The following 1 km you walk on a tarmac road in the river valley, until you arrive at the village Cousset. The signposted route turns right before Cousset's small train station, crosses its single track, and makes a left to go back to the Arbogne River.

On a tarmac road the route passes by Cousset's fire station, soccer field, school, and garbage disposal area.

The Way of St. James briefly follows a small path close to the Arbogne River and crosses the stream on a wooden bridge. This bridge marks the border between Canton Fribourg and Canton Vaud. You are entering protestant **Canton Vaud** at km 20.1. The route passes underneath high-voltage powerlines and crosses through agricultural lands on a concrete farm road for about 700 meters. The route arrives at a tarmac road and turns right. After 150 meters a signpost directs to the right to the Notre-Dame de Tours.

This church stands on a small hill and forms the smallest **enclave of Canton Fribourg**. In 1536 Bernese troops conquered this area and enforced the Reformation in all the churches. However, based on an agreement between Fribourg and Bern, the church and two houses on this hill remained part of catholic Canton Fribourg. So, you are back in Canton Fribourg for 100 meters.

An artistic stained-glass medallion at the foot of the stairs depicts a bright star that lights the way for a pilgrim. The wooden steps up the hill to the church are crooked and eroded. At the top of the stairs you arrive at the catholic Our Lady Church of Tours (at km 21.1).

Our Lady Church, Tours (Eglise Notre-Dame de Tours) P-3

Notre-Dame-de-Tours, 1562 Corcelles-près-Payerne

Our Lady

At the parish office, next to the church

The catholic church is on the site of predecessor churches dating back to the 6th century. The first church was expanded in the 9th/10th century and reconstructed at the beginning of the 12th century. In 1536 Bernese troops conquered the lands of Vaud (to which Tours belonged) and forced the Reformation. However, the church in Tours stayed catholic based on an agreement between Fribourg and Bern, enabling its continuation as a regional pilgrimage destination.

The present church was newly built in 1780 (with new baroque altars) and renovated in 1946.

The church was an important regional pilgrimage destination in the 15th century because of its Virgin Mary statue. This small 'golden rays' statue, dating from 1340, is at the top part of the high-altar. The ceiling fresco in the chancel dates from around the same time.

The legend of the golden Virgin Mary statue made it a place of pilgrimage. After a decision to demolish the chapel of Tours, the small statue was brought to the castle church in Montagny. However, the next day the statue was miraculously back in the chapel. Several more times the statue was brought to the church of Montagny, but each time it miraculously returned. Believing the miraculous return was a sign to not demolish the chapel of Tours, the decision was abandoned, and the chapel and its small statue became a place of regional pilgrimage.

The three baroque altars form a unity in design. Wood carvings representing eight Saints are left and right of the high-altar. One of them is St. James.

From the church the route continues right of the buildings and on the southern side of agricultural fields the path re-enters **Canton Vaud**. The trail descends back to the road, turns right, and passes over road nr. 1. At the fork in the road the route turns left into the *Route du Chêne* and turns left into the *Rue des Moulins* a little later.

The signposted route passes through the outskirts of Corcelles-près-Payerne, without passing by the town's church. This church requires a 300-meter detour. Instead of going left into the *Rue des Moulins*, continue straight. At the town's center turn left, cross the Arbogne River, and turn right into the *Rue du Collège* a little later. You can already see the Romanesque church tower on your right. At km 22.2 you arrive at the reformed Church of Corcelles-près-Payerne.

P-4 Reformed Church, Corcelles-près-Payerne (Eglise Reformée)

- Rue vers l'Eglise, 1562 Corcelles-près-Payerne
- St. Nicholas
- The church contains elements of a small chapel, dedicated to St. Nicholas, that was first mentioned as a subsidiary of the Cluniac monastery of Payerne in 1148. The Romanesque elements probably date from the 11th century: the chancel (in the base of the tower) and tower are the oldest parts of the church. They have

clear Romanesque features such as the three narrow windows in the chancel, and the decorative Lombard arches at the tower and the outer wall of the chancel (walk around the church to see this). The wooden construction and spire on top of the tower date from later centuries.

The church already accepted the Reformation in 1531, before the Bernese invaded the lands of Vaud in 1536. At that time all catholic interior decorations were removed, while the walls were whitewashed to cover the catholic frescos. The left and right transepts were added at the beginning of the 20th century.

The stained-glass windows were created by Yoki (left of the nave) and Eric de Saussure (right of the nave) in the 20th century. The church has a typical protestant interior.

To go back to the signposted route nr. 4, walk to the main road and turn right. About 100 meters later, at the gas station, turn left into the *Chemin du Sansui.* About 200 meters later you cross the railway track (the small Corcelles railway station is to your right), and you are back on the signposted route. The following 1.3 km the route continues on the *Chemin du Sansui* past residential areas with luxurious houses (right) and agricultural fields and a golf course (left).

At the end of the road the route turns right and goes straight over the roundabout. You pass underneath the train tracks north of the Payerne train station and on the other side turn left onto the *Route de la Grosse Pierre.* You pass by a large car park (in front of Payerne's track and soccer fields) and walk on a broad pedestrian promenade towards Payerne's city center.

On your left you pass by a large Coop supermarket. At the roundabout the signposted route goes left and curves to the right towards the Payerne train station.

The signposted route nr. 4 does not pass by the key tourist attraction of Payerne, its 1'050-year-old Cluniac monastery church (instead it passes by the train station).

To end stage P2 in Payerne, you need to leave the signposted route to visit a church, remnants of medieval city walls, and the final two churches and the former Cluniac monastery (none of these are along the signposted route nr. 4). Thus, instead of walking left to the train station, turn right at the roundabout into the *Avenue du Général-Jomini* and after 100 meters you arrive at the German reformed Church of Payerne at km 24.7.

P-5 Reformed Church, Payerne (Deutschsprachige Reformierte Kirche)

Avenue du Général-Jomini 20, 1530 Payerne

The reformed church was built by the German-speaking protestant parish of the Broye valley and Payerne region in 1898. Bernese officials, traders, and craftsmen settled after the Reformation and gradually expanded the community of German-speaking Protestants.

A German-speaking priest already held services in Payerne since 1759, but it took 139 years until they were able to finance the construction of their own church. The parish office at the back was built 54 years later than the church (1952).

The small church has a typical protestant interior.

The doors to the church are generally locked. However, you can gain access by asking at the parish office/community center at the back of the building. Nowadays the church is also frequently used for concerts.

Take the street (*Rue derrière la Tour*) that is opposite the entrance of the church in a westward direction. Behind the carpark you see the only remnants of Payerne's medieval city fortifications.

P-4

Payerne's remaining **medieval City Fortifications** consist of a tower and a short section of wall from 1395. The Barraud Tower is the only one of several towers left standing, together with a part of the fortified city wall. Most of Payerne's medieval city fortifications and towers were demolished to make room for the increasing urbanization in the 1830s-40s. During medieval times the town was an important station along the main route from Lausanne to Bern.

Payerne housed several cigar manufacturers until the 1960s; around town several tobacco plantations existed. Nowadays Payerne has around 10'000 inhabitants and contains one of the major Swiss military air force bases (*Aérodrome Militaire*). Their facilities, including a museum, are about 3 km northwest of the city. The broad and flat plains of the Broye valley provide an excellent, mountain-free, take-off and landing strip for the military jets. For this reason, the **Payerne Airbase** is also the home base of the **Solar Impulse**, Bertrand Piccard's experimental solar-powered aircraft.

At the end of the carpark turn left into the *Route du Chemin Neuf*, cross the *Grand'Rue*, and continue on the *Rue du Temple* to arrive at the reformed Our Lady Church of Payerne at km 25.0.

Reformed Our Lady Church, Payerne (Eglise Reformée Notre-Dame) **P-6**

Place du Marché, 1530 Payerne

Our Lady, St. Marius

The church is on the site of a small chapel, dedicated to Our Lady, consecrated by Bishop Marius of Lausanne in 587. In 1228 the chapel was mentioned as the parish chapel of the Cluniac monastery that was west of the church. The monastery's church was reserved for the monks, whereas the chapel was used by the population of medieval Payerne.

The small chapel was replaced by the current church, of which the chancel and tower were built in 1290-1312 and the nave in 1335. Notice how the church only has a northern bell tower; the southern tower was never finished. Nearly 200 years later, 1505-17, the nave and its windows were enlarged and heightened (from the outside you can clearly see the elevated roof of the center nave).

During the Reformation in 1533 all its catholic interior decorations were destroyed while the walls were whitewashed to cover all frescos. Because the Cluniac monastery church was secularized, the Our Lady church became the parish church of the Protestants from 1533.

In 1625-51 new stained-glass windows were installed in the nave, the wall frescos around the windows were painted, and the northern portal was built. On the outside you can clearly see that two other northern entrances were bricked-up. Major renovations were undertaken in the 1930s and 1990s.

The church has a typical protestant interior. The present stained-glass windows date from 1974-79.

West of the church you arrive at the reformed Church of the former Cluniac Monastery of Payerne (at km 25.3).

P-7 Reformed Cluniac Monastery Church, Payerne (Eglise Abbaye Clunisienne)

Place du Marché, 1530 Payerne

Our Lady

At the Tourist Information Office (inside the *Café du Marché*) at the square west of the church

The church is on the site of a former Roman villa from the 4th century. This villa was the rural residence of a wealthy Roman family from Aventicum. A first church, dedicated to Our Lady (*Notre-Dame*), was built in 950-60 and enlarged as a Cluniac church after 965. This church was again enlarged and received most of its present-day appearance (new nave) in 1070-80. The Gothic tower with the four small round towers in the corners was built a bit later. The abbey and its church, being the earliest large constructions in Payerne, triggered the development of the medieval town Payerne around it.

The City of Payerne was an early adopter of the Reformation. In 1533 it already accepted the Reformation, three years before the Bernese invaded the lands of Vaud. At that time the church was stripped of all its catholic decorations and the walls were whitewashed. The Reformation resulted in the secularization of the church and Cluniac monastery.

To alter the church into a multipurpose building, two elevated floors were constructed that made it a three-level building in 1536. For more than 400 years the church was used for alternative purposes: in the 17th-18th centuries it was used as a granary, in the 19th century as military barracks, gymnastics hall, prison, and archive.

In 1817 the tomb of Queen Bertha was discovered in the abbey's church, after which the relics were ceremoniously transferred to the Our Lady church. After all, the Cluniac church was not serving as a church anymore (it housed a prison), and it was considered appropriate for the remains of the Queen to be reburied in the Our Lady church.

Despite the Reformation and all these changes and different uses, the typical Cluniac Romanesque features are still visible today: massive walls; few and tiny windows; the bell tower on top of the crossing of the transept; the clear footprint of a Latin cross; five apses to the east (of which the chancel in the middle is the largest); and Lombard bands (decorative blind arcades) on the outer walls of the apses. The church still has several frescos dating from around 1200 and 1454.

The church is considered one of Switzerland's most beautiful examples of Romanesque Cluniac architecture from the 11th century. The light sand color of the stones is unique. It is Switzerland's largest and best maintained Cluniac

Romanesque church. The church is undergoing a four-year renovation project and is therefore closed until May 2020. It will be open to the public again from end of spring 2020.

P-1 Former Cluniac Monastery, Payerne (Abbaye Clunisienne)

Place du Marché, 1530 Payerne

Cluniac Order

The Cluniac monastery was established around 965. The House of Burgundy was an important benefactor for the existence and rise of the monastery. The Queen of Burgundy, Bertha, is believed to have founded the first church and priory in 950-60. Queen Bertha was buried in this first church in 961. Her daughter (Empress Adelaide) placed this church and priory under the Cluniac mother Abbey in 965. Konrad II was crowned as the King of Burgundy in the abbey's church in 1033.

Over the centuries the monastery amassed significant lands and rights (15 churches, about 100 towns, and vineyards on the slopes near Lausanne at Lake Geneva), which made it one of the wealthiest monasteries in the region. Significant donations by the House of Burgundy made them wealthy quickly.

The local monks had always sought independence from the mother Abbey in Cluny. They went so far as to create falsified certificates of ownership and rights (including a fake testament of Queen Bertha), which caused conflicts with the mother abbey and the City of Payerne, while the prior of the monastery was also the earthly ruler of the town. Both the mother Abbey and the City aimed to reduce the influence of the monastery. Because of mismanagement the monastery nearly went bankrupt in the 14th century.

By 1444 the monastery was independent from its mother Abbey, but under close supervision of the City of Payerne and the Bishop of Lausanne. By the early 16th century the influence of Bern and Fribourg had increased, against a weakening House of Savoy (who ruled the lands of Vaud). The City of Payerne was an early adopter of the Reformation, seizing any opportunity to be freed from the rule of the monastery. In 1533 it already accepted the Reformation; three years before the Bernese invaded the lands of Vaud. By 1536 the Bernese secularized the monastery, demolished most of the buildings, and seized most of their assets and lands. The remaining catholic monks found refuge in Fribourg.

The Bernese Sheriff had a new residence and offices built. Bernese governors resided at this residence for 262 years, from 1536 until 1798.

At the time of the French invasion (1798) and the Swiss Helvetic Republic (1798-1803) their residence stood empty. After the lands of Vaud became a Canton in 1803, the former residence of the Sheriff was renovated and subsequently housed Payerne's gymnasium school and governmental offices.

Through a narrow arched passage you can access the monastery's former inner courtyard with the old well. On the southern end of the courtyard is the former residence of the Sheriffs of Bern. Look at the red-cobblestoned lines in the courtyard; they mark the location of the former monastery walls.

All that is left of the monastery is its former eastern wing, now housing the **Abbey Church Museum**. Limited guided tours are organized to view the church and its museum while the renovation is ongoing. This will improve from May 2020, after completion of the renovation. A ticket costs CHF 7; open 10:00-12:00 and 14:00-18:00 during summer; closed on Mondays.

On the southern side of the square between the reformed Our Lady church and the former monastery you find the **old town hall** that was built after the Reformation, in 1572. Since 1964 it houses the Cantonal Court.

At the square next to the *Café du Marché* you find the **Banner-Carrier Fountain**, dating from 1542. It bears a large resemblance to the Banner-Carrier Fountain in Bern, both made by the same Fribourg artist Hans Gieng. This figure demonstrates the strong influence of Bern (who placed its Sheriffs in Payerne) over the City. Compared to the statue in Bern, it is rather eroded and pale.

From the ending point

The reformed Church of the former Cluniac Monastery in Payerne is the ending point of stage P1, about 300 meters aside the signposted route nr. 4.

In case you are a day-hiker, you need to walk about 300 meters to the Payerne train station (which is on the signposted route).

In case you are a thru-hiker and spend the night in Payerne, be aware that there are only two hotels (close to the Cluniac church) and a few low-cost accommodations at private residences. There is no pilgrim inn. Check out www.jakobsweg.ch or www.viajacobi4.ch for the accommodation possibilities in Payerne. You can also visit the Tourist Information Office opposite the church (Place du Marché 10; tel. 026 662 66 70; tourisme@estavayer-payerne.ch; www.estavayer-payerne.ch) and have them help you.

The next Stage

Stage P2 guides you along the Broye River in a southern direction to Moudon. Read the next chapter to find out what that entails.

Stage P2:
Payerne to Moudon
29 km

The Way along the Broye River Valley

Route stats

	Distance in km	*Time in hrs:min*
Signposted route nr. 4	23.5	4:40
Churches/chapels	5.6	2:10
Points of interest		0:30
Rest/lunch		1:00
Stage P2	29.1	8:20

In case you hike this stage as a daytrip, you can start the route at the Payerne train station, but need to add 400 meters in Moudon to go to the train station.

Ascent/descent/total	+253/ -173 / 426 altitude meters
Lowest/highest altitude	448 / 537 meters
Pathway/condition	easy / moderate
Churches/chapels	Payerne, Granges-près-Marnand (2), Henniez, Lucens (2), Curtilles, Moudon (2)
Monasteries	none
Points of interest	Henniez Mineral Springs, Former Castle of the Bishopric Kingdom of Lausanne (2), Sherlock Holmes Museum, Historic Upper City Moudon

Route summary

Stage P2 continues in protestant **Canton Vaud**.

Stage P2 guides you from Payerne along the Broye River in a southern direction to Moudon.

After 1 km through Payerne the route reaches the Broye River and follows the embankment next to the river for nearly the whole distance. Hiking is relaxed and easy, in absence of any hills or mountains, through beautiful nature with agricultural landscapes along the river. The Way of St. James follows the eastern (left) embankment of the river, going upstream all the way until Moudon. Road nr.

1 and the railway track also closely follow the river in the valley. The signposted route nr. 4 does not deviate from the eastern embankment. To visit the churches along the route you need to briefly leave the signposted route in Granges, Henniez, and Lucens. The route converges with stage 15 (Romont to Moudon) in Curtilles after nearly 23 km. Most of the remaining 6 km are also alongside the Broye River, until you reach Moudon. A visit to Moudon's 700-year-old church and historic upper city end stage P2.

Getting to the starting point

Today's starting point in Payerne is at the reformed Church of the former Cluniac Monastery. In case you hike stage P2 as a daytrip, you can start following the signposted route directly from the train station, without first going to the church.

Route Map and Profile

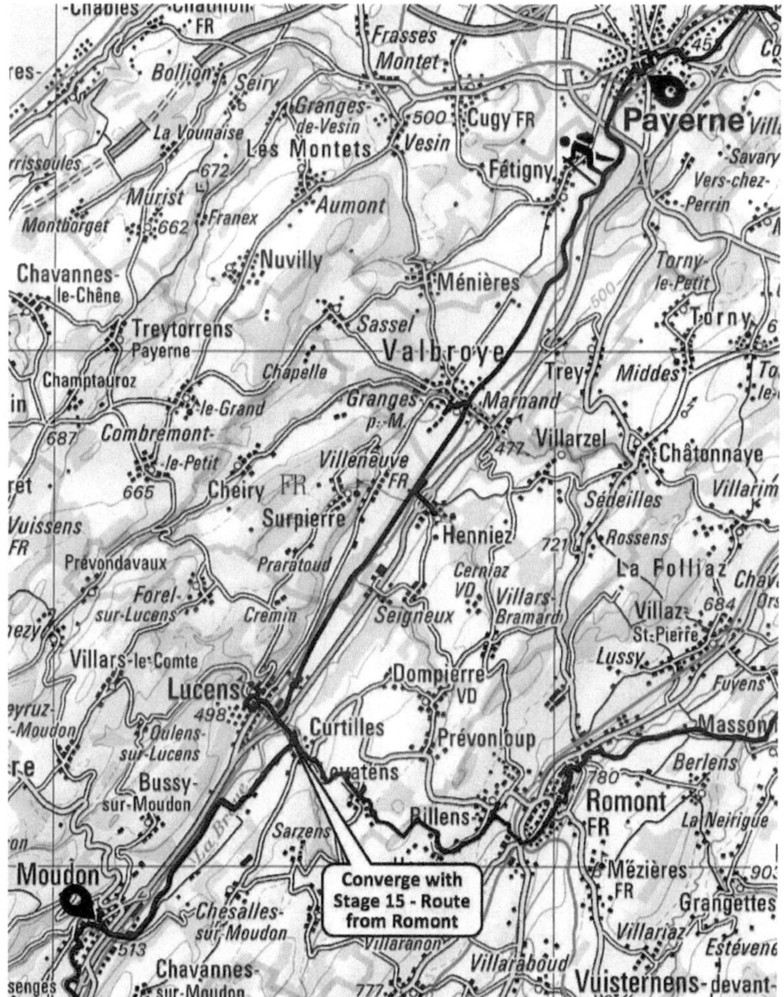

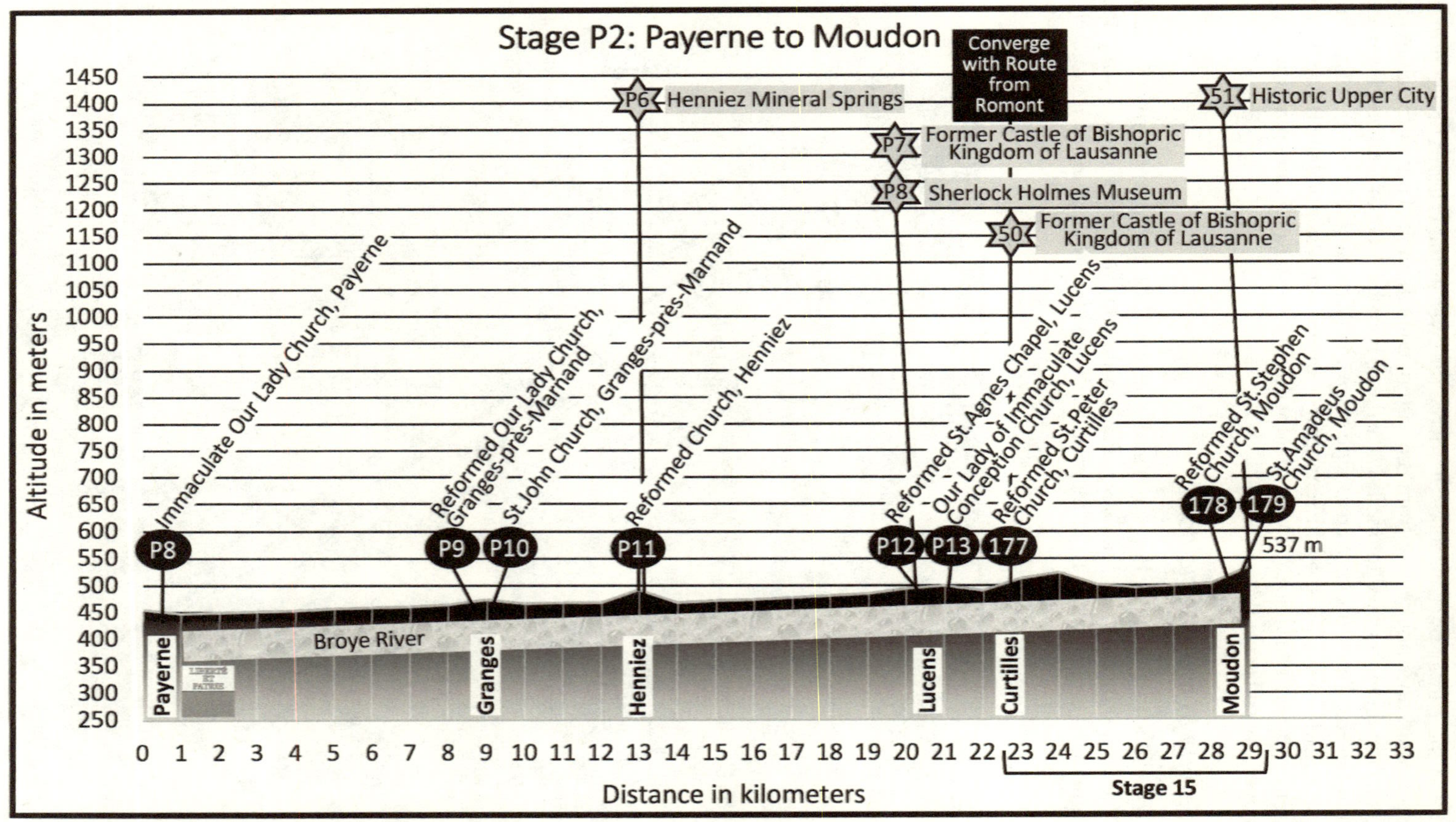
Stage P2: Payerne to Moudon
Converge with Route from Romont
Altitude in meters
1450 1400 1350 1300 1250 1200 1150 1100 1050 1000 950 900 850 800 750 700 650 600 550 500 450 400 350 300 250
P6 Henniez Mineral Springs
P7 Former Castle of Bishopric Kingdom of Lausanne
P8 Sherlock Holmes Museum
50 Former Castle of Bishopric Kingdom of Lausanne
51 Historic Upper City
P8 Immaculate Our Lady Church, Payerne
P9 Reformed Our Lady Church, Granges-près-Marnand
P10 St.John Church, Granges-près-Marnand
P11 Reformed Church, Henniez
P12 Reformed St.Agnes Chapel, Lucens
P13 Our Lady of Immaculate Conception Church, Lucens
177 Reformed St.Peter Church, Curtilles
178 Reformed St.Stephen Church, Moudon
179 St.Amadeus Church, Moudon
537 m
Broye River
Payerne
Granges
Henniez
Lucens
Curtilles
Moudon
0 1 2 3 4 5 6 7 8 9 10 11 12 13 14 15 16 17 18 19 20 21 22 23 24 25 26 27 28 29 30 31 32 33
Stage 15
Distance in kilometers

Hiking the Route

From the monastery church you need to go back to the signposted route nr. 4. Walk down the hill in the *Rue du Collège* that leads to the large car park. Look back; you have a good view of the building of the former Sheriffs of Bern. At the *Rue des Granges* turn right and after 50 meters left. About 200 meters from the church you get to a roundabout, where you are back on the signposted route. Turn right and at the next roundabout go right again onto the *Rue de Guillermaux*. At km 0.4 you arrive at the catholic Immaculate Our Lady Church of Payerne.

Immaculate Our Lady Church, Payerne (Eglise Notre-Dame Immaculée) **P-8**

- Rue Guillermaux 17, 1530 Payerne
- Our Lady
- At the parish office, in the green building right of the church
- The catholic parish in the protestant city of Payerne was established in 1888, 352 years after the Reformation. From 1889 catholic services were held in a small chapel that was established in a house purchased by the parish. From 1895 the building also housed their catholic school, where nuns of the Ursuline Convent of Fribourg taught classes from 1925 to 1984.

  By the beginning of the 20th century the chapel had become too small. For about 25 years the parish collected donations to finance the construction of a new and larger church. The present church was built in 1928-29. Because of limited financing it took 21 years before the bell tower received it clocks (1950) and another 14 years before the four bells were hung in the tower (1964).

The statue representing the Virgin Mary with baby Jesus in the niche above the entrance door was placed in 1956. The church has a modern interior. Notice how the round medallions of the crucifixion way have been integrated in the walls of the nave (above the arches). Look up at the ceiling; it has an unusual design. The interior is austere, reflecting a limited budget for interior decorations; the chancel has no high-altar.

Continue on the *Rue de Guillermaux* for a few meters and you reach the Broye River.

The **Broye River** has a length of 68 km, springs in the Fribourg pre-Alps, and flows into Lake Morat and then in Lake Neuchatel. During medieval times the Broye River regularly flooded its valley, destroying the settlements on its banks. Deforestation of its banks caused increasing damage in case of flooding. Castles and cities were built on the hills (e.g. Lucens, Moudon) to be protected against an unpredictable river. At the end of the 19th century the river was tamed. Nowadays it flows in a nearly straight line with very little gradient between two embankments, while agricultural fields fill the river valley between the forested hills.

The route turns left and follows the eastern riverbank. The route is on tarmac, after 400 meters passes underneath the railway track, and after another 1 km passes underneath a busy road. On your left you pass by an industrial area with a large farm with solar-panels. The path follows the bends of the river. Left of the path the train track follows a straighter line.

At km 8.4 a road crosses the Broye River. The signposted route continues straight, but at this location you need to briefly leave the route to visit two churches in Granges-près-Marnand. Cross the road bridge on the right and take the first road left (*Route de l'Eglise*), and at km 8.7 you arrive at the reformed Our Lady Church of Granges-près-Marnand.

Reformed Our Lady Church, Granges-près-Marnand (Eglise Notre-Dame) **P-9**

Route de l'Eglise 34, 1523 Granges-près-Marnand

Our Lady

It is believed that a first chapel was already built in the 7th century, on the foundations of a utility building that belonged to a 4th century Roman villa. In the 9th or 10th century a second church replaced the old chapel. A third Romanesque church was built in the 12th century, which was first mentioned in 1173. The fourth and present church was built from the 13th century onwards, retaining part of the former building. From 1453 the church was mentioned in official documents under the name Our Lady (*Notre-Dame*).

During the Reformation in 1536 the church converted to Protestantism and all its catholic interior decorations were destroyed and the walls and ceiling whitewashed to cover the frescos.

The church tower with its colored tiles was newly built in 1808. Major renovations were undertaken in 1912-13 (when the front portico was refitted), in 1933-34 (when the stained-glass windows were placed in the chancel), and in 1970-74 (when most historical elements were restored and the frescos were uncovered).

The first thing you notice when entering the church is its differing shapes: the nave is positioned slightly angled to the chancel; a side-chapel protrudes into the nave; the ceiling of the nave is flat, of the side-chapel vaulted, and of the chancel arched; and the nave is nearly square, the chancel rectangular. The church had additional side-chapels in medieval times, but these were demolished over the centuries. The irregular shapes demonstrate the many changes that took place during the middle ages. The partially uncovered fresco in the nave dates from around 1300 and the fresco on the chancel's ceiling from the second half of the 14th century. The front-left small side-chapel is called the 'Loys de Marnand' chapel, built in the middle of the 15th century, with ceiling frescos dating from 1683. The tomb and choir stalls date back to the 16th century.

The church has a typical protestant interior limited to a pulpit, cross, baptismal font, and organ. The doors to the church are closed outside the times of services.

The building with the striped shutters next to the church is the parish house. It was rebuilt in 1591, but its present appearance dates from reconstruction in 1767-72 and a complete renovation in 1988-91. The right side of the building was a former barn, which is nowadays in use as a meeting- and event-room.

From the church continue up the hill and take the first street on the left (*Route des Vuarennes*), and at km 9.1 you arrive at the catholic St. John the Evangelist Church.

P-10 St. John Church, Granges-près-Marnand (Eglise Saint-Jean-Evangéliste)

- Route des Vuarennes 11, 1523 Granges-près-Marnand
- St. John the Evangelist
- The catholic church was built in 1963. Before that catholic services were held in the local school. The church has a typical 1960s appearance with concrete and a modern shape: its northern facade curves round and ends upward close to the top of the bell tower. This outer shape also determines its inner footprint.
- The interior is austere without any large altars.

From the church walk back the same 600 meters to the signposted route. Turn right and keep following the gravel footpath on the embankment. Trees are lined along the river and the path is straight for 2 km.

P-6

At km 11.7 you are west of the town Henniez. **Henniez** is well-known for its **mineral springs** already since Roman times. The Roman town Aventicum may already have used water from these springs. Its first underground spring in the forest was called 'Bonne Fontaine' (Good Fountain). In 1688 the first public bathing house was built at the mineral springs. In 1880 the quality of the water was analyzed for the first time and declared to contain minerals.

The bathing houses were modernized and experienced a boom in visitors after the health aspects of the water were scientifically confirmed. At the beginning of the 20th century the popularity of public bathing declined, and the last facilities were closed in 1930.

The first bottling plant was opened in 1905, which sold the mineral water to pharmacies based on their medicinal qualifications. In 1948 the branding of the water changed from medicinal to general health.

Nowadays the only remaining forest-spring bottling company selling the brand Henniez is owned by Nestlé. These old springs are situated east of the town Henniez, up the hill into the forest. The original small bottling plant is still in the town Henniez, close to these springs. The larger industrial bottling plant is outside town in an industrial area (you pass by it later).

At this location you need to leave the signposted route again to go to the church of Henniez. To do so, you need to cross the railway track, requiring a short detour. Continue east, cross road nr. 1, and walk straight into the town Henniez. You can see the tower of the church on a hill in front of you. At the crossing in town turn right, immediately left, and keep left. At km 13.0 you arrive at the reformed Church of Henniez.

Reformed Church, Henniez (Eglise Reformée) **P-11**

Impasse de la Condémine, 1525 Henniez

The protestant church was built in 1939-40. Until the beginning of the 20th century Henniez was too small to have its own church; the local Protestants visited the 12th century church of Granges-près-Marnand, less than 3 km away.

After the town Henniez began to grow due to the water-bottling plants, an own church was built.

The church has a typical modern protestant interior.

From the church walk back the same 1.2 km to the Broye River and the signposted route. Continue south along a 1.6 km straight section of the river, after which you see the industrial Henniez bottling plant on your left.

The Cantonal border lines between Vaud and Fribourg are not always logical. An example is here at the industrial bottling plant of Henniez, where **Canton Fribourg** has taken a 'bite' out of Canton Vaud. At km 15.9 you pass from Canton Vaud into Canton Fribourg and 1 km later you pass back into **Canton Vaud** (at the underpass of the train track).

About 500 meters before the underpass the trail changes from gravel to a narrow sandy path. After the track the route is straight again for 1.7 km, until you reach the industrial outskirts of Lucens (past a metal scrapyard).

On a road bridge the signposted route changes to the other side (west) of the Broye River (at km 18.7). The route follows a tarmac road and you pass by a large industrial plant of the glass manufacturer Isover-Saint-Gobain on your right. At a T-crossing after the company's parking lot you find a confusing signpost of route nr. 4.

Have a closer look at the signpost. Both nr. 4 signs point in the **wrong directions**. The nr. 4 sign with the blue border (normally directing towards Santiago de Compostela) should point towards Moudon, but points back to Payerne instead. The green nr. 4 sign (normally directing away from Santiago de Compostela) points towards Moudon, instead of to Payerne from where you came. This is confusing. The right direction of the arrows should be: the green/blue nr. 4 directing to the east, over the road bridge in the direction of Curtilles; the green nr. 4 directing to the north, to the street past the Isover-Saint-Gobain glass factory (direction Payerne). Hopefully this will soon be corrected.

At this location you need to leave the signposted route to go into Lucens to visit two churches and the castle that you already saw from afar. Turn right and follow the *Route de Payerne* past the Lucens train station (right), and follow the *Avenue de la Gare* around the left curve. About 600 meters after leaving the signposted route you arrive at the municipal office of Lucens (the building with the protruding red-lined window on the 3rd floor; opposite the COOP supermarket). To visit the St. Agnes chapel of the castle of Lucens you will need to ask for the key there (Place de la Couronne 1, 1522 Lucens; only possible on weekdays; 08:00-11:30, 14:00-16:30). From the municipal office walk towards the hill with the castle towering high above the small town. From the *Rue du Marché* you have a great view of the castle and can see that the chapel of St. Agnes is located a little to the right, separated from the castle.

The Castle of Lucens has two different architectural styles: on the eastern side (right) the light-brown bricked round watchtower and high walls that comprised the residence of the Bishops of Lausanne from the 12th century; on the western side (left) the white residential expansions of the Bernese Sheriffs from the 16th century.

The **former Castle of the Bishopric Kingdom of Lausanne** was built as a fortified summer residence for the Bishops of Lausanne (which is about 30 km south of Lucens). The castle was destroyed and rebuilt several times in the 12th century (last in 1170). Although the castle already belonged to the Lausanne Bishops from the 10th century, they did not use it as their residence until 1230. Until that time, they maintained their residence at the Castle of Curtilles (on the other side of the Broye valley). That castle, and the whole village, were destroyed by a great fire in 1230. The Bishop's Castle of Curtilles was never rebuilt (and nothings remains of it nowadays), because the Bishops transferred their summer residence to the Castle of Lucens.

The Bishops used the castle to control traffic and trade through the Broye valley and to oversee the extensive properties of their Kingdom in the region.

That abruptly ended with the Reformation in 1536. Bernese troops invaded the Broye valley (part of the lands of Vaud under control of the House of Savoy) and seized the castle. From 1536 until the invasion of Napoleon's French troops in 1798, Bernese Sheriffs occupied the castle. The Sheriffs made significant changes and additions to the castle but preserved the 12th century tower and fortifications.

After the French occupation in 1798, the castle was sold to private persons. From 1800 it changed ownership many times; each owner leaving their own mark at attempting to carry out interior restorations. Nowadays it is still in private ownership, but rooms in the castle can be rented for events, weddings, and banquets.

To go to the St. Agnes chapel, turn right and follow the small road up the hill. You pass by the **Sherlock Holmes Museum** on your left.

Sherlock Holmes is the fictional London private detective created by Sir Arthur Conan Doyle. He wrote over 50 short stories and four novels between 1887 and 1927 (he died in 1930). It is rather unusual to find a Sherlock Holmes museum at this location. Switzerland actually has two Sherlock Holmes museums: one in Meiringen (at the eastern valley below the Brünig Pass) and one in Lucens. The museum in Meiringen commemorates the location where the character of Sherlock Holmes died (in the last detective novel he plunges down the Reichenbach Waterfall of Meiringen).

The museum in Lucens was created by Adrian Conan Doyle, the son of the famous author. Between 1965 and 1970 Adrian Conan Doyle owned the Castle of Lucens, where he created a small museum inside the castle. After his death in 1970 the castle was sold and the collection stored, until the museum was re-established in the 'red house' (*Maison Rouge*) in 2001.

The museum has two rooms: a replicated room of Sherlock Holmes' house on 221B Baker Street and a room dedicated to the author Sir Arthur Conan Doyle. A ticket costs CHF 7. The museum is only open on weekends from 14:00 to 17:00.

From the museum continue up the hill to the castle. At km 20.6 you arrive at the reformed St. Agnes Chapel of Lucens.

Reformed St. Agnes Chapel, Lucens (Chapelle Sainte-Agnès) P-12

Rue du Chateau, 1522 Lucens

St. Agnes

The chapel was first mentioned in 1365 and served as the Bishop's private castle chapel (the ordinary people of Lucens visited the church in Curtilles). At that time the chapel stood in the small upper village, outside the upper eastern walls of the castle. The chapel has meter-thick walls on its eastern side and massive buttresses on its southern side.

The story goes that the chapel was built by the Baulmes family (who owned several buildings near the castle) as penance for killing the keeper of the Bishop's castle in 1359.

During the Reformation in 1536 the chapel's catholic decorations were destroyed and the walls were whitewashed. From then the Bernese Sheriffs used it as their private protestant chapel. In 1578 the Sheriffs extended the outer defensive walls and included the chapel in the second layer of fortifications. An attic and gallery (from the gate) were added. Although Protestants do not use the name of saints for their churches, the chapel is nowadays known as St. Agnes.

On the facade above the entrance door you can see remnants of frescos (1588) that did not survive the erosion over the centuries.

The stained-glass windows date from 1952. The frescos on the left wall date from around 1420-30 (the right-wall frescos did not survive the centuries). The two coat-of-arms shields below the fresco are of the Baulmes family.

From the chapel walk back down the hill, turn right at the square, and then left into the *Avenue de la Vignette*. Take the first street on the left (*Rue Champ-Min*) and you arrive at the catholic Our Lady of Immaculate Conception Church of Lucens at km 21.2.

P-13 **Our Lady of Immaculate Conception Church, Lucens** (Eglise Notre-Dame de l'Immaculée Conception)

Rue Champ-Min 1, 1522 Lucens

Our Lady

After the Reformation in 1536, it took the Catholics of Lucens 400 years to establish their own church. From 1921 until 1935 the owners of the Castle of Lucens allowed the catholic parish to use a cellar of the castle as a temporary chapel. Between 1935 and 1953 the catholic community turned an abandoned workshop into a chapel. A small wooden chapel, dedicated to St. Agnes, was built in 1953. Soon this chapel became too small and a large national collection brought in part of the finances to build a church. It took several more years of collections before the funding was sufficient to have their own stone church built (on a plot of land that had already been acquired in 1911). The church was built in a modern design in 1962-65, and serves the Catholics of Lucens and the villages around it.

The church has two special features: the stained-glass windows designed by Yoki and the bronze plaque next to the entrance.

The stained-glass windows cover the full length of the nave and light up the interior in a kaleidoscope of colors.

The bronze plaque represents the Bishops' transferred residence from Curtilles (represented by a depiction of the St. Peter Church – see below) to their Castle of Lucens.

From the church walk back to the municipal office (to return the key in case you borrowed it), and from there the same way back to the signposted route near the Broye River. As explained before, from this signpost at the bridge you need to continue straight (east) across the Broye River, across road nr. 1, and up the hill towards Curtilles.

The reformed St. Peter Church of Curtilles is at km 22.6, and is close to the location of convergence with stage 15 (the route from Romont to Moudon). This church is also visited in stage 15; for the details of the St. Peter Church, please see church nr. 177, as described on page 69.

Converge with Route from Romont

From the church continue 190 meters east to the nr. 4 signpost at the corner of the *Route de Lucens* and *Chemin de Prévondens*, where the signposted route from Payerne converges with the route from Romont.

Hiking the Route from the Converge point in Curtilles (km 23-29)

In case you are a thru-hiker (or a day-hiker who wants to continue to Moudon), continue your pilgrimage to Moudon. This is another 6 km of easy trails along the Broye River, making the total distance 29 km. For the details of the last 6 km of the route, please continue reading on pages 69-74 of stage 15.

In case you are a day-hiker and want to end in Curtilles, you need to go to the nearest train station. This is in Lucens, which is about 700 meters back the same way you came. In case you have already visited the reformed St. Peter church of Curtilles when you pilgrimaged stage 15, you can also consider to end stage P2 at the train station of Lucens and not walk to Curtilles at all. This would make stage P2 21.9 km.

MOUDON TO GENEVA/FRENCH BORDER

Stage 16: Moudon to Lausanne 30 km

The Way to the Bishopric Kingdom

Route stats

	Distance in km	*Time in hrs:min*
Signposted route nr. 4	29.2	6:10
Churches/chapels	1.1	1:30
Points of interest		
Rest/lunch		1:00
Stage 16	30.3	8:40

In case you hike this stage as a daytrip, you need to add 400 meters from the train station in Moudon. In Lausanne you end 200 meters from the metro station; the metro can take you to the train station.

Ascent/descent/total	+745 / -731 / 1'476 altitude meters
Lowest/highest altitude	511 / 876 meters
Pathway/condition	easy / moderate
Churches/chapels	Syens, Vucherens, Montpreveyres, Vers-chez-les-Blanc, Les Croisettes, Lausanne
Monasteries	Former Great St. Bernard Monastery Montpreveyres, Former Carmelite Monastery Jorat
Points of interest	Former Castle of the Bishopric Kingdom of Lausanne (2), Olympic Museum

Route summary

Stage 16 continues in protestant **Canton Vaud.**

Stage 16 guides you from the Broye River valley over the Jorat mountain to the Lake Geneva basin.

The route closely follows main road nr. 1 that connects Moudon to Lausanne. After leaving Moudon you only pass by small villages, until reaching Lausanne's northern agglomerations. Most of the day is spent in the relative remoteness of agricultural fields and forests. The remainder of the Swiss Way of St. James from

Lausanne to Geneva/French border is along densely populated areas, so that stage 16 is the last long section in the quietness of nature.

The signposted route nr. 4 follows the eastern bank of the Broye River for 3 km. The trail is easy; it is flat. The route enters the foothills of the Jorat mountain and ascends over 3.6 km from 520 to 700 meters on farm roads through open fields. The route reaches a highland plateau (between 700-749 meters) where it stays for 3 km. Though there are some gradual ascents and descents, the trail on the highland plateau makes the hiking relaxed. Agricultural fields provide wide views over the rolling foothills and the Alps at the eastern horizon. After some descents to cross streams, the route ascends through the forests over 5 km to the next highland plateau. The route stays on this highland plateau (between 850-876 meters) for nearly 5 km. The route is in the Jorat mountain forests and reach the highest point of the day (876 meters) at km 19. This location marks the watershed between the Rhine (north) and Rhone (south) rivers, and from there the rest of the way is basically downhill. At km 23 the route enters the northern agglomerations of Lausanne. For 3 km the route is through residential areas, after which it reaches the Flon River valley. The route descends through a narrow green valley along the Flon River in a southern direction over 1.5 km. After passing underneath Highway A9 the route crosses through the plateau of the Sauvabelin Park and finally descends more steeply into the upper city of Lausanne.

Getting to the starting point

Today's starting point in Moudon is at the reformed St. Stephen church, directly on the signposted route. In case you hike stage 16 as a daytrip, you need to walk 400 meters from the Moudon train station to the church.

The Tourist Information Office offers a pilgrim snack pack that includes a drink and a snack, which can be obtained free of charge at the *Kiosque du Pont*, *Place de d'Hôtel-de-Ville 2*, 150 meters west of the St. Stephen church at the bridge over the Broye River.

Route Map and Profile

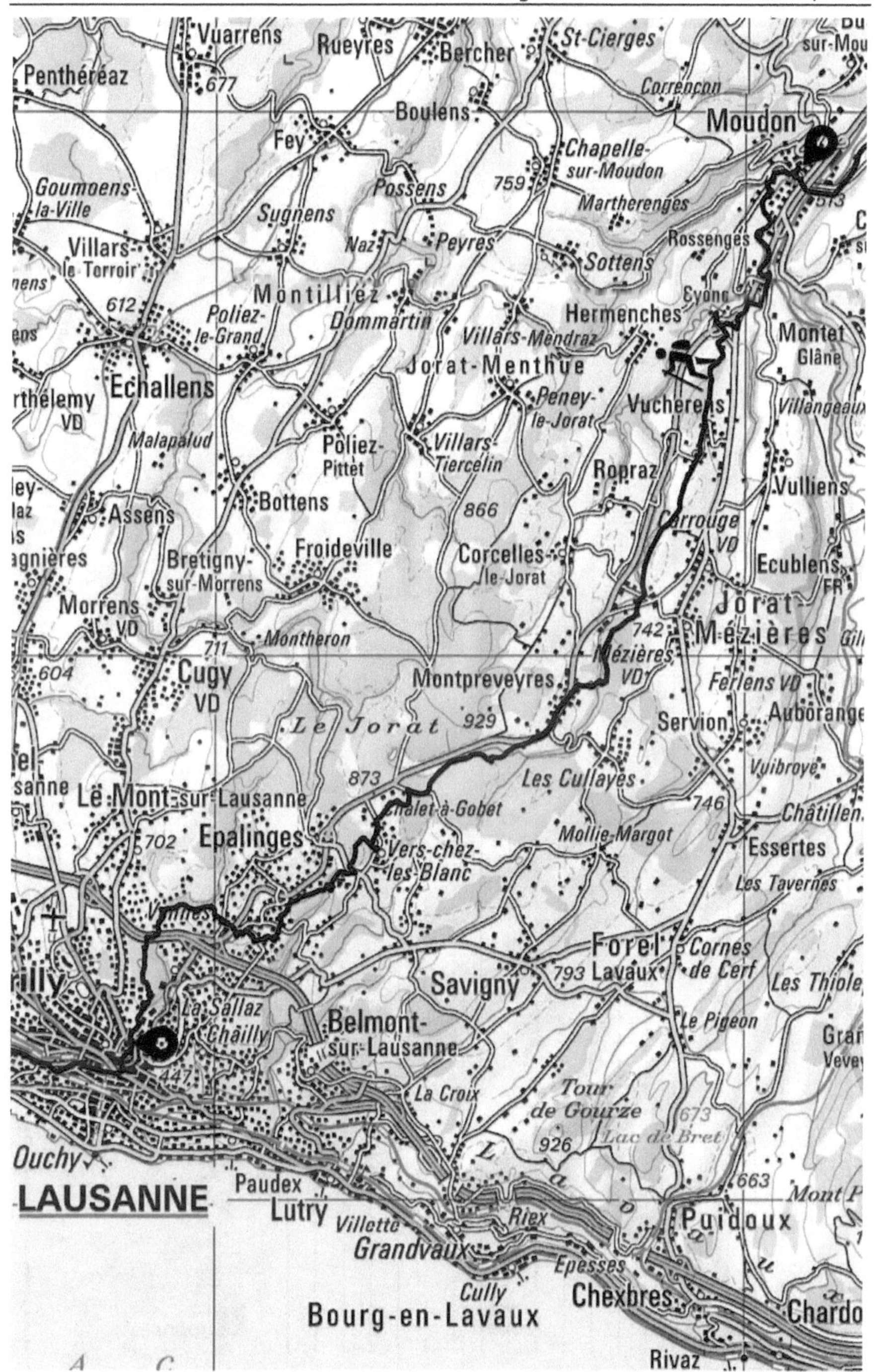
Vuarrens
Rueyres
Bercher
St-Cierges
Penthéréaz
677
Correnon
Boulens
Moudon
Fey
Chapelle-
sur-Moudon
Goumoens-
la-Ville
Possens
759
Martherenges
Sugnens
Villars-
le-Terroir
Naz
Peyres
Sottens
Rossenges
Montilliez
Syens
612
Poliez-
le-Grand
Dommartin
Hermenches
Villars-Mendraz
Montet
Glâne
Jorat-Menthue
Echallens
Peney-
le-Jorat
Vucherens
VD
Malapalud
Poliez-
Pittet
Villars-
Tiercelin
Ropraz
Vulliens
Bottens
Assens
866
Carrouge
VD
Froideville
Bretigny-
sur-Morrens
Corcelles-
le-Jorat
Ecublens
FR
Morrens
VD
Jorat-
Mézières
742
Montheron
711
Mézières
VD
604
Cugy
VD
Montpreveyres
Ferlens VD
Servion
Auboranges
Le Jorat
929
Vuibroye
873
Les Cullayes
Le Mont-sur-Lausanne
Chalet-à-Gobet
746
Châtillens
702
Epalinges
Mollie-Margot
Vers-chez-
les-Blanc
Essertes
Les Tavernes
Forel
Lavaux
Cornes
de Cerf
793
Savigny
Les Thioleyres
La Sallaz
Châilly
Belmont-
sur-Lausanne
Le Pigeon
447
La Croix
Tour
de Gourze
673
926
Lac de Bret
Ouchy
LAUSANNE
Paudex
Lutry
Villette
663
Grandvaux
Riex
Puidoux
Epesses
Cully
Chexbres
Bourg-en-Lavaux
Chardonne
Rivaz

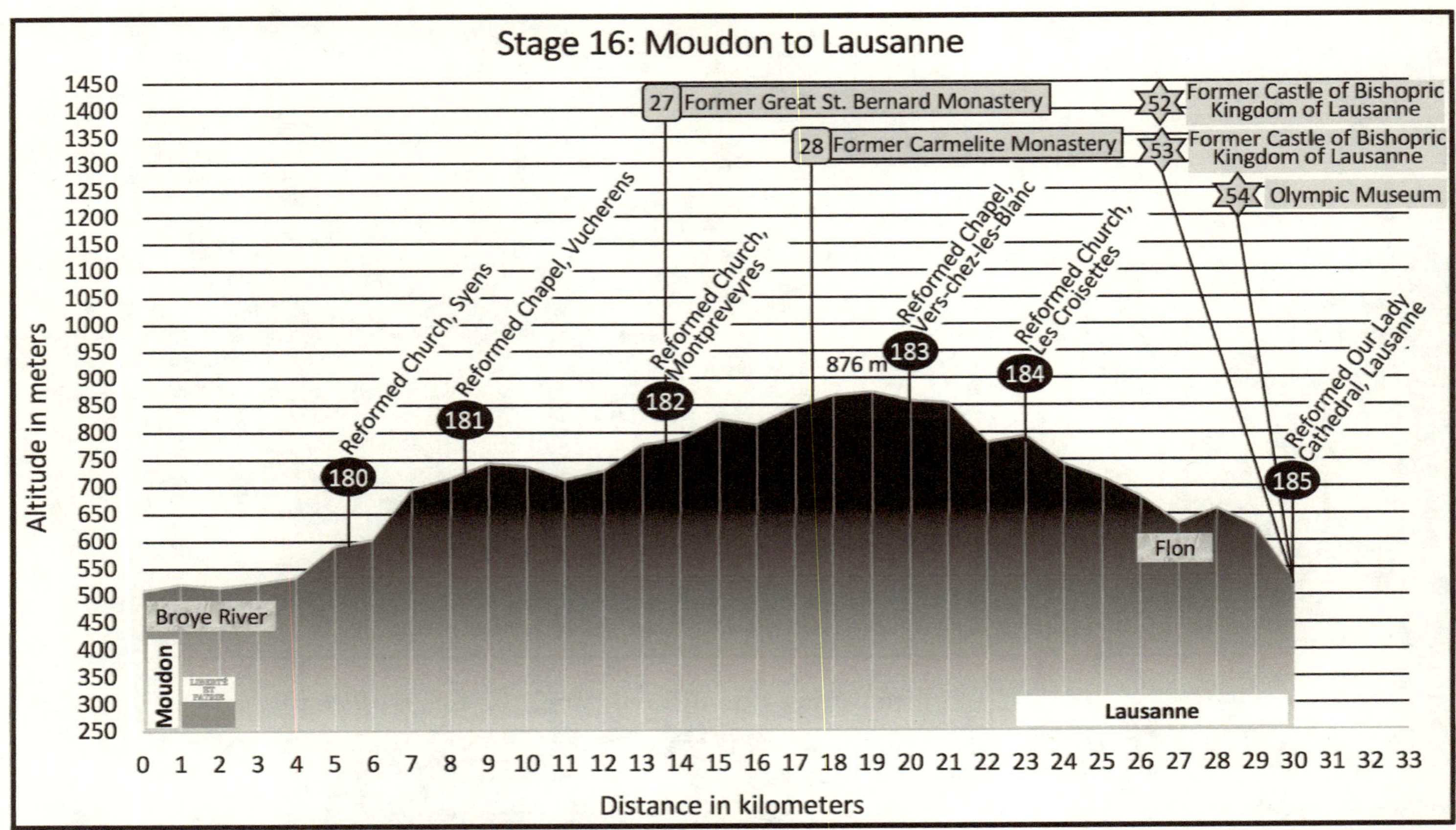
Stage 16: Moudon to Lausanne
Altitude in meters
1450
1400
1350
1300
1250
1200
1150
1100
1050
1000
950
900
850
800
750
700
650
600
550
500
450
400
350
300
250
0 1 2 3 4 5 6 7 8 9 10 11 12 13 14 15 16 17 18 19 20 21 22 23 24 25 26 27 28 29 30 31 32 33
Distance in kilometers
27 Former Great St. Bernard Monastery
28 Former Carmelite Monastery
52 Former Castle of Bishopric Kingdom of Lausanne
53 Former Castle of Bishopric Kingdom of Lausanne
54 Olympic Museum
180 Reformed Church, Syens
181 Reformed Chapel, Vucherens
182 Reformed Church, Montpreveyres
183 Reformed Chapel, Vers-chez-les-Blanc
184 Reformed Church, Les Croisettes
185 Reformed Our Lady Cathedral, Lausanne
876 m
Broye River
Moudon
LIBERTÉ ET PATRIE
Flon
Lausanne

Hiking the Route

From the reformed St. Stephen church, the Way of St. James sign directs to the Historic Upper City (where you might have already walked at the end of stage 15/P2). It goes up the hill via the *Rue de Château* where you see the 17th and 18th century mansions. Along a narrow street the route descends out of the Upper City, turns left along a moss-overgrown wall, and further descends to the Broye River. When you look back across the soccer field, you have a great view of the high walls of the Upper City. After 50 meters along the river's western bank, the path crosses the river on a wooden footbridge to continue along the eastern bank.

The next 2 km the route follows the s-curving Broye River in a southern direction. Walking is easy and relaxed on a tarmac footpath next to the river. You pass by the Moudon open-air swimming pool, camping grounds, and an industrial area. For a few hundred meters the route is parallel to road nr. 1, after which the route passes underneath this road, and crosses the Broye River on a narrow road bridge. The route continues south, parallel to a small stream (*Le Carrouge*), first on tarmac, then on grass. The trail crosses the stream on a narrow footbridge and through a grass field converges back to road nr. 1. The route briefly follows road nr. 1, turns south, and then back again to this road. In the distance you can see the short steeple of the church in Syens, in the middle of a small cluster of houses. Parallel to road nr. 1 the route nr. 4 sign directs to the south. At this location you need to briefly leave the signposted route. Cross road nr. 1 and head north for 320 meters to arrive at the reformed Church of Syens (at km 5.3).

180 Reformed Church, Syens (Eglise Reformée)

Rue du Village 18, 1510 Syens

A church in Syens was first mentioned in 1228. Being in the lands of Vaud, the church converted to Protestantism during the enforced Reformation in 1536. At that time all catholic decorations such as altars, frescos, paintings, and statues were removed.

In 1786 a fire caused by lightning destroyed most of the nave and bell tower. The church was reconstructed a year later: the nave was enlarged, but the chancel was maintained as it was. Originally the nave had the same width as the chancel; since the reconstruction of 1787 it is wider. The chancel originates from this older church and dates from around 1300. The tuff bricks and arched shape of the chancel give it an old appearance, though it dates from the restorations undertaken in 1897-98. The stained-glass windows date from this time too. The wooden choir stalls date from around 1700.

The church has a typical protestant interior, limited to a communion table, pulpit, pews, and a single cross.

From the church walk back the same 320 meters to the signposted route. Continue straight. Through open fields the route turns right, shortly afterwards left, and then right again, gradually ascending a hill. When you look back you can see Moudon in the valley.

The route continues to ascend through a small patch of forest and then on the eastern edge of the forest. You hike through grass, between bushes, and past agricultural fields.

To the east you overlook small villages dotted in the rolling hills, with the Alps at the horizon. The route is on a highland plateau and the ascent becomes more gradual.

The trail changes to tarmac road on the outskirts of Vucherens, and at km 8.4 you arrive at the reformed Chapel of Vucherens (50 meters right of the signposted route).

Reformed Chapel, Vucherens (Chapelle de Vucherens) 181

- Route de la Râpe 1, 1509 Vucherens
- On a small board attached to the wooden wall left in the front portal
- A predecessor catholic chapel was first mentioned in 1523. It stood at another location and was turned into a house in 1593. For 144 years (1593-1737) the village had no place of worship, until this protestant chapel was built in 1737. From then the Protestants in the area did not have to go to Syens anymore to attend a service. The chapel also served as a summer school in 1737-77. The last renovation was undertaken in 1957.
- The chapel has a typical protestant interior without decorations.

The following 2.6 km the route stays on the highland plateau, with only some gradual descents. You have wide views all-around. The trail is easy, on tarmac roads between agricultural fields. The Alps keep accompanying you at the eastern horizon.

The route crosses a patch of forest and descends to the outskirts of the settlement Ecorcheboeuf, crosses two roads, and goes into a forest. The trail ascends on a stony and gravel path through the forest over 1.3 km. The route turns right and makes a short but steep descent to the Bressonne stream. Wooden steps make the descent easy. A poorly maintained concrete footbridge crosses the shallow stream in the valley of the forest.

A narrow forest trail ascends out of the valley. The path leads over a crooked boardwalk consisting of nearly rotten boards covered with chicken wire to hold them together and make them less slippery. Coming up the hill on grass you see the steeple of a church appearing on the right and the roof of a fortified mansion on the left. The fortified mansion (with gun loopholes and elevated windows) was the former Monastery of the Order of Great St. Bernard.

27 Former Monastery of Great St. Bernard, Montpreveyres (prieuré de l'ordre de celui du Grand Saint-Bernard)

Chemin de l'Eglise 12, 1081 Montpreveyres

Great St. Bernard Order

The former monastery dates from before 1160. The Order built the priory as a hospice for travelers along the medieval road from Moudon to Lausanne. The small town Montpreveyres was under the rule of the Order and derived its name from them. Mont Preveyres means Mount of Priests (Priests from the Mountains, as the Order of Great St. Bernard originated at the Alp Pass named after the Order). The coat-of-arms of the town, as depicted on the pilgrim stamp at the church (see below), has two columns that represent the two pillars of the former Bishopric of St. Bernard.

When Canton Bern conquered the lands of Vaud and enforced the Reformation in 1536, they secularized this catholic priory. Their building was reused as a reformed parish house 40 years later (1576).

On the other side of the street is the reformed Church of Montpreveyres (at km 13.6).

Reformed Church, Montpreveyres (Eglise Reformée) 182

- Chemin de l'Eglise 12, 1081 Montpreveyres
- On a shelf at the wall in the front portal
- The church was first built as a catholic church belonging to the Priory of the Great St. Bernard. Not much is known of this first church. It was probably built around the time of the establishment of the priory, before 1160.

  During the enforced Reformation in 1536, the church was plundered and all its catholic decorations destroyed. The first church may have survived the Reformation, but it did not survive a revolt of peasants against their feudal rulers in 1757. They destroyed the church, after which it was rebuilt in 1757-58. This is the church you are in today. Restorations were undertaken in 1818, 1895, and 1949.
- The church is small, the size of a chapel, with the typical austere protestant decorations. The pulpit, communion table, and bell (1483) still date from the old church. During the renovations the original pulpit was placed against the back wall of the chancel. Notice the stained-glass windows, particularly the one with the Savoy flag and the reference to the Priory of Great St. Bernard, with the dates 1167 and 1536.

The brown signpost in front of the church directs the St. James pilgrims (*Chemin de St-Jacques*) on their way to the cathedral of Lausanne. According to the sign it takes 3hr:50min to get there. Following the sign, the route turns to road nr. 1 (*Route de Berne*) through Montpreveyres and follows the road uphill for 800 meters. Shortly after a restaurant (*Les Balances*) the route forks to the left, away from road nr. 1, and enters the Jorat forest (*Bois du Grand Jorat*).

After a short decent to cross a small stream, the trail ascends on an easy path through the Jorat forest. The trail stays relatively close and parallel to road nr. 1. You can regularly hear the sounds of traffic coming from your right. The trail alternates between broad gravel path, narrow grass trail, and tarmac forest road.

At a resting place (at km 17.5) a **brown information table** (in French) explains the history of the route through the Jorat forest and highland. It indicates that the pilgrimage trail you are following is the oldest route between Moudon and Lausanne, dating from before the 6th century. This was the main route for trade, traffic, and pilgrims connecting the valley of the Broye River (Moudon) to the Lake Geneva basin (Lausanne). The route gained in importance after Bishop St. Marius transferred the diocese from Avenches (15 km northwest of Fribourg) to Lausanne, after becoming Bishop in Avenches in 574. Nearly a 1'000 years later, after the Reformation and the annexation of the lands of Vaud by Bern in 1536, traffic on the route increased even more. Since 1865 road nr. 1 (*Route de Berne*) has been the main connection between Moudon and Lausanne. Nowadays the trails you are on are only used by hikers, mountain bikers, and pilgrims.

During the early middle ages, the Jorat highlands were densely forested without possibilities for shelter. Dark forests, cold weather, bandits and robbers made traveling this area a dangerous undertaking until the 18th century. The closest shelters were the Priory in Montpreveyres (in the north) and some isolated houses (*Chalets*) set up by residents of Croisettes and Épalinges (in the south); in the middle ages the forests extended from Moudon to Lausanne. Documents from

1228 mention a hospice, and documents from 1387 a St. Catherine chapel, at a location 50 meters southeast of the resting place with the information board.

Former Carmelite Monastery, Jorat Forest 28

Jorat Forest, 1000 Lausanne

Carmelite Order

The Bishop of Lausanne, Aymon de Montfalcon, established a small Carmelite monastery on the site of the former chapel in 1497. It was also dedicated to St. Catherine, and continued to provide shelter and safety in the treacherous forests. It housed five monks in 1522. When Bernese troops enforced the Reformation in 1536, the small monastery was secularized and abandoned. It subsequently fell into ruins and was completely demolished in the 19th century; nowadays nothing remains.

Continuing from the resting place, the route curves to the right and reaches the highest point of stage 16 at 876 meters (at km 19 km). At the corner of the forest and a horse farm the route makes a sharp left.

A **light-blue information table** draws attention. The table has a map that shows your current position in the Jorat forest in relation to the Way of St. James. It states 10 km to go to Lausanne, 90 km to Geneva, and 1'965 km to Santiago de Compostela. At the highest point of 876 meters you are crossing a **watershed**: north of this location water flows towards the Rhine River and North Sea; south towards the Rhone River and Mediterranean Sea.

The route follows a broad gravel path back into the forest and passes by a golf course. You arrive at the *Route du Jorat*, which you follow south for 200 meters. You pass by a residential area and a camping site. The trail turns right onto a broad gravel path that goes into another patch of forest. About 250 meters into the forest you arrive at a three-way split of the path. The nr. 4 signpost directs to the right.

At this location you need to briefly leave the signposted route to visit the next chapel. Turn left and walk 170 meters out of the forest to the east. As you leave the forest, the view opens up and across the fields you see the Alps at the horizon. Behind the cemetery and across the *Route du Jorat* you arrive at the white modern building of the reformed Chapel of Vers-chez-les-Blanc (at km 20.0).

183 **Reformed Chapel, Vers-chez-les-Blanc** (Chapelle des Râpe)

Route du Jorat 76, 1000 Vers-chez-les-Blanc

The chapel was built in 1960. It belongs to the protestant parish of Les Croisettes and serves the cemetery on the other side of the road. The chapel, in a modern 1960s design, stands a bit lost alongside the road, opposite the forested hill.

Its interior is simple. The doors are only open during services.

From the chapel cross the road and go back into the forest to the signposted route.

The gravel path curves to the left (south) and shortly before another three-way split there is another **brown information table** (in French) at the hiking signpost. In addition to the information provided at St. Catherine, it explains that after the Reformation in 1536 the chalets (houses) of Goblet and de la Croix Blanche took over the role of providing shelter for travelers on the southern side of the Jorat forests. The table further explains the existence of several sunken lanes in close vicinity, though none can be seen along the route.

At the three-way split take the middle path underneath the horizontal tree-barrier. About 500 meters later you exit the forested hill and cross road nr. 148 (*Route de Marin*). The route turns right and follows a gravel path on the edge of the forest. The route makes an s-curve around a large building complex called *Chalet à Matthey*, housing Nestlé's biggest Research Center in Switzerland, with more than 600 employees.

The route turns back into a long patch of forest called the chapel forest (*Bois de la Chapelle*). A curving rocky gravel path leads down to a footbridge crossing the *Flon Morand* stream. The path ascends out of the small valley and continues on a tarmac road on the western edge of the chapel forest. You pass by a residential area, a school, and a cemetery. In front you see the reformed Church of Croisettes on top of a hill (at km 23.2).

Reformed Church, Les Croisettes (Eglise des Croisettes) **184**

- Chemin de Sylvana, 1066 Épalinges
- On a shelf left of the front portal
- The protestant church was built in 1661-62, as an initiative of the protestant authorities in Bern to provide a protestant place of worship north of the city of Lausanne. As the lands of Vaud were forcefully subjected to the Bernese occupation since the Reformation in 1536, Lausanne refused to cooperate with the financing and construction of this church.

  It is the first protestant church in the lands of Vaud that received a flattened three-sided ceiling, matching other Bernese churches built at that time. The bell tower and chancel were remodeled in 1915, and further renovations were undertaken in the 1970s and 2012. The chancel is aligned to the west instead of to the east.
- The brown wooden ceiling and floor make the interior rather dark. The restored wooden pulpit originates from 1662. The stained-glass windows are in an Art Nouveau style dating from 1915 and 1947.

The hill of the church provides the first view of Lake Geneva and the Savoy mountains to the south (with good weather you can see the Mont Blanc south of the lake). From this church the remainder of the route is basically all downhill until you reach Lausanne. The following 2.4 km you hike through the residential areas of the northern agglomerations of Lausanne. The district is called Les Croisettes and is part of the town Épalinges. You walk on residential roads, zigzag past backyards, and cross a small patch of forest. When you arrive at a large grey building complex, the route becomes confusing.

You enter the campus of the **University of Lausanne** (UNIL) in Épalinges, comprising of a dozen buildings occupied by medical faculties, research centers, and laboratories. Nestlé's R&D Center in close vicinity must be beneficial for the cooperation between the University's and Nestlé's research teams. The route crosses the campus and zigzags between the buildings. There is no route signaling; it is best to follow the signs to the metro station M2 Croisettes (the terminal station of Metro line M2). At the station the Way of St. James sign nr. 4 reappears. You walk through the metro's pedestrian tunnel with photos of faces on the walls and ceiling. It does not get more urban than this.

After the tunnel you cross road nr. 1 (*Route de Berne*). This crossing is also confusing. On the other side follow the *Chemin de Croisettes* for 200 meters until the roundabout. Turn right and the first left (*Chemin du Bois Murat*). After 200 meters turn right and you enter a forested area along the Flon River gorge.

The **Flon River** flows down the Jorat mountain range towards Lausanne. Over the millennia it cut a deep gorge in the landscape while flowing into Lake Geneva. As the Flon valley became populated and industrialization steered the urban development of Lausanne, its valley was leveled from the upper parts of the city down to the lake level. In 1875 tunnels were dug for a railway line between Lausanne and Ouchy; the excavated soil was used to fill up the Flon valley. The river valley you are entering is the last preserved section north of the city of Lausanne, now serving as recreational escape for the urban population.

For 1.6 km the Way of St. James follows this narrow valley of the Flon River, nowadays a tame stream flowing from the west to the south. It is an easy trail on a broad gravel path. After crossing to the other side of the stream, the path goes up and signposts direct to make a sharp left, going steeply down a short hill back to the level of the stream. The path alternates between the left and right bank of the stream. The trail climbs out of the valley towards Highway A9. The highway bridge is high above you; temporary wooden stairs (because of maintenance of the bridge) take you to the level of the highway. After 150 meters alongside the highway, the route turns south into a park.

The **Sauvabelin Park** was developed to provide the population of Lausanne a green escape from the city in 1888. The plateau used to be meadows and bushes; trees were planted, an artificial lake was created, a restaurant was built, and in 1899 a funicular was inaugurated that provided easy access from the city of Lausanne to the park. Nowadays Metro line M2 transports tourists to the park. A 35-meter watchtower was added to the attractions of the park in 2003. Nowadays the park has farm- and forest-animals, walking paths, rowing boats on its lake, a tower to view the surroundings, playgrounds, picnic areas, and a Swiss chalet serving as a restaurant. It is mostly visited by families on weekends.

The Way of St. James crosses straight through the park, from north to south, past the lake (*Lac de Sauvabelin*), restaurant, and watchtower (*Tour de Sauvabelin*) to the southern point. The small building that resembles a chapel is not a chapel. It was originally built in 1821, as a storage room (for drinks, chairs, and tables) for the bourgeoisie of the city visiting the viewpoint. During the mobilization of 1939 the storage room was remodeled by the military to make it look like a chapel; its walls are 40 to 50 cm thick. A plaque above the door refers to the mobilization of 1939-45. Nowadays the storage room is empty; it cannot be accessed.

From the southern viewpoint you overlook Lausanne and Lake Geneva, and see the Alps at the horizon. You can already see the destination of stage 16, the cathedral of Lausanne. From the viewpoint a steep descent over 700 meters leads down from the plateau, out of the green, into the city. The first part of the descent zigzags down the hill on tarmac. The second part descends on gravel and is a straighter path through a park.

Two-thirds into the descent you pass by the **Fondation de l'Hermitage** (Heritage Foundation). In 1853 a banker built a mansion with park-like gardens on the hill overlooking Lausanne and Lake Geneva. Since 1984 the restored mansion has housed a charming museum of fine arts, with over 600 paintings from the 19th and 20th centuries. It is one of the top cultural attractions of Lausanne, being situated on an elevated location and surrounded by a park.

The final meters of the descent are on a narrow street between houses. You have reached the city of Lausanne. Be aware that from here on, while passing through the city, the **Way of St. James signposting** changes. Like in Fribourg, the yellow signs are replaced by the square dark-blue signs with the yellow scallop imprint and the text *Chemin de St-Jacques* with a small arrow indicating the direction. Like in Fribourg, locating these dark-blue signs on lampposts or against walls in the busy streets of Lausanne can be quite challenging.

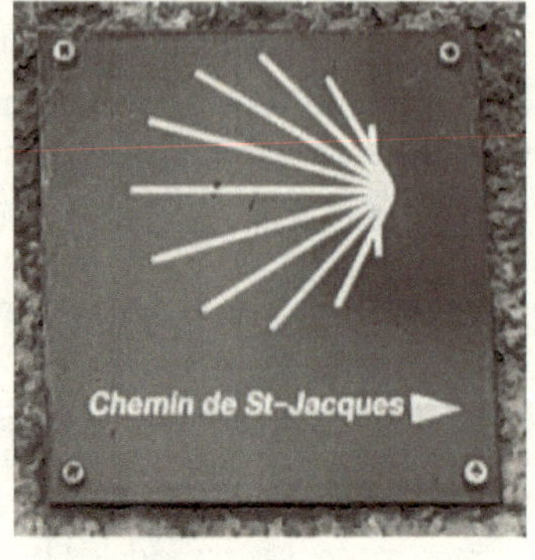

At the *Rue de la Barre* turn left, go straight across the roundabout, and you arrive at the castle square (*Place du Château*) with the St. Marius Castle.

The **former Castle of the Bishopric Kingdom of Lausanne**, also called St. Marius Castle (*Château Saint-Maire*), was built by the Bishops of Lausanne between 1397 and 1425. It was named after the first Bishop of Lausanne, St. Marius. The castle served as a fortified Bishop's residence until 1536, when Bernese troops conquered the lands of Vaud from the House of Savoy and enforced the Reformation.

Bern exiled the bishop, occupied the castle, and used it as armory. The Bernese Sheriffs resided at the castle for more than 260 years until 1798 (when French troops occupied Switzerland). The castle has housed the Cantonal Governmental offices since the establishment of Canton Vaud in 1803.

The original castle had the shape of a cube. The lower building on the western side was built by the Bernese in 1789. This now is the entrance. A fortified city-gate tower stood separate from the castle, but was demolished to make room for a road in 1890.

From the early middle ages, the **Bishopric Kingdom of Lausanne** amassed significant wealth, lands, and religious and earthly power. Until the occupation by the Bernese in 1536, the Bishopric of Lausanne was a small Kingdom, encompassing the city of Lausanne and several other territories. They struck coins, were feudal owners of the city, lands, and peasants, and set up a military defense system, including extensive fortifications (walls and 50 watchtowers and gates) around their city. Two of their castles stood at the northern end of the Jorat forests (Curtilles and Lucens), while three stood at the southern end of their territory (Lausanne, Ouchy, and Saint-Prex). They occupied their castle in Curtilles from the 10th century until 1230 (see stage 15), their castle in Lucens from 1230 until 1536 (see stage P2), their St. Marius castle in Lausanne from 1397 until 1536, their Castle in Ouchy from 1159 until 1536 (see below), and their castle in Saint-Prex from 1234 until 1536 (see stage 17).

The Bishopric of Lausanne (lasting nearly a 1'000 years) started when St. Marius relocated from Avenches at the end of the 6th century, and ended with the military enforced occupation and Reformation by Bern in 1536. The Lausanne Bishops were exiled for 127 years (1536-1663), after which they have settled in Fribourg (1663 until today). The Diocese of Lausanne was combined with Geneva in 1821-1925, and has encompassed Lausanne, Geneva, and Fribourg since 1925 (with the St. Nicholas Cathedral in Fribourg as the Bishop's seat).

Continue straight, and 200 meters later (at km 30.3) you arrive at the reformed Church that was the former catholic Our Lady Cathedral of Lausanne until 1536.

185 Reformed Our Lady Cathedral, Lausanne (Cathédrale de Notre-Dame)

Place de la Cathédrale 13, 1005 Lausanne

Our Lady, Twelve Apostles, St. James the Greater, St. Marius

At a special pilgrim corner in the southern transept

The cathedral was built on the site of predecessor cathedrals, dating back to the end of the 6th century, when the Bishop's seat of St. Marius was transferred to Lausanne. The first cathedral was replaced by another one in the 2nd half of the 9th century. The second cathedral was replaced by a Romanesque one in the first half of the 11th century. The present fourth cathedral was built in three stages from east to west by three master builders between 1150 and 1235. Fires, changes in plans, and changes of master builders resulted in the 85-year construction time. The cathedral was consecrated 40 years later (1275), after the construction of the attached monastery was completed.

North of the nave and the transept once stood a monastery, built between 1220 and 1270, providing the monks direct access to the cathedral. The monastery was secularized at the time of military occupation and enforcement of the Reformation by Bern in 1536. It fell into disrepair and was demolished in the 17th century.

The Reformation had a big influence on the interior of the cathedral: all traditional catholic altars, paintings, and statues were removed or destroyed; the noses or heads of statues were cut-off; the stained-glass windows were removed; and many of the interior's colorful walls and statues were whitewashed. Liturgical vestments (robes worn during services), tapestries, and other church treasures were taken to Bern in 1537. The high-altar was dismantled and shipped to Bern in 1563. A golden statue representing the Virgin Mary, which attracted many thousands of pilgrims each month during the middle ages, was smelted and struck into coins by the Bernese troops.

Restorations were undertaken during the 18th to 21st centuries, partly uncovering the original interior colorings. Reformed churches usually do not have a name reference to a catholic Saint, but because of the long history of this church its former name of Our Lady and Cathedral were maintained (though it has not been a cathedral, with a bishop's seat, since 1536).

The cathedral was an important pilgrimage destination throughout the middle ages and one of the important stops along the way to Santiago de Compostela. During the middle ages more than 60'000 pilgrims visited the cathedral every year, on a local population of 5'000 to 6'000. Can you imagine how overwhelmed the ordinary medieval pilgrims from the countryside must have been by the sheer size and magnitude of this cathedral. Even today it is still impressive. It is one of the great architectural accomplishments of the 12th century in Switzerland, nowadays receiving nearly half a million visitors every year.

The cathedral is the largest Gothic building in Switzerland (length 100 meters; height of the bell tower 80 meters) and was designated as a historical monument in 1900.

The most interesting features are the missing bell tower, the night watchmen, the history of the access portals, the rose window, the pilgrim corner, the old choir stalls, the knight's tomb, and the views from the bell tower.

You may not have noticed it when you approached the cathedral, but the bell towers are asymmetrical. Two towers stick out above the roof of the nave: a tower above the chancel and a tower south of the western entrance. **Missing** is the twin (second) **Tower** north of the western entrance. It was never built for financial and structural reasons.

Did you know that **Night-Watchmen** have been calling out the times every night since 1405? In the past they called out every hour; nowadays they only call out the hours between 22:00 and 02:00. Lausanne has been the only European city upholding this night-watchmen tradition without interruption for more than 600 years. Originally they served the purpose of fire-lookout, at the time the medieval houses surrounding the cathedral were made of wood.

The **West Portal** (main entrance) through which you entered the cathedral is not the original entrance. The present portal was built in 1892-1909 on the foundations of the first portal dating from 1515. The outside statues resemble the people who worked on the restoration in 1982-1909. Until 1515 there was a public passage in between the (former) western end of the nave and the (current) western front portal with the two side-chapels (Montfalcon chapel (north) and Tourist Information (south)). At the width of the cathedral the passage was covered by a vaulted ceiling (forming a tunnel), further connecting to an open street (*Rue Cité-Devant*) to the north to the Saint Marius Castle (*Château Saint-Maire*) and to the south to the old South Portal. The street and passage provided the bishops a straight-line access to the cathedral's southern access portal for 100 years. Bishop Montfalcon had this passage closed in 1515, the nave's western wall removed, and a new western entrance built. When you stand at the western end of the nave (*Grande Travée*), you are at the location of the former north-south passage; when you look up you can still see the vaulted ceiling of the former tunnel. This extension made it the largest Gothic building of Switzerland. The original entrance from before 1515

lies to the south, in the middle of the nave. These have the original stone sculptures representing prophets, apostles, and evangelists from 1235 (the lower ones restored, the higher ones heavily eroded). Once they were colorfully painted, which gave it its name of the **Painted Portal**. Most colors have long since faded, leaving pale stone statues. You can only access this former South Portal from inside the nave.

Most iconic of the cathedral is its **Rose Window**: a circular stained-glass window with a diameter of eight meters containing 105 medallions depicting the medieval cosmological view of the world (Imago Mundis), built between 1205 and 1220. The rose window you see nowadays is a version that was restored several times over the centuries: medallions were rearranged, replaced, and refilled during the last major renovation in 1894-99; there are still 78 original medallions left. The artwork is extraordinary: the shape and cut of the medallions resemble a collection of sparkling colorful diamonds. Most medallions depict a scene (some are gap fillers), telling the story from the inside out. The tilted middle square depicts God (medallion created in 1899) and His four creations: separating light from darkness; separating land from sea; separating day from night, creating birds and fish; and creating animals and mankind (Adam and Eve). This square is surrounded by: the four seasons (spring, summer, autumn, and winter), each surrounded by the three months corresponding to the season; the four natural elements (earth, water, air, fire), each surrounded by the three signs of the zodiac corresponding to the element; the four rivers of Paradise (of the Garden of Eden: Pishon, Gihon, Tigris, and Euphrates), and the monsters outside of paradise; and the four corners of the earth (winds; north, east, south, west). It is really a pity that you cannot see them up-close. At the Tourist Information desk, you can pick up a brochure that explains the rose window in greater detail.

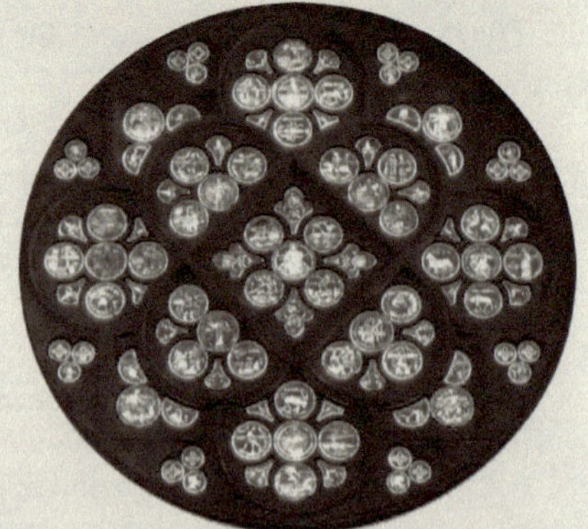

The cathedral has a special **Pilgrim Corner** in the southern transept, dedicated to both St. James pilgrims on their way to Santiago de Compostela and English pilgrims from Canterbury on their way to Rome. The corner is situated in the Virgin chapel. Its walls once had colorfully painted decorations; they faded over the centuries. At the back wall in a recess two eroded sandstone statues represent the Virgin Mary and the angel Gabriel. Two stained-glass windows reflect colored light. The pilgrim stamp is neutral, as the cathedral's stamp is used for both pilgrimages. The stamp depicts the pattern of the iconic rose window.

Two further features may be of special interest to a St. James pilgrim: a choir stall with the carving of St. James the Greater and the tomb effigy of Knight Othon de Grandson.

You find the **Choir Stalls** in the Montfalcon chapel (named after the bishop of 1509) left of the entrance. The chapel has a thick iron grating blocking the entrance, but you can easily look through it. What you see is a massive u-shaped choir stall comprising 17 seats. The walnut wooden stalls date from 1509 and are richly decorated with carvings representing the Twelve Apostles. Unfortunately, the carving of St. James is not visible from the fence, because it replaced another stall that was destroyed during the Reformation in 1536.

Othon de Grandson (1238-1328) was a prominent Savoy knight, born in Grandson (pronounce in French), a town about 45 km north of Lausanne. He spent much of his time in England, serving King Henry III and later King Edward I. He went on two crusades (Acre and Jerusalem) and established a Franciscan convent and Carthusian monastery. His relatives served as Bishops of Lausanne and oversaw the cathedral where he was buried. The Grandson family coat-of-arms has three scallops, also displayed on the tomb effigy, referring to the pilgrimages and crusades to Jerusalem. You can find his tombstone between the arches at the northern side of the chancel.

The tourist shop and information counter are right of the entrance. They sell the tickets (CHF 5) to climb the bell tower and have information brochures in several languages (including English). A narrow spiraling staircase, with 220 eroded stone steps, leads you to the top viewing platform. Along the climb you pass by exhibitions of additional historical items, such as the original choir stalls dating from 1275 (they were still in use until the beginning of the 19th century). Higher up you see the giant bells. Better not to be near them when all seven (two on the first level, five on the second level) are tolling the full hour. From the **viewing Platform of the Bell Tower** the sights are magnificent. To the southeast you overlook Lausanne and

Lake Geneva, and on the southern side of the lake see the Savoy Alps (including the Mont Blanc mountain range) and France.

To the southwest you overlook Lausanne and the western lake shore, where you will continue in stages 17, 18, and 19, curving south to Geneva, at the most southern point of the lake. The church tower right in front of you belongs to the St. Francis church that you will visit at the beginning of stage 17.

The Our Lady Cathedral marks the end of stage 16. But there is more to see in Lausanne, in case you have time and are interested. After Geneva (stage 19), Lausanne is the second-biggest city along the Swiss Way of St. James, with a population of around 145'000. The number of medieval buildings in Lausanne is limited, despite the town having its roots in Roman times. The Bishopric Kingdom and Cathedral of Lausanne attracted many monastic Orders during the middle ages. After 1142 the Cistercians, Augustinians, Dominicans, Franciscans, and Knights of St. John of Jerusalem settled in Lausanne, and built their churches and monasteries. During the Bernese invasion in 1536 and subsequent occupation during the Reformation, they underwent the same fate as all other monasteries in the lands of Vaud: they were looted, closed, secularized, and their buildings either re-utilized (as a warehouse, hospital, or offices) or demolished. Apart from the cathedral, the remaining medieval buildings are the St. Marius Castle (which you passed shortly before arriving at the cathedral), the St. Francis Church (which you will visit in stage 17), the Ale Tower (1340), and the Castle of Ouchy (1177).

The Ale Tower (*Tour de l'Ale*) is just a free-standing tower, not so interesting; it is the last remaining tower of the medieval fortifications that once used to comprise 50 towers (they were all destroyed in the 18th century to make room for expanding urbanization). The Castle of Ouchy was the residence of the Bishops of Lausanne from 1177. It is worthwhile to visit this castle, which nowadays houses a hotel.

From the upper city of the cathedral it is easiest to take the metro down to the lake level (Metro station *M2 Riponne-M. Béjart*). The lakeside promenade of Ouchy is the right place to end a long hiking day. The marina, passing cruise boats, blue water, fresh air, and wide views over the lake towards the Savoy Alps and Mont Blanc ensure a refreshing end. Many restaurants and terraces invite to sit down and enjoy the evening. From the *Ouchy-Olympique* metro station at the lakeside you see the castle on your left.

The **former Castle of the Bishopric Kingdom of Lausanne** (*Château d'Ouchy*) was built by Bishop Landry of Durnes as a stand-alone fortified residential tower protecting the Bishopric Kingdom at the lakeside in 1159-77. Around 1207 the tower was destroyed in a battle with the Duchy of Savoy, which tried to extend their influence to the north. Bishop Roger of Vico Pisano rebuilt the tower after 1212. By around 1273 additional low buildings were constructed around it, together with a fortified wall around the compound. Until 1536 the Bishops of Lausanne used the castle as residence and gradually extended the compound with other residential buildings and a prison.

When the Bernese occupied the lands of Vaud they took over the castle and used it as a prison (1536). The tower was destroyed by a fire in 1609 and rebuilt immediately. In the 17th century the low buildings and fortified walls fell into ruins. In the 18th century new low buildings used for offices and shops were built around the tower.

In 1885 Canton Vaud sold the compound to a private person (Jean-Jacques Mercier), who had the low buildings and remaining ruins demolished. The tower was modernized and the hotel was built in the design of a neo-Gothic chateau in 1889-93. Nowadays it is still a four-star hotel, called Chateau d'Ouchy.

From the castle follow the road (*Place du Port*) and promenade in an eastern direction. On your left you pass by the Grand Hotel Beau-Rivage Palace and 500 meters from the castle you arrive at the bottom of a flight of stairs with a fountain and the five Olympic rings. From there you cannot yet see the Olympic museum, which is at an elevated position, away from the street. You need to go up several flights of wide stairs to its elevated position, overlooking the lake and the Savoy Alps in the south.

54

Lausanne made its name as the Olympic Capital. It has been the home of the International Olympic Committee (IOC) for more than 100 years. After the reformed Our Lady Cathedral, the **Olympic Museum** (Quai d'Ouchy 1, 1006 Lausanne; www.olympic.org) is the second-most visited tourist attraction in Lausanne. Spread over three floors it has the world's largest Olympic collection with more than 1'500 objects such as torches, medals of all the games, and equipment used by famous athletes. The museum, with library, study centers, auditorium, and restaurant with panoramic views, is interactive and presents the history and development of the Olympics since the Antiques. It is open from 09:00 until 18:00; a ticket costs CHF 18; information is available in many languages.

From the ending point

The reformed Our Lady Cathedral of Lausanne is the ending point of stage 16, directly on the signposted route nr. 4. In case you have time and are interested, a visit to the lakeside of Lausanne and the former Bishop's Castle and Olympic Museum in Ouchy may be an alternative ending of stage 16.

In case you are a day-hiker, it is easiest to take the Metro line M2 (station *Riponne-M. Béjart*, 200 meters from the cathedral) to the Lausanne train station (CHF 2.30; 3 min; 2nd stop).

In case you are a thru-hiker and spend the night in Lausanne, there are many hotels which are, however, relatively expensive, the city being a major tourist destination. There is no pilgrim inn, but low-priced accommodation can be found at the Youth Hostel or Backpackers Guesthouse. Check out www.jakobsweg.ch or www.viajacobi4.ch for the accommodation possibilities. Lausanne has three Tourist Information Offices (tel. 021 613 73 73; www.lausanne-tourisme.ch; info@lausanne-tourisme.ch): at the cathedral; at the Lausanne train station (central hall); and at the lakeside Ouchy Metro station. They can help you find the appropriate accommodation. When you check-in at a hotel in Lausanne, you will receive a free of charge Lausanne Transportation Card for the duration of your stay. It gives you free and unrestricted access to Lausanne's public transportation, in addition to discounts at several museums. It is worthwhile to first check into your accommodation, and then continue exploring the city and lakeside.

The next Stage

Stage 17 guides you from the upper city of Lausanne down to Lake Geneva, and directly along the lake's shore to the west. Read the next chapter to find out what that entails.

Stage 17: Lausanne to Rolle 33 km

The Way along Lake Geneva

Route stats

	Distance in km	*Time in hrs:min*
Signposted route nr. 4	31.6	6:10
Churches/chapels	0.9	1:30
Points of interest	0.5	1:20
Rest/lunch		1:00
Stage 17	33.0	10:00

In case you hike this stage as a daytrip, you need to add 200 meters in Lausanne and 500 meters in Rolle (from and to the train stations).

Ascent/descent/total	+296 / -436 / 732 altitude meters
Lowest/highest altitude	372 / 422 meters
Pathway/condition	easy / moderate
Churches/chapels	Lausanne (3), St-Sulpice, Morges, Saint-Prex, Buchillon, Perroy, Rolle (2)
Monasteries	Former Franciscan Monastery Lausanne, Former Cluniac Monastery St-Sulpice, Former Benedictine Monastery Perroy
Points of interest	Stairs of the Market, Roman Archaeological Site, Castle of Morges, Medieval City of Saint-Prex, Former Castle of Bishopric Kingdom of Lausanne, Castle of Rolle, Harpe Island

Route summary

Stage 17 continues in protestant **Canton Vaud**.

Stage 17 guides you from the upper city of Lausanne down to Lake Geneva, and directly along the lake's shore to the west.

The route closely follows main road nr. 1 that was the historical trade and pilgrimage route along the northwestern shore of the lake, connecting Lausanne to Geneva. This northwestern shore was already populated by the Romans and increased in importance for trade and settlements around 1200. Several castles were built at strategic locations directly at the lake, new cities were founded under the protection of these castles, new monasteries were established in charge of the religious and social well-being of the local population, and new catholic churches were built. Many of these medieval remnants have been beautifully restored and are still visible today. They are situated along the Swiss Way of St. James, hence the many points of interest in this stage.

From the reformed Our Lady Cathedral in the upper city of Lausanne the signposted route nr. 4 descends through the agglomerations of Lausanne to the shore of Lake Geneva over 4 km. For the remaining 29 km the route stays directly along or in close vicinity of the shore. The trails are easy; it is all flat, except for a few low hills in the second half of the stage. The route passes by small yacht ports, small beaches and swimming areas, vineyards, medieval churches, historic cities, and fortified castles. The lakeside route provides nice views and with clear weather views of the Mont Blanc. This large variation of scenery and the lake make it one of the nicest stages of the Swiss Way of St. James. Like a string of pearls, the medieval towns line up along the shoreline. The longest section in nature (3.5 km) is through the forested Aubonne River delta, a nature protected area (between Buchillon and Perroy – km 24.4 to 27.9).

Getting to the starting point

Today's starting point in Lausanne is at the reformed Our Lady Cathedral, directly on the signposted route nr. 4. In case you hike stage 17 as a daytrip, you can get there from the Lausanne train station with metro line M2, station *Riponne-M. Béjart* (CHF 2.30; 3 min; 2nd stop; 200 meters from the cathedral).

Route Map and Profile

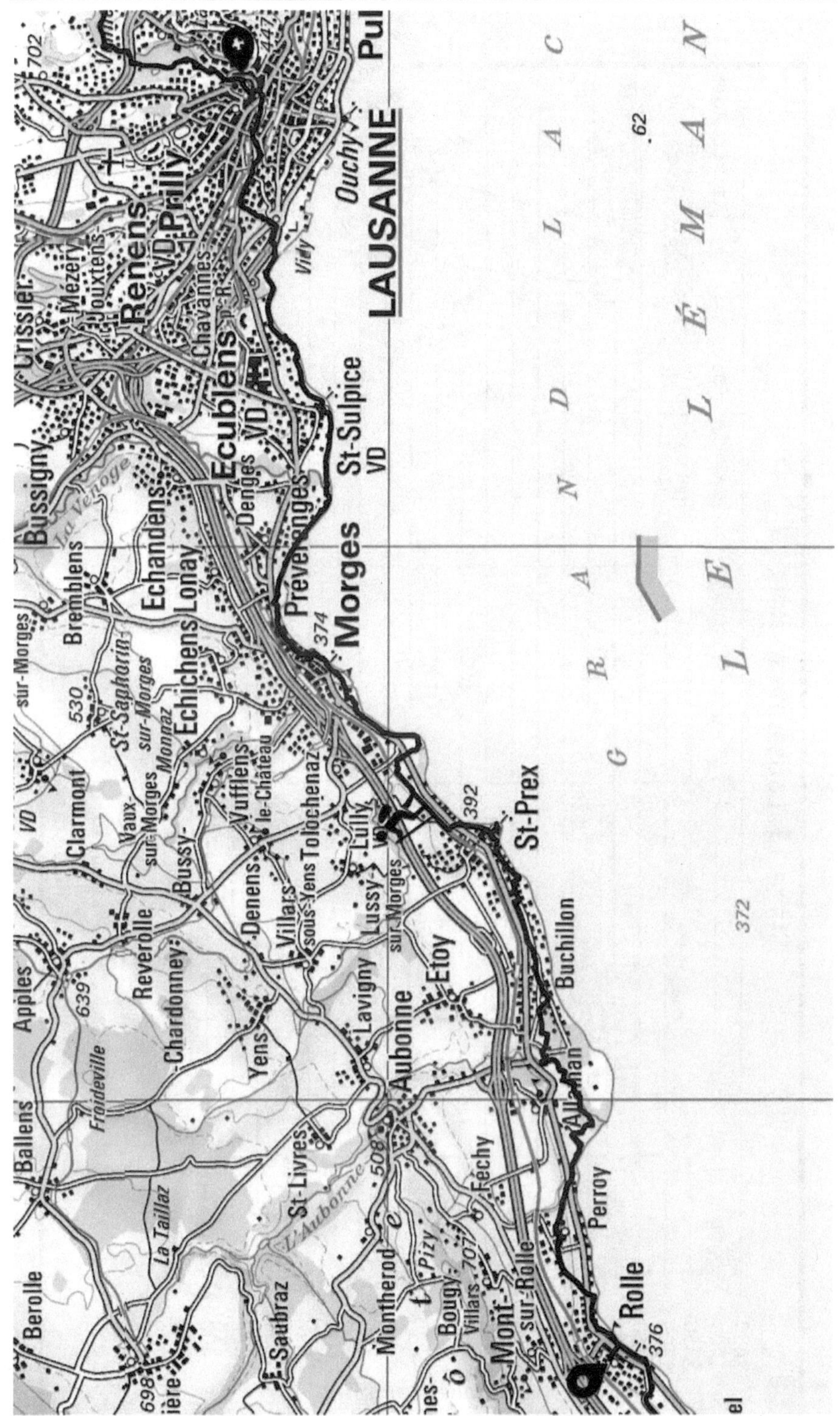
LAUSANNE
Ouchy
Vidy
Renens
Prilly
Crissier
Mézery
Jouxtens
Chavannes
Ecublens
St-Sulpice
Bussigny
La Venoge
Echandens
Denges
Préverenges
Morges
Lonay
Bremblens
Echichens
St-Saphorin sur-Morges
Monnaz
Clarmont
Vaux-sur-Morges
Bussy
Vufflens-le-Château
Tolochenaz
Lully
Denens
Villars-sous-Yens
Lussy-sur-Morges
St-Prex
Buchillon
Etoy
Lavigny
Aubonne
Yens
Reverolle
Chardonney
Apples
Froideville
Ballens
La Taillaz
St-Livres
L'Aubonne
Saubraz
Montherod
Pizy
Bougy-Villars
Féchy
Allaman
Perroy
Mont-sur-Rolle
Rolle
Berolle
L A C   L É M A N
G R A N D   L A C
702
447
62
530
374
392
372
639
508
707
376
698

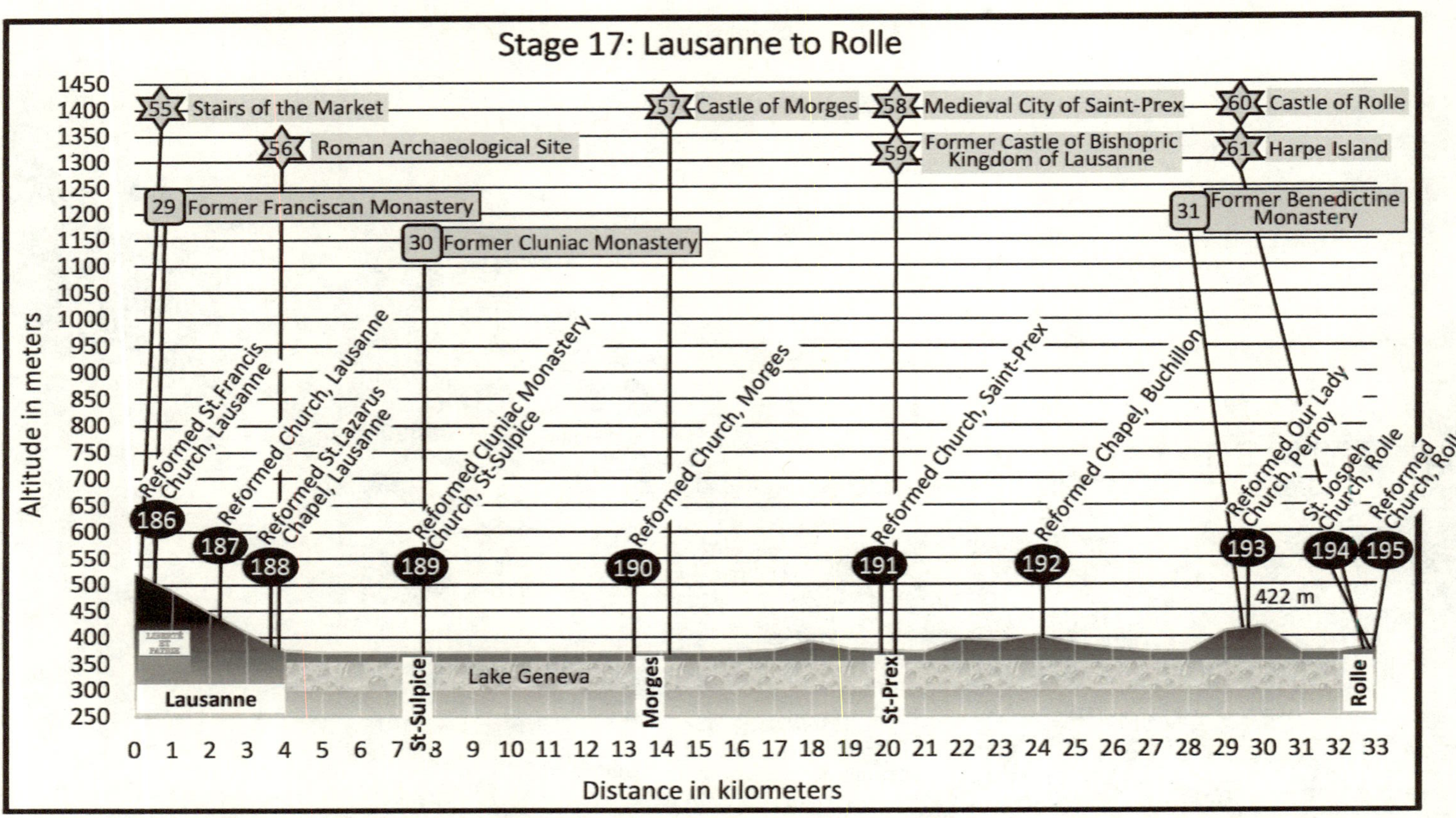
Stage 17: Lausanne to Rolle
Altitude in meters
Distance in kilometers
55 Stairs of the Market
56 Roman Archaeological Site
29 Former Franciscan Monastery
30 Former Cluniac Monastery
57 Castle of Morges
58 Medieval City of Saint-Prex
59 Former Castle of Bishopric Kingdom of Lausanne
60 Castle of Rolle
61 Harpe Island
31 Former Benedictine Monastery
186 Reformed St.Francis Church, Lausanne
187 Reformed Church, Lausanne
188 Reformed St.Lazarus Chapel, Lausanne
189 Reformed Cluniac Monastery Church, St-Sulpice
190 Reformed Church, Morges
191 Reformed Church, Saint-Prex
192 Reformed Chapel, Buchillon
193 Reformed Our Lady Church, Perroy
194 St. Jospeph Church, Rolle
195 Reformed Church, Rolle
422 m
Lausanne
St-Sulpice
Lake Geneva
Morges
St-Prex
Rolle

Hiking the Route

Be aware that in Lausanne the yellow Way of St. James signs are replaced by the square dark-blue signs with the yellow scallop imprint and the text *Chemin de St-Jacques* with a small arrow that indicates the direction. Locating these dark-blue signs on lampposts or on walls in the busy streets of Lausanne is quite challenging. They are easy to overlook.

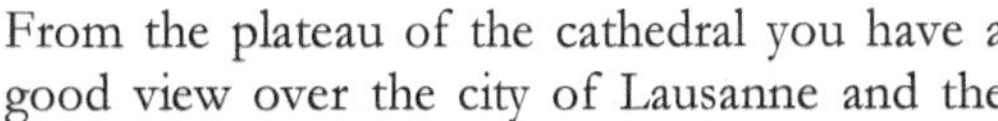

From the plateau of the cathedral you have a good view over the city of Lausanne and the Savoy mountains behind the lake. Above the rooftops you can already see the bell tower with the green steeple of the St. Francis church. Opposite the entrance of the cathedral a flight of stairs, below a dilapidated light-grey construction, leads down the hill. At the top of the stairs a brown Way of St. James sign indicates 3hr:20min to Morges; graffiti and abrasions make the sign almost illegible.

The flight of stairs, covered with a wooden roof, lead to an underpass of a busy road. The covered gallery continues downhill, until you arrive at a square called *Place de la Palud.* These 177 steep steps date back to the 13th century. Their present appearance with the wooden roofing and alignment to the steep paved street dates from 1717-19. They are called the **Stairs of the Market** *(Escaliers du Marché)*, as the city's market was held on the flat part to the left, about halfway down the stairs, until the 14th century. The covered gallery was designated Vaud Heritage Site in 1900. When you look back you can see the bell tower of the cathedral rising high above the stairs.

At the square *Place de la Palud* turn left into the *Rue du Pont.* You walk downhill on the cobbled stones of a shopping street. At the zebra crossing of the *Rue Centrale* (road nr. 1) continue straight onto another cobbled shopping street (*Rue Saint-François*); this time uphill. At the end, on top of the hill, turn right and you arrive at the square *Place Saint-François* with the reformed St. Francis church right in front of you.

The church is surrounded by large buildings, Hotel des Postes, banks, stores, and busy streets. Together with the cathedral, the reformed St. Francis Church (at km 0.4) is the only remaining medieval church in the city of Lausanne from before the Reformation.

186 **Reformed St. Francis Church, Lausanne** (Eglise Saint-François)

Place Saint-François, 1003 Lausanne

St. Francis of Assisi

The church was built as part of a Franciscan monastery (hence the name of the church) in 1270-75. Its original construction was a bit different from the other churches established in the 13th century: the nave had no stone vaulted ceiling (it was flat and made of wood); the chancel was square instead of semicircular; and there was no bell tower. At that time the church was located on the southern outskirts of the city. The church was surrounded by wooden houses and a city fire destroyed most of the church in 1368; only the chancel survived because of its stone vaulted ceiling. Remodeling to a Gothic architecture was undertaken in 1383-87, while the bell tower (designed after the tower of the Our Lady Cathedral) was constructed at the beginning of the 15th century.

The church converted to Protestantism after the annexation of the Bishopric Kingdom of Lausanne by Bern and the Reformation in 1536. All catholic icons and artefacts were destroyed, removed, or taken to Bern, and all interior colors were whitewashed.

During the 19th and 20th centuries many renovations and changes were undertaken, giving the church the different shapes.

The oldest interior treasures are the choir stalls dating from 1387. The stained-glass windows date from 1907-38. The latest interior redesign was undertaken in 2011, significantly changing the look of the interior. Classical concerts and organ recitals are frequently held at the church.

29 **Former Franciscan Monastery, Lausanne** (Couvent de Cordeliers)

Place Saint-François, 1003 Lausanne

Franciscan Order

The monastery was established at the southern fortified walls of the city in 1258. The Franciscan Order settled in Lausanne to provide religious services and care for the poor in the growing city. During the occupation by the Bernese and the following Reformation in 1536, the monastery was secularized and their buildings were given a different use. In 1895-1902 the former monastery buildings were demolished to make room for the expansion of the city; nothing is left of it nowadays.

From the square turn east along the *Rue du Grande Chêne* where you pass by the large 5-star Lausanne Palace Hotel. After the hotel take the street forking to the left (*Avenue de Montbenon*). Along a promenade and a small park overlooking Lake Geneva you pass by two large buildings from the beginning of the 20th century: the Courthouse (*Palais de Justice*) on the right and the Casino Montbenon on the left. The **Casino Montbenon**, though called casino, never was a gambling hall; built in 1908-09, it now houses a café-restaurant, concert hall, winter garden, and the Swiss Film Archive. Stately rooms can be rented for banquets, seminars, conferences, and exhibitions.

At the T-crossing turn right and then left, and you are on the *Avenue Jules Gonin*. After a large road crossing take the first left and then right into the *Chemin des Croix Rouges*. At the end of this street (T-crossing) turn right on the *Avenue du Belvédère* alongside the lowered railway tracks. At the crossing of a main road (*Avenue de Tivoli*) turn left to cross over the tracks. About 200 meters later you arrive at the reformed Church of Sévelin (at km 2.2).

Reformed Church, Lausanne (Le temple de Sévelin) **187**

Avenue de Tivoli 74, 1007 Lausanne

The church was built in 1961, in the typical urban style of that decade, with much use of concrete and a modern free-standing bell tower. The church was built on the site of a wooden chapel, which stood there from 1947 to 1961. This chapel was relocated to a northern part of town; nowadays it does not exist anymore.

The interior of the church is modern and austere. The door to the church is locked; you can only access the church during the service hours.

Continue down the main road (*Avenue de Provence*) for 500 meters. The small blue signpost directs to the left, onto a small path into a park and then onto a broad tarmac road. You are in the **Youth Valley Park** (*Parc de la Vallée de la Jeunesse*), sloping down the hill from north to south. You pass by an indoor swimming pool, skateboarding grounds, and playgrounds. The route zigzags down the hill through the park. At the foot of the hill is a small educational science museum for young children. The building is run-down and looks like a concrete flying saucer.

On the right (west) of the park is **Lausanne's largest cemetery** (*Cimetière du Bois-de-Vaux*) with over 26'000 graves. Several famous people are buried there, one of which is Coco Chanel. Concessions are granted for an initial term of 30 years (costing up to CHF 5'700), after which they need to be renewed (and paid again).

The route descends towards one of Switzerland's largest roundabouts, the *Rond-Point de la Maladière*. It has 10 entry- and exit-points, a road underpass coming from the park, and connects the district of Ouchy to Highway A1. Its name La Maladière means disease. In this case it refers to the leprosarium of Lausanne that was moved to this area in 1450. After an underpass you arrive at the reformed St. Lazarus Chapel (at km 3.6), which stands lost and isolated west of the roundabout, in between the tarmac jungle of connecting roads with heavy traffic.

Reformed St. Lazarus Chapel, Lausanne (Chapelle de la Maladière) 188

Route de Chavanne 1, 1007 Lausanne

St. Lazarus

The chapel was built in 1461 and restored in 1924. Excavations revealed that it was built on the foundations of older Roman buildings. The chapel was dedicated to St. Lazarus (of Bethany), the patron Saint of the ill, particularly lepers, and hospitals. In the middle ages the people with contagious diseases, such as leprosy, were moved outside the city. In 1450 the leprosarium of Lausanne was moved to this area, where a hospital and chapel were built to isolate and take care of the lepers. They lived in communities of around 15 to 20 lepers. Once a person was in such a leper house they often stayed there for the rest of their life, until they died.

The chapel was in use until 1638 (when the leper house closed), after which it was used for storing torture instruments of the nearby gallows. The condemned said their last prayer at the chapel before being taken to the gallows. The leper house itself fell into ruins and was demolished in the 17th century.

In the 19th century the chapel was used as a shed for farm equipment and for storage of road-work equipment when the roads around it were built.

The chapel was completely renovated and was made into a place of worship again. The chapel's door is locked.

This is one of only two former Leper House Chapels along the Swiss Way of St. James. The other one is in Burgdorf (see stage L3, in Volume II).

From this location the yellow Way of St. James signs are back. The descent out of the city has ended: you reach the level of the lake and from here on the route will be flat. The route passes underneath Highway A1a and turns right.

56

You enter a **Roman Archaeological Site** revealing the foundations of the first Roman settlement in this area, called Lousonna. It is the open-air part of a Roman Museum (*Musée Romain de Lausanne Vidy*). An information board explains what the grounds must have looked like 2'100 years ago. The settlement, housing traders, fishermen, and craftsmen, had between 1'500 and 2'000 inhabitants and had city-like features such as a street grid, a forum and theater, houses with inner courts, and a small lakeside port. From the 1st century BC until the 4th century AD the

Romans occupied this town as a strategic station on the trade routes that connected between the Rhone (south) and the Rhine rivers (north).

From the 4th century the development of Lousonna shifted to the higher grounds, where the medieval and modern-day city of Lausanne developed. The old settlement was abandoned and fell into ruins. Nowadays hardly anything is left of the old town; the present visible foundations make up less than 15 percent of the original city. Apparently, it is not such a popular tourist attraction: the grass and weeds are high. You can barely see the footprint of the 2000-year-old foundations.

Lake Geneva is the largest of the Swiss lakes, with a length of 73 km, a maximum width of 14 km, and an average depth of 154 meters (maximum depth 310 meters). Its surface is at 372 meters altitude. The lake is shared between Switzerland (60 percent) and France (40 percent), and is named after the biggest town on its shore, Geneva. The primary inflow comes from the Rhone River at the northeastern end of the lake. On its southwestern end lies Geneva, from where the Rhone River flows out of the lake.

Over a parking lot and past a large camping ground the route arrives at the shore of Lake Geneva. Pink colored Hello-Kitty pedal boats wait to be rented by tourists at the lakeside. The next 1.5 km the route closely follows the shore, curving to the west. Along the way you pass by lakeside recreational areas for swimming, water sports, and picnicking. Tree lined broad gravel paths make the hiking easy and relaxed.

The views over the lake are splendid. The path turns to tarmac when you arrive at a small port for sailing- and fishing-boats. The route enters the *Parc des Pierrettes*. It is a narrow stone-paved/concrete footpath with a length of 500 meters directly along the shore of the lake. The path is in between the lake and the backside of the gardens of houses, on the residential outskirts of the town St-Sulpice. To the left you see the clear water of the lake, to the right the gardens of stately mansions.

The route enters another small park (*Parc du Pelican*) and continues on gravel in between the lake and gardens. The path along the shore ends and changes to a tarmac street, first between houses, then along the lake, and between houses again. Many of the stately houses are hidden behind high hedges or walls. At the boat pier of St-Sulpice the road makes a right curve and you arrive at the reformed Church of the former Cluniac Monastery of St-Sulpice (at km 7.7).

Reformed Cluniac Monastery Church, St-Sulpice (Eglise St-Sulpice) **189**

- Chemin du Crêt 10, 1025 Saint-Sulpice
- St. Sulpicius, St. James the Greater, St. Nicholas
- At four locations: at the church, at the hotel/restaurant opposite the church, at the municipal offices, or at a kiosk in the village
- The church was built as part of the Cluniac monastery (see below) around 1111. The Cluniac church replaced an old church, dedicated to St. Sulpicius, which is believed to have been built around the year 1000. The village of St-Sulpice was named after this patron Saint. The Abbey of Molesme (France) established a Cluniac priory and remodeled the church to the typical 11th century Romanesque architecture of the Cluniac Order: massive walls; few and tiny windows; the bell tower on top of the crossing of the transept; the clear footprint of a Latin cross; three apses to the east (of which the chancel in the middle was the largest); and the Lombard bands (decorative blind arcades) on the outer wall of the chancel. The two side-apses contained altars dedicated to St. James and St. Nicholas.

  After the Cluniac Order abandoned the monastery in 1413, a small Benedictine priory continued to exist, but they neglected maintenance of the church, which fell into disrepair and near ruins.

  In 1536 the Bernese secularized the priory and made significant changes to the church. They destroyed all catholic artefacts and turned it into a protestant place of worship. They did not try to restore the nave as they considered it too big for the small village. The already half-ruined nave was demolished and the large arched gap on the western side was walled up (you can still see the outline of the different types of bricks). Only the chancel, transept, and tower were restored. The roof of the tower (originally much flatter) was made pointed. A larger window opening was broken into the wall of the chancel's apse to let in more light (the bricked-up wall to the former nave made the interior very dark) and the 14th century wall frescos were whitewashed. A small chapel was built on its northern side (which is also walled up nowadays).

The main architectural restorations to the original state of the chancel and transept were undertaken in 1897, but the restorers decided against replacing the 16th century larger window in the chancel's apse with the original smaller one.

Interior renovations were undertaken in 1974: the stained-glass windows were renewed and the whitewash was removed to reveal parts of the original 14th century frescos. In absence of the nave, you enter the church at the northern transept. The interior of the church is still very dark; limited light comes in through the small windows.

30 Former Cluniac Monastery, St-Sulpice (Abbaye Clunisienne)

Chemin du Crêt 10, 1025 Saint-Sulpice

Cluniac Order

In 1094 the Lords of Bex donated the lands, including the already existing St. Sulpicius church, to the Benedictine Abbey of Molesme (France), which was part of the Cluniac Order. In 1111 the Bishop-King of Lausanne approved the establishment of a small priory and based on donations of sources of income the church was rebuilt, with a Cluniac monastery next to it. Typical for the Cluniac Order, the mother Abbey closely supervised the priory.

The Cluniac Order abandoned the monastery by 1413. The monastery changed ownership several times and became a commendatory priory; it was supervised remotely and represented by an administrator on location. A Benedictine priory continued to exist, but under the remote supervision it was neglected and maintenance of the buildings was minimized; they fell into disrepair.

After the Bernese annexed the lands of Vaud and enforced the Reformation, they closed the priory in 1536. All their assets and lands were secularized by the City of Lausanne. The monastery buildings were turned into a farming estate and leased to local noble families. Nowadays the buildings next to the church are in private ownership.

From the church look back to the boat pier and the lake with the Savoy Alps at the horizon. A beautiful view.

On a small gravel path along the backside of the former monastery the route turns back to the shore of the lake. For 1.5 km the Way of St. James follows a gravel path along the lake in a westward direction. You pass by small boat piers belonging to the private properties with their gardens on your right. Some of these properties have their boat stored in a garage on land. Rails from the garage to the lake are used to lower the boats into the water.

You walk between hedges, pass by a small port, a recreational swimming area, and at the end of a small patch of forest you cross the Venoge stream that flows into the lake. From this location the route continues on tarmac for the following 1.2 km, passing by recreational areas and sandy beaches along the shore. While the road makes a curve to the right, the trail continues straight on a small gravel path directly along the lake's shore.

The following 1.5 km lead you to the outskirts of the next town, Morges. The shore curves to the northwest and then to the southwest; the Way of St. James follows it closely. The underground alternates between gravel, earth, woodchips, and tarmac. In the curve of the shore you can already see the next church tower, beyond the sailing boats anchored in the bay. Back on tarmac you pass by the Hotel Fleur du Lac (flower of the lake). In the garden of the hotel a brown plate in a large stone explains the Way of St. James in French. A broad tarmac promenade curves along the shore towards the center of Morges. To visit the reformed Church of Morges you need to briefly leave the signposted route. After a right turn you arrive at the church at km 13.2.

190 **Reformed Church, Morges** (Temple de Morges)

- Place de l'Eglise, 1110 Morges
- At the church or at the Tourist Information Office (opposite the Castle of Morges)
- The church is on the site of an old catholic village chapel that was first mentioned in 1306. It was built against the city's fortification walls and a fortified watchtower served as the bell tower.

  Upon the invasion of the Bernese the church converted to Protestantism and all its catholic icons and altars collected over the preceding 230 years were destroyed in 1537. By the 18th century the chapel had become too small for the growing population of Morges, and plans for a new and larger church were made by the protestant parish.

  In 1769 the chapel was demolished to make room for the new protestant church as you see it today. The church was built in a French baroque style in 1769-76. Nowadays it is one of the Swiss baroque architectural master pieces built after the Reformation.
- Only the communion table, choir stalls, and one bell (all dating from around 1645) from the old chapel were taken to the new church. The stained-glass windows were renewed in 1896. During the 18th to 21st centuries regular renovations were undertaken; the latest interior renovations were ongoing in spring 2019. Classical concerts and organ recitals are frequently held at the church.

From the church cross the parking lot on the right to go back to the signposted route at the lake's promenade, and continue in a southward direction. You pass by the boat pier of Morges, the Hotel Mont Blanc (because of the view of that mountain across the lake), and the yacht port. At the southern outskirts of the medieval town, close to the lake, is the Castle of Morges.

57

The **Castle of Morges** (*Château de Morges*) was built by Duke Louis of Savoy, the first ruler of the lands of Vaud, to defend the newly founded city in 1286. The castle was situated at the northern territory of the lands of Savoy to counter the growing power of the Bishopric Kingdom of Lausanne.

Morges quickly developed into a regional trade and administrative center along the shore of Lake Geneva. Due to its port it became an important regional transshipment station for goods. Together with its markets it became an economic stronghold during the middle ages. Emperor Sigismund stayed at the castle in 1416.

The castle has typical Savoy features with a square inner courtyard and four round towers at the corners. Note that one of the towers is taller than the others; it served as the main tower. Military battles resulted in the damaging and plundering of the castle and city in 1475 and 1530. The castle was dilapidated by the time of the Bernese occupation of the lands of Vaud in 1536.

In 1539 Bern made Morges the regional governmental seat and restored the castle when the Sheriff of Bern moved in. The medieval town Morges had several city gates and fortified walls. In 1769 and 1803 these were demolished to make room for broader roads and urbanization. Bernese Sheriffs resided at the castle from 1539 until 1798.

After the French invasion in 1798 and the establishment of Canton Vaud in 1803, the castle was turned into a Cantonal armory and served as a prison until 1844. In 1925 the castle was converted to a military museum. Nowadays the castle is open to the public and you can visit the cellars, the top of the walls, and the towers. It houses four regional historical museums: artillery (40 cannons from the Burgundy Wars); military (medieval armor, uniforms, and weapons, including those of the Papal Swiss guards);

police (from 1803 to present); and small tin military figures (10'000 of them in 50 dioramas). A ticket of CHF 10 provides access to all four museums.

The Way of St. James continues through the castle's gardens, crosses the Morges River, passes by the open-air swimming pool and a camping site, and arrives at another small port. The trail follows the pavement around the port and enters a narrow patch of forest between the lake and a cemetery. For a short stretch the route is on a sandy beach of the lake, before going back on grasslands. You pass by a deserted concrete structure that used to contain a military shooting range, and enter a nature protected park along the shore (*Boisements des Rives du Leman*).

At this location the route follows a forest trail with a narrow and winding path in uncultivated nature directly along the shore. The path turns right (west), away from the shore, and follows the Boiron River through a dense forest for 800 meters. The route follows the vita parkour and passes by a row of large nature photos, before going underneath road nr. 1 via a small concrete ledge next to the river. The route switches to the other side of the river, passes by beehives, and leads to the railway tracks.

For 1.5 km the Way of St. James stays next to the tracks. First on a narrow gravel path, followed by grasslands, and after switching to the northern side of the tracks on concrete and tarmac country roads. For the first time you walk along vineyards, where white and red grapes are ripening in the sun, close to the railway tracks. A

little further along the road a big board (in French) explains the history of the Way of St. James (*Saint-Jacques*) and the European routes.

The route turns east and crosses the railway tracks and road nr. 1 again, going back to the shore of the lake. On an elevated road you pass by the small port of Saint-Prex and enter the town. At the *Rue du Motty* you need to briefly deviate from the signposted route to go to the next church. About 200 meters to the right, up the hill, you arrive at the reformed Church of Saint-Prex (at km 19.8).

Reformed Church, Saint-Prex (Eglise Reformée) 191

- Rue du Motty, 1162 Saint-Prex
- St. Prothasius
- On the windowsill right of the entrance
- The present church is the fifth church in a long history of churches on this site. At the time of the Romans 2'000 years ago, it was a small pagan chapel on a burial mount. The first Christians were buried here and the first church was erected in the 6th century. The 7th century Bishop of Lausanne Prothasius was buried at the church, after he died in a wood-cutting accident around 652 (the town belonged to the Bishopric Kingdom of Lausanne). In the 7th or 8th century the church was demolished and replaced by a larger one with a semicircular chancel. Around the year 1000 the early Christian cemetery building was demolished and replaced by a parish church with two side-naves, a rectangular chancel, and a new bell tower that functioned as access gate (the cemetery was maintained west of the building). Finally, in the second half of the 12th century the Bishop-Kings of Lausanne had the church remodeled with Romanesque features. The two side-naves were bricked up (you can still recognize the bricked-up high arches of the former side-naves on the left and right walls of the nave). The bell tower was renewed and the chancel was rebuilt in a square footprint with decorative arches. This determined the present-day appearance.

  Outside the church, an information table with drawings indicates how the predecessor churches developed into the present one.

  The church converted to Protestantism during the occupation of the lands of Vaud by Bernese troops in 1536. All catholic interior decorations were removed and the frescos on the walls were whitewashed. The front portal to the entrance and the spire on the tower were added in 1663. The present appearance of the building is based on extensive restorations in 1910-13 and 1976-79, when many of the 12th century features were restored.

Typical of the Romanesque churches, the inside is dark: the windows are tiny and high up on the walls. You can switch on the light left of the entrance (switch it off again when you leave). In the light you can recognize many special features: the closed decorative arches in the square chancel; the vertically arranged stained-glass windows (1978) in the chancel; the partly recovered frescos (unrecognizable) on the right side of the nave; the replica gold-colored chandeliers; the absence of a ceiling underneath the roof; the entrance portal (in the base of the tower) that mirrors the shape of the chancel, with a small organ crammed on its gallery; and the stained-glass window (1896) that depicts the medieval city of Saint-Prex as a small island.

The view from the elevated position of the church, overlooking the medieval village and the lake with the Alps at the horizon, is marvelous.

From the church go down the hill, back to the signposted route nr. 4. At the *Rue du Pont-Levis* turn right and you arrive at the medieval city of Saint-Prex. At this location it is worthwhile to leave the signposted route and explore the medieval city (it is only 240 meters to the boat pier at the eastern point of the peninsula).

The **Medieval City of Saint-Prex** was built on a peninsula with the eastern and southern sides along the shores of the lake. The city was built by the Bishopric Kingdom of Lausanne, which had the previous city (around the church on the upper part of town) moved to the small peninsula for security reasons in 1234. This explains why the old church is outside the historic city.

At that time the House of Savoy regularly attacked the area in their efforts to expand their territory to the north. The city of the Bishopric Kingdom retreated to the small

island that was protected by wooden ramparts with one access gate and a drawbridge over a moat. The village was completely surrounded by water (as depicted in the stained-glass window at the church).

The rather strange name Saint-Prex was derived from the name of the 7th century Bishop of Lausanne Prothasius, who was buried at the church around 652. The village on the peninsula was named after him, but Saint Prothasius became Saint-Prothias, which became Saint-Pré, and finally Saint-Prex.

The square thick-walled fortified tower is the Castle of Saint-Prex that was the **former Castle of the Bishopric Kingdom of Lausanne**. It was built in 1234, but the Bishops did not make it their residence. From 1240 onwards, they leased the castle and city to regional Lords who were favorable to the Bishopric Kingdom and helped them protect the Kingdom's southern territories against attacks from the House of Savoy. Othon de Grandson (remember him from the tomb in the reformed Our Lady Cathedral in Lausanne) leased it from 1240, followed by other noblemen.

Over the centuries the castle was expanded with the rectangular building on the side. You can still recognize that the ground floor was also fortified without windows and doors. Some of these were added in later centuries. The fortifications stood no chance against Bernese troops in 1536. They set the wooden ramparts on fire and took possession of the town. The castle was subsequently used for storage. In the 16th century the Bernese built new stone fortifications (walls, access gate, and clock tower). Most of the stone ramparts were demolished and the moat was leveled in the subsequent centuries. Nowadays the castle houses the municipal offices.

From Saint-Prex follow the *Rue du Pont-Levis* to the lake's shore south of the historic city. For 800 meters the path is directly at the lake, on a boardwalk above the water. After a small port the route turns away from the lake and continues westward on a broad tarmac road through a residential area with villas. For about 1 km the route is parallel to the lake (400 meters away) on a tarmac country road.

From this location onwards, you will regularly notice **blue arrows or dots** sprayed on streets, stones, and on trees in forests. The arrows and dots help with the direction of the Way of St. James. Though they are not the official route markers, they do confirm the direction where the official yellow signs are far apart. But be aware that in a few cases they misdirect, leading away from the signposted route.

Upon entering the village Buchillon you pass by vineyards and the village's fountain underneath a roof. At km 24.1 you arrive at the reformed Chapel of Buchillon.

192 Reformed Chapel, Buchillon (Chapelle Buchillon)

- Rue Roger de Lessert 10, 1164 Buchillon
- Right of the entrance
- The chapel was built in 1924-25. There was no predecessor church; for many centuries the population of Buchillon was deemed too small to have its own church or cemetery. They had to go to the church in Etoy, about 2.5 km to the north. The first school in Buchillon was built in 1863, and since then a school room was used for protestant services. By 1905 the municipality started the planning for its own chapel. As Canton Vaud did not support the village having its own place of worship, the community was dependent on donations to finance its chapel. It took nearly 20 years to collect the funds; construction was completed in 1925, with the support of the local community (200 inhabitants).

  Being the largest building in the village, it was also used for conferences, school festivals, concerts, and theater performances. Major renovations were undertaken in 1950-57, also financed by donations. The stained-glass windows of the chancel, bell, and pulpit date from this period. It took many more years to collect financing for the organ, which was installed in 1975.
- Wood dominates the interior: floor, ceiling, sides, pews, organ housing, and pulpit. It gives the typical protestant and austere interior a warm appearance.

From the chapel the route turns right and 300 meters later left. You enter the **Aubonne river-delta**. For 1.2 km you walk westward through a patch of forest and along a tarmac road on the edge of the forest, until you reach a concrete footbridge over the Aubonne River. The route turns left and follows the curving river southward for 1.7 km until it flows into Lake Geneva. This is a nature protected area, where nature is allowed to take its own course. You walk through a narrow patch of forest on a sandy trail that closely follows the curving river. Along the way you pass by a sand pit and, surprisingly, a kiwi farm.

As the river flows closer to the lake, the riverbed becomes wider and the trees open up. Some uprooted trees fell into the river as a result of a storm. Shortly before the river flows into Lake Geneva, the route turns right (west). At this location in the forest the signs are rather confusing. It seems as if some yellow signposts are missing, and the blue arrows/dots on the trees do not lead in the right direction (there is no clear path). You may need to search a bit to stay on the right track (the App of SwitzerlandMobility helps).

The route leaves the forest and passes by another kiwi farm. On a tarmac street the route turns back to the lake's shore. You pass by vineyards and cross road nr. 1 again. In between vineyards the route goes up the hill, diagonally away from the lake towards the town Perroy. The town lies at an elevated position with vineyards on its southern slopes. Decommissioned wine presses and large wine barrels indicate that the small town has a long history in winemaking. On your left you pass by a building that looks rather neglected. It is the former Benedictine Priory of the winemaking monks of Perroy (at km 29.8).

31 Former Benedictine Monastery, Perroy (Chateau de Perroy)

Grand'Rue, 1166 Perroy

Benedictine Order

The former monastery, nowadays called the Château of Perroy, was established by the Benedictine Abbey of Tournus, France (about 120 km to the west) from the middle of the 10th century. The monks established vineyards in Perroy and the lands north of town, and started a winemaking business. They built the monastery between 1132 and 1172.

From the end of the 15th century the monastery was in decline, as the number of monks successively decreased. By 1518 all monks had left and the monastery was converted to a winery estate.

The former monastery buildings were burned down and the estate secularized during the Bernese invasion of the lands of Vaud in 1536. The winery estate and ruined buildings were sold to a private family (de Senarclens), who reconstructed the mansion and continued the winemaking business. The mansion and wine business changed owner several times over the centuries. In 1914 the last private owners sold the mansion to the municipality of Perroy, which housed a school and the town's administrative offices in the buildings.

About 100 meters later (at km 29.9) you arrive at the reformed Church of Perroy.

Reformed Our Lady Church, Perroy (Eglise Notre-Dame) 193

Grand'Rue, 1166 Perroy

Our Lady

On a table behind the last pew

The church was built as part of the Benedictine monastery in 1132. It is believed that the church was built on the fundaments of an earlier church, dating from 1013-14. The chancel and bell tower received their present appearance from construction work in 1481-87. The nave was widened on both sides in 1538.

During the invasion of the Bernese troops in 1536, the church converted to Protestantism, upon which all catholic icons and decorations were removed.

The nave was renovated in a neoclassical style and the front porch was built in 1828. The stained-glass windows date from 1959. Major renovations, restoring the church to its original 15th century appearance, were undertaken during the 20th century, last in 1985.

You can clearly see the architectural differences between the neoclassical nave (with its columns) and the Gothic chancel (with its vaulted ceiling). The chancel has a relatively large size; the space behind the communion table is used for additional rows of chairs for parishioners.

The typical protestant interior decorations are limited to the communion table, pulpit, baptismal font, and a cross.

In Perroy you reach the highest point of stage 17 at 422 meters. For 1.4 km the route follows the village road down the vineyard slopes, across the roundabout of road nr. 1, back to the shore of Lake Geneva. You enter the outskirts of Rolle (population of around 6'000) and walk past a recreational swimming area and a camping site along the shore of the lake. After a soccer field, parking lot, playground, and skate park, you arrive at the Castle of Rolle.

The **Castle of Rolle** (*Château de Rolle*) was built by the Dukes of Savoy around 1264. They planned to establish a city in competition with Saint-Prex. The Dukes of Savoy established the town Rolle around the castle in 1319, to close a gap in their northern territories along Lake Geneva (they had already established the castle and town Morges in 1286-95). The castle stood directly at the shore of the lake, while a moat surrounded the land-side of the castle. The town itself had minimal fortifications (the castle served as a place of refuge).

From 1291 the Dukes of Savoy leased the castle to regional noble families. In 1484 Amédée de Viry became the Lord of Rolle, after the Duke of Savoy granted him fiefdom.

The castle was plundered and burned down when the Bernese invaded the lands of Vaud in 1536. In 1558 a rich Bernese patrician (Jean de Steiger) purchased the castle and rebuilt and restored it. The de Steiger family owned the castle for 240 years, until the French invasion in 1798.

One year later (1799) the municipality of Rolle acquired the castle. They used it to house a school, prison, library, and municipal offices. Nowadays the building still houses the municipal offices, Tourist Information, and a historical library with 13'000 books. Some areas are used for exhibitions and events.

The castle has several unusual architectural features. The main tower is round, the tower at the side of the lake is square, and the two other towers are half-round. The castle and its inner courtyard are V-shaped. At the opening of the V, on the western side, there is no fortification anymore (nowadays just a thin concrete wall). From the lakeside square tower, a roofed elevated wooden footbridge leads to a smaller tower standing in the water. It is unclear why this Savoy castle is so different from all the other medieval castles along the shores of Lake Geneva. It had many different owners over the centuries and it is likely that each made changes to the design of the buildings. The western fortification might have been destroyed during the battles with the Bernese.

When you walk along the gravel lakeside promenade (*Quai-Promenade*) you pass underneath the wooden footbridge. In old times this area was part of the castle's inner gardens and shielded by high walls towards the east and the lake.

In front you see a small island covered by trees, about 70 meters from the shore. It is called the Harpe Island (*Ile de la Harpe*).

61 **Harpe Island** is man-made; it was built by local merchants to protect the port from the lake's waves in 1835. Originally the island was an embankment built on the shallow sandy bottom of the lake. A small village on poles existed there, used by traders to ship wine and wood from Rolle to Geneva. The embankment was strengthened by rocks and rubble to become an island in 1837.

The island was named after **Frédéric de la Harpe**, an internationally connected political leader of that time, who was born in Rolle. In 1782-95 he was a teacher to the grandchildren of the Russian Tsar Alexander I in St. Petersburg (Russia). Upon his return from Russia, de la Harpe became one of the major political influencers striving for the lands of Vaud to become an independent Canton. This made Rolle the center for revolutionaries, who were inspired by the French Revolution and wanted to achieve freedom from the oppression of Bern. De la Harpe was part of the Board of the Helvetic Republic in 1798-1803, and enabled the establishment of the lands of Vaud as an independent Canton in 1803. Through his connections with the Russian Tsar Alexander I he secured that Vaud remained an independent Canton in 1815, when Bern reclaimed possession of the lands of Vaud. This made Frédéric de la Harpe a Cantonal hero. A 13-meter-high white obelisk memorial (1844) dedicated to de la Harpe stands in the middle of the island.

Terraces and restaurants under magnificent trees occupy most of the promenade. They look inviting for dinner and relaxation after you complete stage 17 (only 500 meters to go).

After 100 meters along the promenade you need to depart from the signposted route nr. 4 (which continues straight along the promenade) to visit the two churches of Rolle at the end of stage 17. Enter right into the *Ruelle des Halles* and 50 meters later you arrive at the catholic St. Joseph Church (at km 32.6).

The location of the church seems a bit strange. It is on a stretched patch of land with a garage partly below the chancel; it looks like it was crammed into this location.

194 St. Joseph Church, Rolle (Eglise Catholique St. Joseph)

- Ruelle des Halles 1, 1180 Rolle
- St. Joseph
- In a black box on a small white table left of the entrance
- The catholic church was built in 1843. It was one of the first catholic churches built in Canton Vaud, after the Canton allowed freedom of religion in 1810. The church was renovated in 1929-30, from which period the stained-glass windows and the ceiling vaults of the chancel date.
- It has an austere interior with limited decorations. Most interesting are the colorful stained-glass windows of the chancel.

From the catholic church continue 400 meters slightly up the hill to the north (away from the lake). After a passage underneath a building you cross road nr. 1 (*Grand-Rue*) and via the *Rue du Temple* arrive at the reformed Church of Rolle (at km 33.0).

195 Reformed Church, Rolle (Eglise Reformée)

- Route des Quatre Communes, 1180 Rolle
- On the pulpit
- The church is on the site of a predecessor catholic church that was built in 1520-21. Before that time the catholic parishioners of Rolle had to attend services at the church in Perroy, less than 3 km away. Upon the enforced Reformation in

1536, this first church converted to Protestantism. As the community of Rolle grew in the 18th century (and outgrew Perroy), the reformed parish saw the need for a larger church.

In 1789-90 the old nave and chancel were demolished and remodeled into a hall church, maintaining the bulky square bell tower (in a Romanesque style) of the previous church (1521).

Typical for a protestant hall church, the grey gallery at the back of the nave (holding the organ and additional pews) is supported by columns and curves forward to the left and right sides of the nave. Its interior is modern and austere. The stained-glass windows in the chancel date from renovations in 1878, the ones in the nave from 1920-24. The grey pulpit, accessible from two sides, at the center of the chancel dates from 1790.

From the ending point

The reformed Church of Rolle is the ending point of stage 17, about 450 meters aside the signposted route nr. 4.

In case you are a day-hiker, you need to walk 500 meters (north) to the Rolle train station.

In case you are a thru-hiker and spend the night in Rolle, there is no pilgrim inn but reasonably-priced accommodations are offered by a hostel (L'Hôtel by Hostellerie du Château; Grand-Rue 16; tel. 021 822 32 62; www.lhotel-rolle.com; info@lhotel-rolle.com) opposite the Castle and several private accommodations. Check out www.jakobsweg.ch or www.viajacobi4.ch for the accommodation possibilities in and around Rolle. You can also visit the Tourist Information Office in Rolle (Grand-Rue 1; tel. 021 825 15 35; www.tourisme-rolle.ch; tourisme@rolle.ch) located at the castle and have them help you.

The next Stage

Stage 18 guides you along Lake Geneva, past vineyards from chateau to chateau. Read the next chapter to find out what that entails.

Stage 18:
Rolle to Coppet
32 km

The Way along Vineyards and Chateaus

Route stats

	Distance in km	*Time in hrs:min*
Signposted route nr. 4	29.0	5:40
Churches/chapels	3.0	2:20
Points of interest		1:00
Rest/lunch		1:00
Stage 18	32.0	10:00

In case you hike this stage as a daytrip, you need to add 800 meters in Rolle and 600 meters in Coppet (from and to the train stations).

Ascent/descent/total	+361/ -359 / 720 altitude meters
Lowest/highest altitude	373 / 440 meters
Pathway/condition	easy / moderate
Churches/chapels	Bursinel, Prangins, Nyon (2), Crans-près-Céligny, Céligny, Bossey, Commugny, Coppet
Monasteries	Former Augustinian Monastery Nyon, Former Dominican Monastery Coppet
Points of interest	Chateau of Bursinel, Chateau of Dully, Toblerone Trail, Chateau of Prangins, Castle of Nyon, Roman Archaeological Site and Museum, Chateau of Crans, Chateau of Céligny, Chateau of Bossey, Chateau of Coppet

Route summary

Stage 18 continues in protestant **Canton Vaud**.

Stage 18 guides you along Lake Geneva, past vineyards from chateau to chateau.

Similar to stage 17, the route closely follows main road nr. 1 that was the historical trade and pilgrimage route along the western shore of the lake, connecting

Lausanne to Geneva. Compared to stage 17, though, the route is not directly along the shore of Lake Geneva anymore. Instead, it trails between 1 and 2 km distance from the shoreline. The route briefly touches the shoreline only three times (at km 1, 14, and 32). Being away from the shoreline has the advantage of great views, walking along vineyards that cover the hills, and passing by beautiful chateaus that were built on the hilltops overlooking Lake Geneva. Stage 18 has the highest number of points of interest of all stages due to the 17th and 18th century chateaus. Like a string of pearls, the chateaus quickly follow after each other between the vineyards. Each of these chateaus has an interesting history. Most of these chateaus are still in private ownership (not accessible), though some of them have been turned into a museum (accessible). Stage 18 from Rolle to Coppet is one of the most beautiful stages of the Swiss Way of St. James, hiking past vineyards from Chateau to Chateau.

From Rolle the signposted route nr. 4 goes up the hill, inland, away from the lake. The first km 5 the route is mostly between agricultural fields, until it enters the first town Bursinel. A road lined with houses leads to the next town, Dully. After a patch of forest and vineyards, the trail passes by the train station of the larger town Gland. It then takes 5 km through patches of forest along a stream and agricultural fields to the next town, Prangins. This town and Nyon make up one agglomeration. The signposted route passes by the train station of Nyon without entering into town. Because Nyon has a 750-year-old castle, a 900-year-old church, and 2'000-year-old Roman ruins, it is worthwhile to make a 1.5 km detour into the city. From Nyon the route goes along fields and through patches of forest to Crans, followed by a straight road to Céligny. After 2.5 km past agricultural fields, apple orchards, and vineyards, the route enters Founex, which is close to Commugny. From Commugny the signposted route continues southward towards Geneva. The end of stage 18 is 1.4 km aside this signposted route. This deviation is required to visit the chateau and church of Coppet at the lakeside.

The small town Coppet does not have accommodation possibilities; as a thru-hiker you may consider an alternative earlier ending of stage 18 (avoiding backtracking to an earlier point on the route that does offer accommodations). This earlier ending could be at the Chateau of Bossey or in the town Commugny. As a day-hiker Coppet is a good ending point, since it is near a train station.

Getting to the starting point

Today's starting point in Rolle is at the signposted route nr. 4 along the lake's shore (at the level of Harpe Island). In case you hike stage 18 as a daytrip, you need to walk 800 meters (downhill) from the Rolle train station to the lakeside.

Route Map and Profile

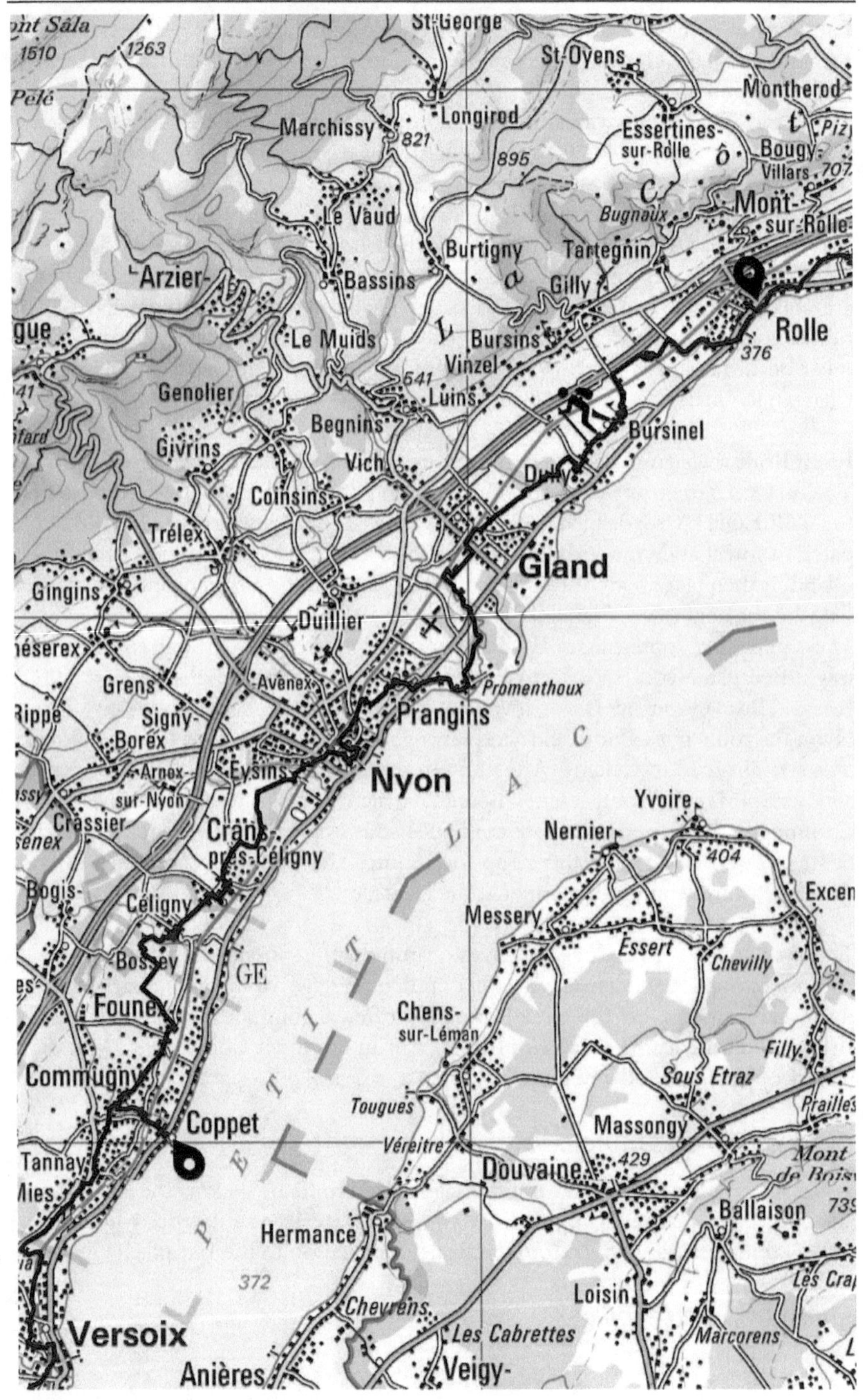
St-George
St-Oyens
Montherod
Longirod
Marchissy
821
Essertines-sur-Rolle
Bougy-Villars
895
Le Vaud
Bugnaux
Mont-sur-Rolle
Burtigny
Tartegnin
Arzier
Bassins
Gilly
Le Muids
Bursins
Rolle
376
Vinzel
641
Luins
Genolier
Begnins
Bursinel
Givrins
Vich
Dully
Coinsins
Trélex
Gland
Gingins
Duillier
Grens
Avenex
Promenthoux
Signy-Borex
Prangins
Arnex-sur-Nyon
Eysins
Nyon
Crassier
Crans-près-Céligny
Yvoire
Nernier
404
Bogis-
Céligny
Messery
Bossey
GE
Essert
Chevilly
Founex
Chens-sur-Léman
Commugny
Filly
Sous Etraz
Tougues
Coppet
Massongy
Tannay
Véreitre
Douvaine
429
Mies
Ballaison
Hermance
372
Loisin
Chevrens
Versoix
Les Cabrettes
Marcorens
Anières
Veigy-

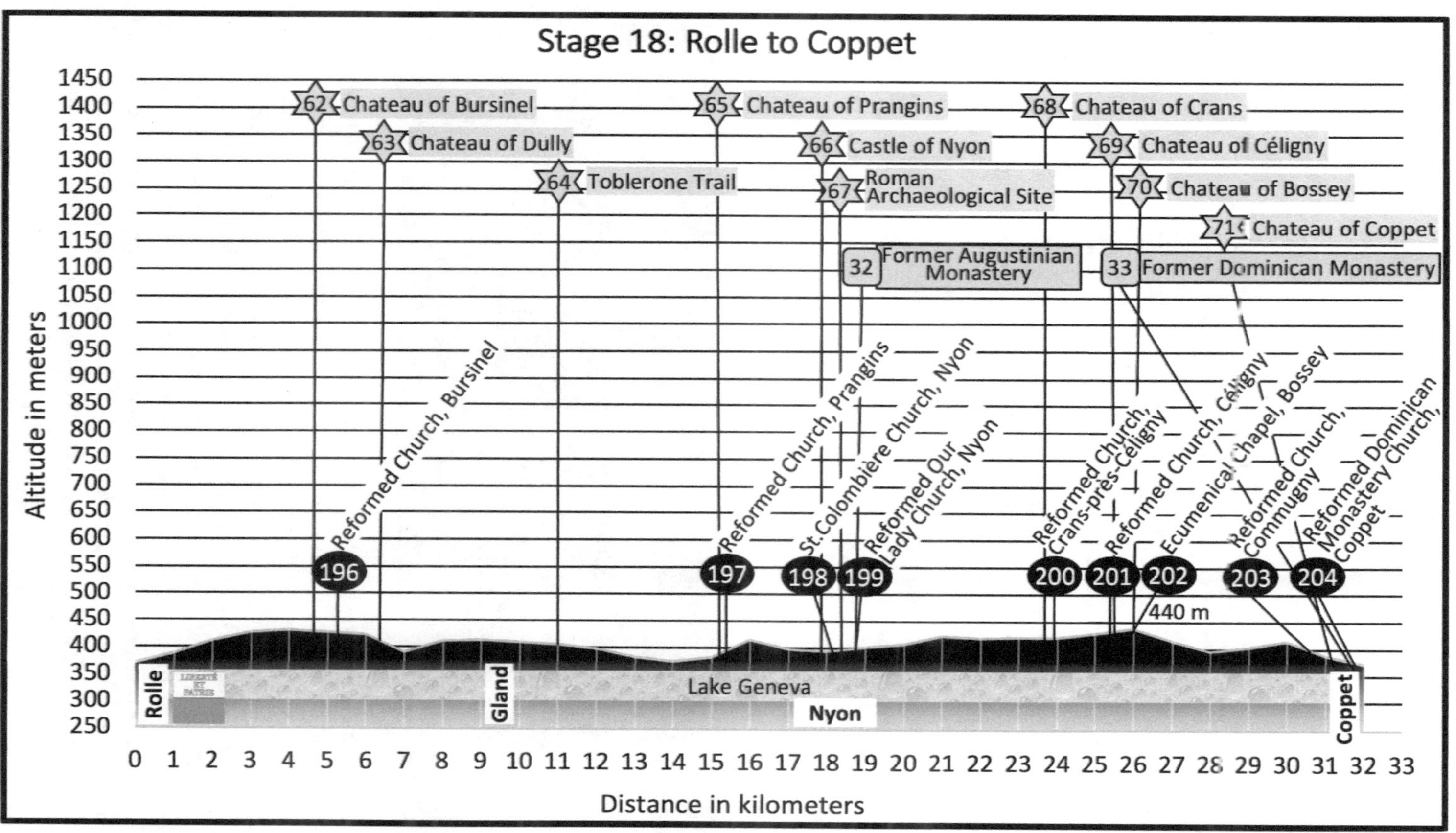
Stage 18: Rolle to Coppet
Altitude in meters
1450
1400
1350
1300
1250
1200
1150
1100
1050
1000
950
900
850
800
750
700
650
600
550
500
450
400
350
300
250
62 Chateau of Bursinel
63 Chateau of Dully
64 Toblerone Trail
65 Chateau of Prangins
66 Castle of Nyon
67 Roman Archaeological Site
68 Chateau of Crans
69 Chateau of Céligny
70 Chateau of Bossey
71 Chateau of Coppet
32 Former Augustinian Monastery
33 Former Dominican Monastery
196 Reformed Church, Bursinel
197 Reformed Church, Prangins
198 St.Colombière Church, Nyon
199 Reformed Our Lady Church, Nyon
200 Reformed Church, Crans-près-Céligny
201 Reformed Church, Céligny
202 Ecumenical Chapel, Bossey
203 Reformed Church, Commugny
204 Reformed Dominican Monastery Church, Coppet
440 m
Lake Geneva
Rolle
Gland
Nyon
Coppet
0 1 2 3 4 5 6 7 8 9 10 11 12 13 14 15 16 17 18 19 20 21 22 23 24 25 26 27 28 29 30 31 32 33
Distance in kilometers

Hiking the Route

Along the lake promenade (*Quai-Promenade*) you pass by the Rolle boat pier and port, where the route turns right to cross road nr. 1 (*Route de Genève*). The route continues up the hill along the *Route de Gilly* for 600 meters and turns left at the roundabout. On an ascending tarmac road curving to the right you hike past a vineyard, after which you pass underneath the railway tracks. Shortly afterwards the route turns left and the path becomes a gradually ascending concrete farm road between agricultural fields. Due to the elevated position you have good views over the lake (left side). The route passes through a small patch of forest, where it crosses the Gillière stream. You are near Highway A1 and can hear the busy traffic speeding by.

For 700 meters a straight concrete farm road is parallel between the highway (north) and the railway tracks (south). You pass by corns fields and apple orchards. The route makes a sharp left and follows the *Route de la Gare* southward. It would have been easiest to continue on the overpass over the train tracks, but the signposted route forks left, where you need to take a pedestrian underpass to the other side of the tracks. After the underpass the route converges back to the road that went over the tracks. Following an s-curve in the road you arrive in Bursinel. Brown signs point to the several winemakers in town. The route along vineyards provides splendid views over the lake and the mountains on the other side. Hidden behind a high wall and trees you pass by the Chateau of Bursinel (on your right).

62

The **Chateau of Bursinel** was first built in 1143, and expanded in phases from the 12th until the 15th century. The chateau has an interesting story of historical importance.

In 1527 several Lords of the lands of Vaud and the House of Savoy established the 'Brotherhood of the Knights of the Spoon' during a banquet at the chateau. The members had to wear a gold or silver spoon around their neck. This may sound funny, but it was a serious organization that was well organized and accumulated wealth contributed by its rich members. The organization's mission was to free the town Geneva from the authorities who favored close relationships with Bern. The Knights of the Spoon wanted to re-establish a Savoy/Vaud-oriented government in Geneva. They terrorized the population around Geneva for years, trying to isolate the city. In 1530 they were at the city gates of Geneva with 4'000 men, determined to 'free' the city. The authorities of Geneva had already asked Cantons Bern and Fribourg to help defend the town (which was mostly populated by merchants). The armies of Bern marched south, invaded the lands of Vaud along Lake Geneva, and on their way burned down the mansions of the members of the 'Brotherhood of the Knights of the Spoon'. The Chateau of Bursinel was also burned down in 1530. The Knights of the Spoon had lost and their organization was dissolved.

The importance to Swiss history is that the Brotherhood had provided Bern the justification to invade the lands of Vaud and conquer the territory from the House of Savoy. This was completed in 1536, upon which the Bernese ruled the lands of Vaud for 262 years.

The chateau was rebuilt around 1535, much to its original state, and was the property of the family de Sacconay for more than 300 years. In the 18th century the building was in disrepair and poor condition when it changed hands between family members. Considerable renovations were undertaken in 1760-70. It regularly changed ownership in the 20th century and an Italian billionaire put it up for sale in 2014 (it had been uninhabited since 2006). An anonymous buyer purchased it in 2015. The chateau cannot be accessed.

About 400 meters after the chateau you arrive at the reformed Church of Bursinel at km 5.2.

196 Reformed Church, Bursinel (Eglise Bursinel)

- Route de Village 13, 1195 Bursinel
- On a shelf left of the front portal
- The church was first mentioned as a chapel in 1139. It became a parish church in the 13th century. During the invasion of the lands of Vaud in 1536, the Bernese enforced the Reformation and the catholic church converted to Protestantism, as a result of which all catholic icons were removed. The church was enlarged in 1732. By 1822 the building was dilapidated and the old church was demolished. The present hall church was built in 1828-29.
- Its interior is typical protestant, limited to a pulpit, large cross, communion table, and organ.

After the church, the Way of St. James keeps following the main road, along vineyards and residential bungalows with large gardens, in a southern direction. You pass by a villa with a beautiful iron front gate, sculpted with peacocks and orange, blue, and purple colored metal flowers; a unique creation. The elevated route continues to provide panoramic views over vineyards and the lake. About 1.1 km from the church you reach the Chateau of Dully. To see it you need to enter the driveway behind the gate (it is private property).

63 The **Chateau of Dully** was first mentioned in official documents in 1463. The estate consisted of two buildings, from different periods, belonging to two different families. The buildings were connected by a gallery in the 17th

century. In 1837 the chateau was purchased by the Swiss industrialist Auguste de Meuron, who had made his fortune from Tobacco plantations in Brazil. He renovated the chateau in 1841-46, and differentiated between the historical appearances of the two buildings (one neo-Gothic and the other neo-Renaissance style). The view from the driveway is on the back of the chateau, whereas the architectural differences are mostly visible at the front or lakeside of the building. The chateau changed ownership several times and is still privately owned; it cannot be accessed.

From the chateau the route turns right for 50 meters, then left for 200 meters, after which it turns southward (left). On a farm road the route descends to a forested river valley, where three rivers converge. In the small patch of forest, you cross the Duville stream on a small footbridge. The typical Swiss triangular anti-tank obstacles are lined up alongside the stream. After crossing the Lavasson stream the trail turns right and follows the stream for about 500 meters. On a sandy path the route trails out of the valley and passes by apple orchards and vineyards. This is one of the most beautiful views along the Swiss Way of St. James.

A sandy/gravel tractor trail leads to Gland. The route continues straight, passes by the Gland pilgrim inn, and after a short right reaches the Gland train station. The route signaling at the train station is not very clear; you need to stay on the tarmac on the eastern side of the station (do not pass underneath the tracks).

At the end of the station the route turns left (*Chemin de la Crétaux*) and passes by the modern Swissquote building in an industrial area. At the end of the street turn right to follow the *Route des Avouillons* for 600 meters. At the T-crossing turn right towards the train tracks. Shortly before the train tracks a narrow path leads you to a long patch of forest along the Promenthouse stream. Shortly before this stream the signpost directs to the left (south).

The next 1 km you follow a section of the **Toblerone Trail** (*Sentier des Toblerones*). This trail has nothing to do with the triangular Swiss chocolate, other than being named after it because of its shape. The Toblerone Trail refers to the typical Swiss triangular concrete anti-tank obstacles that are lined next to each other for about 10 km from Lake Geneva to the Jura Mountain slopes. This defense line was built during the mobilization in 1939-45. The trail is a curving narrow sandy path between low bushes and overhanging trees alongside the Promenthouse stream. Most anti-tank blocks are overgrown with climbers or mosses. About halfway, a wooden plateau with a bench provides a view over the fields towards the north.

The Toblerone Trail is interrupted by road nr. 1. The Way of St. James passes underneath the road on a small concrete ledge through a tunnel next to the Promenthouse stream. In case of high water, you would not be able to walk there. On the other side of the tunnel the sign directs up to the road, and the route crosses the stream over the bridge and follows road nr. 1 for about 50 meters. The route turns back into the forest through a narrow opening in the bushes (easy to overlook, as the signpost nr. 4 is on a low pole).

The route stays on the western side of the Promenthouse stream and leaves the Toblerone Trail. After a small patch of forest, you walk along the tree line and turn back into the forest. About 1 km after road nr. 1 you leave the forest and walk on a tarmac road between agricultural fields. You pass by a residential area with several big villas and large gardens.

Along the *Route de Promenthouse* you briefly walk along the shore of Lake Geneva, pass by a hotel, and after 1.4 km the trail converges with road nr. 1. Shortly before road nr. 1 the route turns left and is parallel to the road, crosses a parking lot, and passes by a soccer field, before turning right and crossing road nr. 1. A footpath leads up the hill and you can see the Chateau of Prangins right in front of you above a high wall. The route circles around the left side (south) of the chateau and after a short ascent leads to the side entrance of the Chateau of Prangins.

The **Chateau of Prangins** is on the site of a former medieval fortress that was first mentioned in official documents in 1096. It was probably built by the Lords of Prangins, who also owned Nyon Castle.

The House of Savoy conquered the castle of Prangins in 1293 (and Nyon at the same time) and rebuilt it after battles had ruined it. The castle was again ruined when the Bernese annexed the lands of Vaud by conquering the Savoy troops in 1536.

Unlike other mansions that stay in ownership of a family for many generations, the Chateau of Prangins changed ownership many times over the centuries. The enormous property was expensive in maintenance (not to mention furnishing) and few owners could afford the high expenditures. The present Chateau of Prangins was built (and furnished) as a mansion in a French classical style by the wealthy Parisian banker Louis Guiguer in 1732-39. As owner of the chateau he received the title Baron of Prangins.

Since its remodeling to a French styled mansion in the 1730s, it attracted the attention of well-known French people. Voltaire, philosopher and advocate of separation of Church and State, lived there for a while after he was exiled from France (18th century). In 1814 ownership changed to Joseph Bonaparte, older brother of Napoleon Bonaparte.

From 1873 until 1920 the chateau housed a school. Between 1920 and 1974 it changed owner four times. It became the property of Canton Vaud in 1974, which donated it to the Swiss Federal State in 1975. They housed the Swiss National Museum for

French-speaking South-West Switzerland in the chateau in 1998. It seems the chateau found its final owner: the Swiss State, being rich enough to be able to finance the maintenance and care for the immense property.

It is the largest 18th century chateau in Switzerland open to the public, organizing permanent and temporary exhibitions of Swiss history. The park contains Switzerland's largest historical kitchen garden, resembling its original 18th century design. A ticket costs CHF 10. Information guides are available in several languages.

From the southern side of the chateau follow the 100-meter promenade along the walls of the garden to arrive at the reformed Church of Prangins (at km 15.4).

197 **Reformed Church, Prangins** (Temple de Prangins)

- Avenue du Général Guiguer 4, 1197 Prangins
- On a shelf right of the front portal
- Prangins had a Romanesque chapel from around 1184, which stood southwest of the castle at a crossing of several roads. The chapel belonged to the Benedictine Abbey of Saint-Oyens-de-Joux, France until 1210, when it passed to the Bishopric Kingdom of Lausanne. Ownership of the chapel transferred to the protestant parish of Nyon after the Reformation in 1536.

  From 1671 the chapel belonged to an independent parish, being the owner of the chateau. During these times the chapel was neglected and by the middle of the 18th century it was dilapidated. The City Council decided to build a new church and made a land-swap deal with the then owner of the chateau, Baron Guiguer. The Baron received the lands of the old chapel and in return provided the land for the new church. The Baron had the old dilapidated chapel demolished in 1759. Under direction of the administrator of the chateau and with partial financing by the Baron, a new and modern church was built at the present location in 1761.

  The church is now located west of the chateau, opposite its large French garden, at the end of the promenade lined with linden trees.
- The protestant hall church has an interior similar to the ones in Bursinel and Rolle, which were built in the same period.

From the church follow the signs southward for 200 meters to the *Chemin de Trembly*. Follow this road for 800 meters towards the railway tracks. You walk through a stately residential area with large villas behind high walls and hedges, and pass by a vineyard providing wide views over the lake.

At the train tracks follow the nr. 4 signs left (south) on a narrow tarmac footpath next to the tracks for 800 meters. This path takes you to the Nyon train station.

At the Nyon train station you need to leave the signposted route nr. 4. This route continues straight and keeps following the train tracks, without entering the 2'000-year-old city of Nyon. The town has a castle from the year 1272, a church from 1110, and 2'000-year-old Roman archaeological artefacts. It is worthwhile to make a 1.5 km **detour into Nyon** to visit these interesting historical buildings and sites.

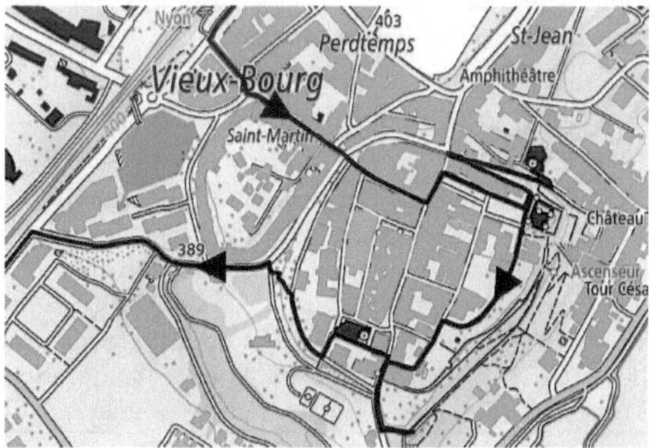

When you are in front of the Nyon train station turn left (east, towards the lake) into the *Rue de la Gare* (instead of going straight, south). Follow the signs to the Chateau/Nyon

Port/Musées. At the end of the road turn left, the first right, and 500 meters from the station you reach the *Place du Château* with the white castle right in front of you.

66 The white **Castle of Nyon** towers high above the city. It was built on top of ruins of a Roman settlement that had occupied the hill overlooking Lake Geneva in the 1st century. The castle was built by the Lords of Prangins and was first mentioned in official documents in 1272. They owned the town Nyon, but lost the town and castle in a battle to the House of Savoy in 1293. The castle was seriously damaged and rebuilt by Duke Louis of Savoy.

The square castle has architectural styles from several centuries. Significant changes to its appearance were made in the 15th century. After the annexation of the lands of Vaud by Bern the castle was converted to the seat of Bern's Sheriff in 1536. The present appearance originates mostly from construction work in 1574-83.

The Bernese Sheriffs occupied the castle for 262 years, until Napoleon's armies occupied Switzerland in 1798. The castle became the property of the Canton, when Canton Vaud was established in 1803. The City of Nyon purchased the castle from the Canton one year later. From 1804 it housed judicial courts, municipal offices, a school, and a prison. The square tower also served as private residence. From 1888 the castle housed a museum.

The castle used to be surrounded by a moat and had a drawbridge, which together with watchtowers and a fortified wall protected the town. The medieval fortified city walls and gates were demolished in 1718, and the remaining fortifications in 1822-25. Wall remnants can be seen at the bell tower of the reformed Our Lady Church and at the *Promenade des Marronniers*. Together with this church (see below), the castle is the last remaining medieval building in Nyon.

The square in front of the castle was created in 1822-25, when all houses there were demolished to create a better view of the castle. Comprehensive renovations were undertaken in 1999-2006.

Nowadays the historic fortress houses a museum. The museum has permanent as well as temporary contemporary art exhibitions, focusing on the town and region. A tour of the permanent exhibition includes a visit to two floors with famous neoclassical Porcelain collections (made in Nyon until 1813), a floor with prison cells (built after 1804 and in use until 1979), and a floor under the roof to see the wooden structures built 400 years ago. A ticket costs CHF 8 and also provides access to the Roman Museum (both museums are closed on Mondays).

North of the castle is the modern catholic church of Nyon. Follow the *Terrasse de Bonstetten* westward, make a sharp right into the *Ruelle des Moulins* (downhill), take the stairs down on the left, and you arrive at the catholic St. Colombière Church of Nyon (at km 18.2).

St. Colombière Church, Nyon (Eglise de la Colombière) 198

Rue de la Colombière 18, 1260 Nyon

St. Colombière

In 1810-30 the laws for catholic churches in Canton Vaud were very restrictive. Though catholic services were allowed after 1810, neither bells, nor other external signs were allowed, nor were any processions outside the building, until 1830.

From 1810 the chapel of the local hospital, outside of town, was used for catholic services.

In 1832 a new catholic parish was established, which initiated plans to build an own church in the city of Nyon. This first church was built in 1837. The parish started planning for the construction of a replacement church in 1948, as the old church had become too small. It lasted another 27 years before sufficient funds were available to start this construction.

The old church was demolished in 1975, and the new (present) church was built in 1975-77 (renovated in 2012).

The church and its interior have a modern 1970s design. Most interesting is the pyramidal roof. From the window in the pyramid's top, light shines in the chancel and on the altar table. When you look up you can see three bells integrated in the windowsill. The artistic stained-glass windows were made by Yoki.

From the catholic church retrace the same 200 meters to the front side of the Castle of Nyon. Cross the square and continue straight into the *Rue Maupertuis.*

After about 50 meters you pass by a **Roman Archaeological Site** on the right. Julius Caesar established the first Roman colony (Colonia Iulia Equestris) in Switzerland in Nyon in 46-45 BC. Its center town was called Noviodunum and was occupied by the Romans for nearly three centuries. Together with Lousonna, Noviodunum was one of the important Roman settlements along Lake

Geneva. The archaeological site comprises: the remains of an amphitheater (discovered in 1996); a statue representing Julius Caesar (replica from Rome); and a Roman Museum (built around the remains of a Roman Basilica, discovered in 1974).

The Roman Museum is an **Archeological Site Museum** with many artefacts from the Roman occupation of Nyon: sculptures, religious objects, and objects of crafts and trade. Most interesting are the footprint and 2-meter-high walls of the old Basilica. A ticket costs CHF 8, and also provides access to the museum of the Castle (both museums are closed on Mondays).

You should see one more Roman archeological object: three **Roman Columns**, about 300 meters from the museum. Keep following the *Rue Maupertuis,* at the T-crossing turn left into the *Rue du Vieux-Marché*, and at the next T-crossing again left into the *Grand'Rue.* After a few meters you arrive at a large gravel square (left), where you see the Roman Columns. The columns were excavated at a nearby location and placed at the square in 1958. They were part of a subterranean passageway (cryptoporticus) of a Roman Forum (square) built around 50 AD. The gravel promenade that leads towards the castle on the left (with the rows of plane trees) is the *Promenade des Marronniers.* There you see the remnants of the medieval fortification walls.

From the Roman Columns return to the *Grand'Rue,* take the first left (*Rue du Prieuré*), and 60 meters from the columns you arrive at the reformed Our Lady Church of Nyon (km 18.8).

199 Reformed Our Lady Church, Nyon (Temple de Nyon)

Rue du temple 2, 1260 Nyon

Our Lady

The church was first mentioned in official documents when it was part of a Benedictine monastery (see below) in 1110. The church, dedicated to Our Lady, was built with stones and materials from the old Roman settlements in Nyon, and replaced a first Romanesque church, probably from the 8th century. By 1442 the building was dilapidated and the nave was rebuilt in 1448.

During the conquest of the lands of Vaud by the Bernese in 1536, the catholic church was forced to convert to protestant worship. All catholic icons were removed and the walls were whitewashed to cover all frescos. The building was renovated and changed several times in 1661-1718 and in the 19th to 21st centuries.

As you see the church today, the chancel dates from the 12th century, the nave from 1448, and the ceiling and side-chapels from 1470-81. In 1795 the original bell tower was demolished, as its size and weight endangered the structural stability of the chancel beneath it. It was remodeled with a reinforced concrete frame in the old Romanesque style 141 years later (1936). The last renovations were undertaken in 2012-16.

Special features of the church are: the chancel's wall frescos depicting Pentecost and the Last Supper from the end of the 13th century (they were whitewashed multiple times after the Reformation, uncovered in 1925-26); the blue and red colored stained-glass windows from the renovations in 1926 and 1951; the ceiling vaults with arabesque decorations; the small chancel with the Lombard arches and pillars around the small windows, in the base of the bell tower; and the 8th century eroded sandstone memorial.

The front portico has a modern electronic information table that provides additional information (in French) about the history of the church.

Former Augustinian Monastery, Nyon (Couvent de Augustines) 32

Rue du temple 2, 1260 Nyon

Augustinian Order

The Benedictine Abbey of Saint-Oyens-de-Joux (France) established a subsidiary priory in Nyon and built the church around 1100. In 1244 ownership of the monastery and its church changed to the Augustinian Order. By then the Benedictine Orders were in decline and new mendicant Orders, such as the Augustinians, were on the rise. The Augustinian Order specifically sought out 13th century developing cities, such as Nyon, for preaching and helping the poor. The Augustinians occupied the monastery and church until the Reformation.

The last prior of the Augustinian monastery, before the military enforced Reformation in 1536, was Aymon de Gingings, who was also the abbot of Bonmont and Bishop of Geneva. Upon the conquest of Nyon by Bernese troops, the Augustinian monastery was closed and all their properties secularized.

The church converted to Protestantism and the town's hospital moved into the monastery's buildings in 1539.

The Reformation caused two more medieval religious buildings in Nyon to be destroyed. In 1296 Duke Louis of Savoy established a Franciscan monastery, where several members of the House of Savoy were buried. During battles with Bernese and Fribourg troops the monastery was plundered and all catholic artwork was destroyed by the Bernese army in 1530. When the Savoy troops could not prevent the annexation by Bern in 1536, they burned down the monastery as they retreated from Nyon. It was never rebuilt; nothing is left of it today.

Outside the medieval city walls another church existed, dedicated to St. John the Baptist. This church was first mentioned in official documents in 1346, and was under the authority of the Augustinian monastery latest from 1412. The church was a medieval pilgrimage destination with relics of the martyrs of the Theban Legion. The church was destroyed by order of the Bernese Authorities in 1537, shortly after the annexation of Nyon. It was never rebuilt; nothing is left of it today.

From the reformed church you need to go back to the signposted route nr. 4 along the Nyon railway station. From the entrance of the reformed church go southward and after 30 meters turn right. Follow the street for 100 meters, at the end turn left into the *Rue de la Combe*, and after 300 meters you arrive at the railway tracks on the *Avenue Reverdil.* Cross the road, turn left, and you are back on the official route.

At the T-crossing cross the road and turn right to go over the railway tracks. Immediately turn into the road on the left (*Chemin du Lignolet*) and follow it for 400 meters downhill through a residential area. At a small patch of forest turn left and on a concrete footbridge you cross the Boiron de Nyon stream.

After the bridge the route direction is unclear; keep following the white gravel trail towards the right. The route climbs out of the valley and leaves the small patch of forest along a hedge. At a country road the route turns left and immediately right, where you pass by a farm. After a curve the route follows a straight tarmac road along the edge of a forest for about 600 meters.

Over agricultural fields to the right (north) you have clear views of the forested Jura mountain range with elevations of 1'400 to 1'500 meters. When the road makes a right curve, the Way of St. James turns left into the forest (*Bois Neuf*). On a sandy trail the route goes through the forest in a southern direction. After 800 meters you leave the forest and on a tarmac road pass by a vineyard. From the elevated position you have wide views over the lake and the Savoy mountains. The road turns right, passes by a residential area with villas, and turns left converging with the road (*Route d'Eysins*) that leads into the town Crans. The route does not enter the village center, but turns left and then right into the *Rue Antoine Saladin*. On the left you see a chateau hidden by the trees of its driveway. It is the Chateau of Crans.

The **Chateau of Crans** is on the site of Roman villas from the 1st-4th centuries. After the Bernese occupation in 1536, the Quisard family bought the estate and built a fortified mansion in 1542. Heirs of the Quisard family sold the estate to Antoine Saladin in 1763. He was a wealthy Genevan banker who returned from Paris. Saladin demolished the fortified mansion and built a chateau in French classical style in 1764-69. Many respected architects and craftsmen worked on its design and construction. The chateau was mostly used as a summer residence. It was renovated several times, last in 1987-88. The chateau is still owned by descendants of Antoine Saladin and is not publicly accessible.

Nowadays the chateau is mostly known for the 14 different wines produced from its 1'000-year-old vineyards. They offer wine tasting in the vaulted cellars underneath the chateau.

Continuing on the *Rue Antoine Saladin* you pass by the winemaker's buildings and a pastel-colored house with a short steeple, resembling a church (which it is not). At the crossing the signposted route directs to the right, but you need to turn left to the reformed Church of Crans-près-Céligny. After 50 meters on the *Rue de l'Eglise* with the pastel colored houses, you arrive at the church (at km 24.0).

200 Reformed Church, Crans-près-Céligny (Temple de Crans)

Rue de l'Eglise 11, 1299 Crans-près-Céligny

On the shelf of a cupboard left of the front portal

The church was built before 1500. Upon the enforcement of the Reformation by Bern in 1536, the catholic church converted to Protestantism and all religious icons were removed.

The history of this small church is marked by appearance-changing renovations and partly undoing these again. Major changes were made in 1888, when the floor of the previously round chancel was elevated and made rectangular, the window of the chancel was bricked up, arches were removed, and a front portal was built.

The interior of the church was renovated again in 1936-37, when they tried to restore some of the features of the previous church. Wooden beams were placed at the ceiling to imitate arches. The bricked-up window space in the chancel was broken through the wall again and a new stained-glass window was placed. In 2014 another renovation was undertaken to refresh the interior; this time consistent with the previous renovation.

The ceiling above the chancel and the angels on the walls were painted by a local artist in the typical 1930s pastel colors. This artist, Jean van Berchem, had already participated in creating the artwork in the St. Peter Church in Fribourg (see church nr. 160, stage 14). The ceiling above the chancel looks like a memory game: it has 60 panels painted with biblical themes, each one occurring twice. Notice how grapes are present everywhere, demonstrating the importance of winemaking to the town. Organ music plays upon entering the church.

On a bench behind the church you can rest and admire the view over the vineyards and Lake Geneva, with the Savoy mountains at the horizon.

From the church walk back to the signposted route and keep going straight for about 300 meters, after which the route turns left. You are on a road that connects Crans-près-Céligny to Céligny. Upon leaving Crans-près-Céligny the road slightly descends to cross the Nant de Pry stream.

At this location you change from Canton Vaud to **Canton Geneva**. Between km 24.6 and 25.9 you are crossing a small patch of land that is part of Canton Geneva. The Canton has a plot of land in the shape of a U within Canton Vaud (the open end of the U being in the lake). It is called the '**Corridor of Bogis-Bossey**' and has a historical reason: from the 14th century the Bishopric Kingdom of Geneva owned this corridor of land; upon the invasion of the Bernese troops in 1536 they claimed the corridor to make it part of the lands of Vaud; it remained with Geneva based on an agreement of 1564.

A road sign indicates that it is only 20 km to Geneva; you are getting close to the end of the Way of St. James through Switzerland. The route follows a gravel footpath left of a hedge that separates from the road to Céligny. After 600 meters you arrive in the small town.

With a population of less than 700 the town may be small, but its small size has made up for it with fame. The **village Céligny** had several famous people visiting and staying (forever). Richard Burton (American actor), Alistair MacLean (Scottish writer), and Vilfredo Pareto (Italian economist known for the Pareto-Principle – the 80/20 rule) all lived there and were buried at the village's cemetery. Benito Mussolini (Italian dictator) lived in the village during his years in exile.

In the village the road turns left and right, and you walk straight towards the reformed Church of Céligny (at km 25.4), with the chateau behind it.

201 Reformed Church, Céligny (Temple de Céligny)

Route de Céligny 67, 1298 Céligny

The church is the oldest building of the village, built on the remains of a Roman villa from the 4th century. Two predecessor wooden churches existed before a Romanesque stone church was built around the year 1000. The latter church had a rectangular nave and a square chancel. With the annexation by Bernese troops in 1536, the church converted to Protestantism and all catholic icons were removed. Over the centuries this stone church was destroyed, rebuilt, and reshaped several times until it received its present appearance in 1806. In the beginning of the 16th century the church had a vaulted Gothic chancel, but this was demolished when the present rectangular shape was built in 1806. The arcaded bell tower over the entrance was rebuilt at the end of the 18th century.

The church burned down in 1991, and was rebuilt and reopened in 1993, restored to its original appearance from 1806.

The church has no separate chancel; inside the pews are oriented towards the long northern wall (instead of towards the east, which would have been the case in the predecessor churches). The pulpit, lectern, and communion table came from the Escalade side-chapel of the reformed St. Gervase Church in Geneva (see church nr. 210, stage 19). The organ is set in a beautiful wood-carved housing and dates from 1994. The doors to the church are locked; you cannot access it outside the hours of services.

South of the church, behind an iron gate, you see the Chateau of Céligny.

The **Chateau of Céligny**, also called Chateau de Garengo, was built in 1722 and enlarged as a mansion in the 19th century. The name Garengo was derived from the name of the plot of land on which the chateau was built. Originally the Céligny family built a fortified mansion on the plot of land in the 15th century. Like other large chateaus, it had many owners over the centuries. The famous American pianist and composer Ernest Schelling owned the chateau and used it as his Swiss summer residence from 1910. Other famous pianists regularly played at the mansion's music room, such as Ignacy Paderewski and Nikita Magaloff (who lived nearby). Schelling's widow sold the chateau to Ernst Schmidheiny, a Swiss industrialist, in 1945. The chateau is still privately-owned; the estate cannot be accessed.

From the chateau walk back to the main street, turn left, and 100 meters later left again. You walk on a narrow tarmac road between old walls and hedges. After a right and left curve, the tarmac turns into gravel leading to a small patch of forest. On a wooden footbridge you cross the Nant du Courtenaud stream. At this location you leave Canton Geneva and re-enter **Canton Vaud**.

The route follows a grass trail at the edge of the small patch of forest in the upstream direction of the Nant du Courtenaud stream. About 500 meters later you get to a tarmac road that leads past some houses and other buildings. Towards the right you can see a chateau with a round tower. The route circles around its park to the front side (east), from where you have a great view of the Chateau of Bossey.

The **Chateau of Bossey** is an estate with a long history. It was first mentioned when the Bishopric Kingdom of Geneva transferred the estate to the Abbey of Bonmont (about 10 km northwest of Bossey) in 1125. The Abbey established the estate as a winery for its vineyards and built a fortified castle. Nowadays all that is left of the castle is the round tower.

The Abbey maintained ownership until the Bernese annexed the lands of Vaud in 1536 (and secularized the Abbey). The Bernese sold the estate to a private person, after which it was sold again several times. Most of the present appearance dates from 1722-58, when it was rebuilt as a mansion by a wealthy family. As with the Chateau of Prangins, maintenance and furnishing was expensive. The property changed hands many times since then.

At the beginning of the 20th century its purpose changed from private mansion to public service. From 1930 it housed an American College and from 1939 was an internment for soldiers, until the World Council of Churches bought the chateau in 1946. They made it the permanent seat of their Ecumenical Institute.

The Ecumenical Institute is the international center for encounter, dialogue, and formation of the World Council of Churches. Every year students from all over the world attend an academic year at the Institute for theological formation and education. The campus hosts the library of the World Council of Churches, which contains about 100'000 volumes. Apart from the Ecumenical Institute, it also houses a hotel and conference center for meetings, weddings, conferences, and banquets.

During his visit to Switzerland, Pope Francis attended the celebration of the 70th anniversary of the World Council of Churches at the chateau on 21 June 2018.

The chateau also offers accommodation to passing pilgrims at fair prices (www.chateaubossey.ch; bossey@wcc-coe.org; tel. 022 960 73 00). In case you are a thru-hiker, you may consider making this point an alternative ending of stage 18 (Coppet at the end of the stage does not have accommodation possibilities).

You can visit their Ecumenical Chapel (at km 26.5).

Ecumenical Chapel, Chateau of Bossey, Bossey 202

Chemin Chenevière 2, 1279 Bogis-Bossey

The chapel is situated next to the old tower. The small rectangular chapel is used by visitors of all faiths staying at the Ecumenical Institute. This is the third ecumenical church along the Swiss Way of St. James.

The chapel has rough stone walls, as an extension of the old tower. Stained-glass windows from floor to ceiling on one side of the room let in the light. The interior is austere. The stone walls and low wooden ceiling give it a rustic appearance. The chancel has a small communion table and a large wooden cross against the wall, flanked by two small paintings depicting Mary and Jesus.

Left of the entrance gate you see an old house with a round tower. It must have been the house of the gatekeeper at the former entrance to the chateau.

When you look east towards the lake, you see an unkept driveway. This is the original driveway leading from road nr. 1 to the chateau. It is perfectly straight and lined with trees, with a length of 1.5 km. The old driveway has not been used for a long time: nowadays the railway tracks go across the driveway on the lower side of the hill; the overgrowing trees and bushes are unkept; and the path is a combination of sand, gravel, and loose rocks. The hiking signpost directing the way stands in the bushes and is almost overgrown by the trees.

The route follows the old driveway down the hill for 400 meters, after which it turns right. For 600 meters the route is on a straight tarmac road passing through open fields and an apple orchard. Rows of apple trees stand on the southern slopes in the direction of the lake. The route turns left and for 1 km gradually descends along agricultural fields and vineyards to the residential areas of Fournex. At the village's main street (*Grand'Rue*) the route turns right. Follow this road on a tarmac path for 2 km. You pass by agricultural fields, residential areas, a school complex with soccer fields, and enter the town Commugny.

The route follows the tarmac road through a residential area with stone walls and high hedges protecting the privacy of the houses behind them. A fountain is hardly visible behind the colorful flowers. In front you see the bulky square tower of the reformed Church of Commugny at km 30.6.

Reformed Church, Commugny (Temple de Commugny) 203

Chemin du Clos, 1291 Commugny

In a small side-chapel (*Chapelle de Prière*)

The church is one of the oldest in the region, originating around 515. It was built on the foundations of a Roman villa dating from the 1st century, belonging to the Roman colony of Nyon (Colonia Iulia Equestris). A second church replaced the first one in the $8^{th}/9^{th}$ century. This church was first mentioned in official documents in 1026. During the subsequent 1'000 years many alterations and expansions were undertaken: in the 11th century the chancel (in the base of the bell tower) was changed from semicircular to square; and in the 14th to 16th centuries seven side-chapels were successively built into the church. During the 20th century the church was renovated four times. The stained-glass windows date from 1933, 1947, and 1972. In 1998 the bell tower was restored, the roof repaired, and its interior refurbished to modern standards.

Upon the annexation of the lands of Vaud by the Bernese in 1536, the catholic church converted to Protestantism. Judging from the many side-chapels that were constructed before the Reformation, the church must have had many catholic statues, altars, and paintings (probably one side-altar in each side-chapel). Unfortunately, these were all destroyed during the Reformation.

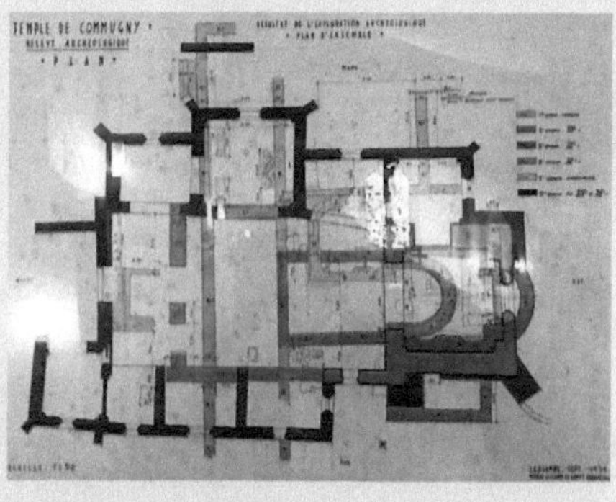

Compared to other churches along the Way of St. James, the most interesting features of this old church are the seven side-chapels. Have a closer look at the map of the floorplan (1931) on the wall right of entrance, outlining the expansion phases of the church.

Left of the chancel is a small side-chapel (*Chapelle de Prière* – prayer chapel) dedicated to pilgrims.

At the square/car park in front of the church you need to **depart from the signposted route nr. 4**. The signposted route continues straight to the south and does not enter the town Coppet. As you can see on the Way of St. James signpost opposite the church, it is only a 4hr:30min hike to the St. Peter Cathedral in Geneva. But that is the route for stage 19. The end of stage 18 is in Coppet at the lake (1.4 km aside the signposted route), because of the 750-year-old Chateau of Coppet and the 500-year-old Dominican monastery church. Be aware that Coppet does not have accommodation possibilities. In case you are a thru-hiker, you may have to return to Commugny that has two inns offering accommodations.

To continue, follow the yellow signs towards the Coppet train station/port. Walk down the hill on the *Chemin du Clos* for 800 meters until you reach the train tracks.

Continue across the tracks down the hill on the *Rue de la Gare*. You pass by the large garden (behind a wall and hedge) and then the Chateau of Coppet.

The **Chateau of Coppet** was first mentioned in official documents in 1268, when it was a fortified castle with a moat and drawbridge, belonging to the Dukes of Savoy. In the subsequent centuries several noble families resided at the castle, such as Othon de Grandson and Amédée de Viry from 1484. When the Bernese conquered the lands of Vaud from the House of Savoy, they burned down part of the castle in 1536. It was reconstructed by the Lords of Viry and subsequently changed owner several times, each time to wealthy French families.

Around 1665 the fortified castle was reconstructed as a mansion. It was expanded to its present appearance in 1767-71. In 1784 Jacques Necker, a Genevan banker who was Finance Minister of King Louis XVI of France, bought the chateau. King Louis XVI was the last King of France, until the French Revolution of 1789; he was married to Marie Antionette of Austria. Under influence of French interior designs of the 18th century, Jacques Necker was responsible for the interior decorations, which you can still see today.

During the 18th and 19th centuries the family received many famous French guests, making the chateau well-known among the international elite. Today the chateau is still owned by the descendants of Jacques Necker.

The chateau has its original furniture, paintings, art, family souvenirs, and interior decorations from the 18th and 19th centuries. Nowadays the chateau is the only one in the region still occupied by descendants. Though it is not a public museum, you can visit the family residence for sightseeing (April until October; closed on Mondays; ticket CHF 10). The foundation that manages the estate regularly organizes cultural and artistic events and exhibitions. Some of the rooms can be rented for weddings, banquets, or other events.

From the chateau continue on the street down the hill towards the lake. At road nr. 1 (*Grand'Rue*) cross the zebra crossing and turn left. You arrive at the old center of Coppet (population of around 3'000) with small stores under the arcades. The small town was established around 1300, under the protection of the fortified Castle of Coppet. Being at the border between Canton Geneva and Canton Vaud, the small town derived much of its business from transportation. In the 18th century it had four inns accommodating travelers (nowadays there are none).

Opposite the arcades is the reformed Church of the former Dominican Monastery of Coppet (at km 32.0). The church and monastery are situated in a row of old houses directly on the busy street. From the outside the buildings look weathered. The short round steeple of the church reveals it being a place of worship (otherwise one might miss it).

Former Dominican Monastery, Coppet (Couvent de Dominicain) 33

- Ruelle du temple, 1296 Coppet
- Dominican Order
- The former Dominican monastery was established by the Lord of Coppet (Amédée de Viry) in 1490. Amédée de Viry was already Lord of Rolle (see point of interest nr. 60, stage 17) and after the Duke of Savoy also granted him fiefdom in Coppet in 1484, he financed the Dominican Order to come to Coppet and set up a monastery and church. The small monastery did not exist longer than 46 years. Upon the conquest of the lands of Vaud, the Bernese closed the monastery and secularized its assets in 1536. The monastery buildings next to the church were put to different uses.

Reformed Dominican Monastery Church, Coppet (Eglise Reformée) 204

- Ruelle du temple, 1296 Coppet

Four Evangelists

On a table at the front-right side-chapel, next to a pilgrim guestbook and information about the Way of St. James in the region

The church was an extension of the Holy Spirit Chapel that was built in 1379. This chapel was part of an institute that cared for the poor and homeless. The church was built in a late-Gothic, or flamboyant, style as part of the Dominican monastery in 1500-10. This was the last catholic church built in Vaud before the Bernese invasion and Reformation in 1536. The church was catholic for only 30 years, after which it was converted to Protestantism. The Reformation caused the destruction of the new statues, interior decorations, and a rood screen. The baroque bell tower was added in 1723, replacing the original small steeple. The church was renovated in 1774 and 1927.

From the outside the church does not look well maintained, but its interior is in top condition. When you enter the church, it is likely going to be dark inside. You can switch on the lights (the three green buttons at the top of the switchboard) in the small front portal. Just do not forget to switch them off again upon leaving the church.

You first enter the small Holy Spirit side-chapel that has a cabinet with information leaflets about the church in several languages. This was the chapel that already existed since 1379, and to which the church was attached.

The interior of the church has several special features. Left of the chancel is a tall recess, framed in masonry, with the date 1484. This recess used to lead to a small tomb chapel where Amédée de Viry was buried (1519). After the Reformation it became a sacristy and later it was sold because the parish needed money. The entrance to the former tomb chapel was bricked up and nowadays holds a black memorial plaque for a later Baron of Coppet (Daniel I of Bellujon – 1630).

The walnut choir stalls and carved main front door are still the originals from the time the church was built (1510).

The small organ in the chancel dates from around 1800, whereas the large organ on the gallery was built in a similar style in 1992. Notice the exact placement of the pipes of the organ so that the stained-glass window remained unobstructed.

The pulpit dates from 1787 and replaced the original one from 1568.

The most interesting aspects of the church are its stained-glass windows (1933-50) from Charles Clément. The windows in the chancel depict the Crucifixion of Christ with the Four Evangelists on the left and right. Most special is the Gothic masonry at the top of the windows. Have a closer look at the middle window.

Notice how the glass was fit in the masonry and how the shooting stars fit in the shapes.

Unique is the masonry and the fitting of the colored glass in the window next to the large organ. See how the angels were shaped to fit the rare shapes of the masonry.

The church is closed on Saturdays and Sundays.

From the ending point

The reformed Church of the former Dominican Monastery is the ending point of stage 18, about 1.4 km aside the signposted route nr. 4.

In case you are a day-hiker, you need to walk back 500 meters up the hill, past the chateau, to the Coppet train station.

In case you are a thru-hiker and want to spend the night in Coppet, be aware that there are no accommodation possibilities. The two closest fairly-priced hotels are in Commugny (about 600 meters west of the church of Commugny). Since Coppet has a station it would also be easy to take the train to a nearby bigger town with more accommodation possibilities. Check out www.jakobsweg.ch or www.viajacobi4.ch for the accommodation possibilities near Coppet. You can also ask the Tourist Information Office in Coppet (Grand-Rue 65; tel. 022 960 87 37; info-coppet@nrt.ch; www.lacote-tourisme.ch) located inside the town hall on the Grand'Rue, 30 meters north of the church (in the building with the blue/white shutters) to help you find accommodation.

The next Stage

Stage 19 guides you along Lake Geneva and across the Rhone River to the historic upper city of Geneva. Read the next chapter to find out what that entails.

Stage 19:
Coppet to Geneva
19 km

The Way to the Center of the Reformation

Route stats

	Distance in km	*Time in hrs:min*
Signposted route nr. 4	18.5	3:40
Churches/chapels	0.8	2:00
Points of interest		2:00
Rest/lunch		0:50
Stage 19	19.3	8:30

In case you hike this stage as a daytrip, you need to add 800 meters in Coppet to go from the train station to the starting point. In Geneva the stage ends about 1.2 km from the train station, where you can take a tram or bus.

Ascent/descent/total	+241 / -261 / 502 altitude meters
Lowest/highest altitude	373 / 452 meters
Pathway/condition	easy / easy
Churches/chapels	Genthod, Bellevue, Pregny-Chambésy, Geneva (6)
Monasteries	none
Points of interest	Chateau of Tournay, Chateau of Rothschild, Chateau of Penthes, Botanical Gardens, Water-Jet Fountain, Medieval Clock Tower, Cathedral Archaeological Museum, International Reformation Museum

Route summary

Stage 19 continues in protestant Canton Vaud and enters protestant **Canton Geneva** after 3.2 km.

Stage 19 guides you along Lake Geneva and across the Rhone River to the historic upper city of Geneva.

From km 1 to 13 the route is on a plateau about 1 km west of road nr. 1 and the lake's shore. This plateau is at around 410 meters. On the plateau the route passes by a few small vineyards and some parks, but most of the time it is on tarmac streets through the northern agglomerations of the city of Geneva. These agglomerations such as Genthod, Bellevue, Chambésy, and Pregny are not the usual residential areas: they are the Beverly Hills of Geneva. The route goes past mansions hidden behind high hedges or iron entrance gates, chateaus owned for centuries by the same wealthy families, foreign embassies, and head offices of international organizations and luxury brand companies.

For 1 km the route descends from the plateau to the Lake Geneva shore at 373 meters. The last 5 km are through the streets of the city of Geneva.

With only 19.3 km, stage 19 is relatively short. Geneva is a 2'000-year-old city that was under the rule of the Bishopric Kingdom of Geneva for 1'000 years, until the Reformation in 1536. The City played a leading role during the Reformation: the reformed St. Peter Cathedral and the nearby International Reformation Museum demonstrate Jean Calvin's reformative influence on churches and society. Together with a 3'000-square-meter Archaeological Museum underneath the reformed St. Peter Cathedral, these points of interest require enough time to take in their significance.

Getting to the starting point

Today's starting point is at the signposted route nr. 4 at the reformed Church of Commugny (see church nr. 203). In case you hike stage 19 as a daytrip, you need to walk 800 meters from the Coppet train station to the church. From the train station of Coppet cross the tracks (west), take the first road right, and then left (*Chemin de Clos*) up the hill to the Church of Commugny.

Route Map and Profile

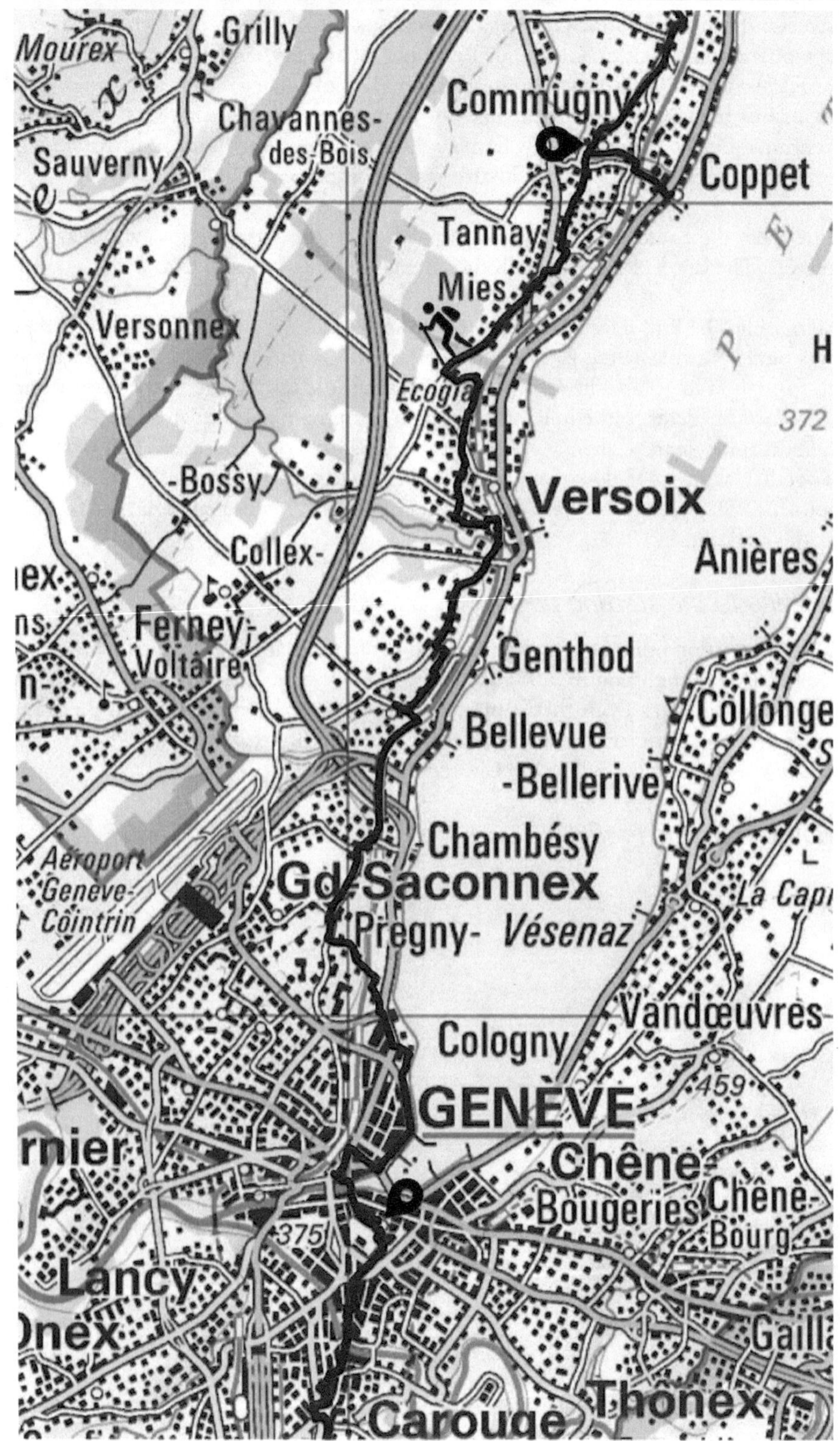
Mourex
Grilly
Commugny
Chavannes-
des-Bois
Sauverny
Coppet
Tannay
Mies
Versonnex
H
Ecogia
372
Bossy
Versoix
Collex-
Anières
Ferney-
Voltaire
Genthod
Bellevue
-Bellerive
Collonge
Chambésy
Aéroport
Genève-
Cointrin
Gd-Saconnex
La Cap
Pregny-
Vésenaz
Vandœuvres
Cologny
459
GENÈVE
Chêne
Bougeries
Chêne-
Bourg
375
Lancy
Gaill
Thônex
Carouge

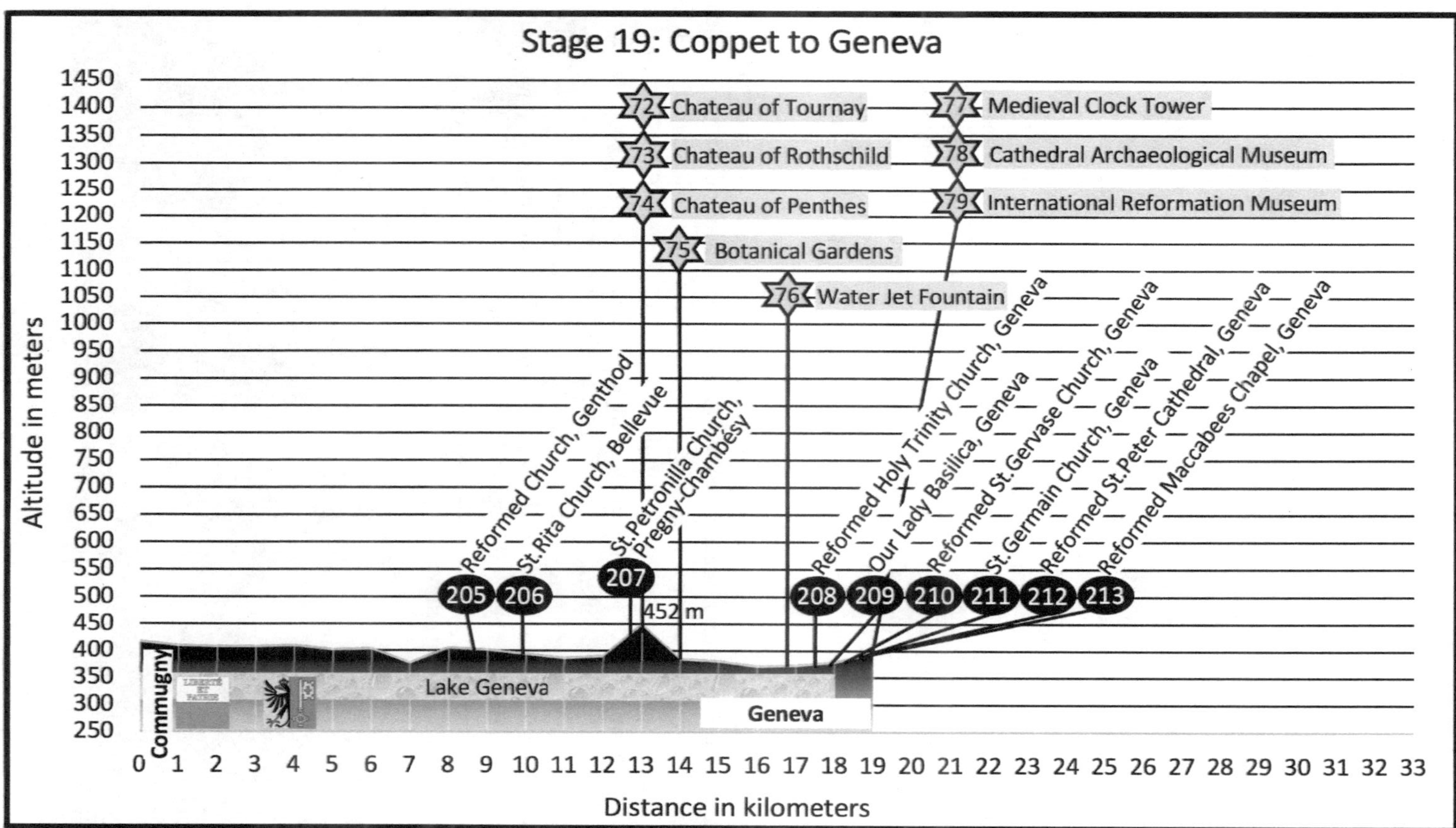

Stage 19: Coppet to Geneva
72 Chateau of Tournay
73 Chateau of Rothschild
74 Chateau of Penthes
75 Botanical Gardens
76 Water Jet Fountain
77 Medieval Clock Tower
78 Cathedral Archaeological Museum
79 International Reformation Museum
205 Reformed Church, Genthod
206 St.Rita Church, Bellevue
207 St.Petronilla Church, Pregny-Chambésy
452 m
208 Reformed Holy Trinity Church, Geneva
209 Our Lady Basilica, Geneva
210 Reformed St.Gervase Church, Geneva
211 St.Germain Church, Geneva
212 Reformed St.Peter Cathedral, Geneva
213 Reformed Maccabees Chapel, Geneva
Commugny
Lake Geneva
Geneva
Altitude in meters
1450 1400 1350 1300 1250 1200 1150 1100 1050 1000 950 900 850 800 750 700 650 600 550 500 450 400 350 300 250
0 1 2 3 4 5 6 7 8 9 10 11 12 13 14 15 16 17 18 19 20 21 22 23 24 25 26 27 28 29 30 31 32 33
Distance in kilometers

Hiking the Route

From the church the route goes south on a walled footpath between vineyards and continues straight on a tarmac street (*Chemin de la Fin)* for 1 km. It passes by agricultural fields and residences behind high hedges. In the town Tannay the route makes a left and 50 meters later at the town's square a right. The route follows the tarmac village road *Chemin des Molards* that makes a curve to the right. The road descends while passing an old wall with an engraving and a plaque. The plaque provides a short description (in French) of the Way of St. James route through Switzerland and how it continues in France. The carving represents a scallop (though a bit difficult to recognize).

The route descends to the Torry stream valley through a small patch of forest. It crosses the stream on a small concrete footbridge, after which the route ascends out of the valley to the town Mies. For 400 meters the route follows road nr. 121 (*Rue de Village*), after which it forks to the right into the *Route de Pénys*. This road is followed for 1.4 km. You walk on the road or pavement next to the road with little traffic. It is flat, so hiking is easy. You pass by some smaller agricultural fields and residential areas behind high hedges. Towards the east trees block the views to the lake. The blue arrows painted on the road help with the direction where the yellow hiking signposts are missing. At km 3.2 you enter protestant **Canton Geneva**.

At a large sports area with an outdoor swimming pool, soccer and tennis fields, athletics track, and a large parking in front of it, the route turns left (*Chemin de Braille*). You walk on the road and after a curve to the left pass by a large parking with trailers, cars, and machinery of traveling funfairs and carnivals (carousels, amusement rides, games, food vendors, and so forth). Before reaching the railway tracks the route turns right onto a white gravel path through a small patch of forest. This trail goes up a flight of wooden stairs, converges with the tracks, and continues next to them in a southern direction for about 400 meters.

The train tracks are lowered; you look down on the passing trains. The route crosses a street and continues south on a gravel footpath along a small stream in a narrow patch of forest for 400 meters. In the mean time you have arrived in the town Versoix. The route crosses another street and continues its way on the gravel footpath along the small stream, aligned by bushes and trees, for another kilometer. You hear airplanes fly over every two minutes. The following 4 km you will be directly below their landing/take-off air corridor to/from Geneva Airport.

At the end of the trail the route turns left and follows a tarmac street (*Chemin des Colombières*) down the hill through residential areas. After a left and right you arrive at the Versoix train station, where the route turns right. The signposts are a bit difficult to make out, but you should not follow the road through the underpass below the train tracks; stay on the right side of the road and continue straight, parallel to the train tracks. The tarmac road you are following is at the back of a large office building housing the company Coty (a multinational beauty company); it feels a bit like trespassing on an industrial area. At this location the train tracks are elevated and you cross over the Versoix River below the train's bridge. The route passes by some apartment blocks and along the *Route de Malagny* it crosses through some agricultural fields, before getting to the town Genthod.

As you will notice, Genthod is mostly a residential town for the rich people of Geneva. Since the 18th century they have built their summer residences in this area to escape the city. You pass by an estate that houses the Geneva English School and a little later the watch factory of Franck Muller, hidden behind a large advertising billboard.

Left and right of the road you see large mansions, with iron front gates and driveways, behind high hedges and old trees. At the crossing with a school and its playground on the right, the route turns left (*Route de Rennex*). About 100 meters later you arrive at the reformed Church of Genthod (at km 8.7).

205 **Reformed Church, Genthod** (Temple de Genthod)

- Route de Rennex 1, 1294 Genthod
- At the parish office
- The church was built in 1867-69, and is the third church on this site. A first church was built in the 16th century, probably soon after the Reformation of 1536. About 100 years later this first church was in ruins and was replaced by another church in 1648-49. Another 100 years later this church was also in poor condition, and the City Council decided to demolish it and built a new one in its place in 1869. This is the neo-Gothic hall church you are looking at now. Another 150 years later this church was also in poor condition; this time the City Council decided on a renovation project. In 2017-18 the church was renovated, just in time for its 150-year celebration in 2019.
- The church has the typical austere protestant interior. Unusual is the high arch at the back wall of the chancel. It seems that there used to be a semicircular chancel that was bricked up. The wooden door at the back wall indeed accesses a low and small chamber, which has a stained-glass window. Maybe this indeed used to be the chancel; nowadays it is used as sacristy/storage. The restored interior frescos date from 1938. One of the bells in the tower is the oldest in the Genevan countryside. It dates from 1421 and was brought back by Genevan

troops as spoils of war from the church of Ballaison (a French town north of Geneva, on the southern side of the lake) in 1589. Six stained-glass windows date from the early 20th century, whereas another four date from the church's original construction in 1869. The doors of the church are usually locked outside the hours of services.

The route continues south on the *Route de Village* and passes by historic houses and the village fountain, covered with flowers. The route turns left and 50 meters later right.

On the left you overlook vineyards and the train tracks, and in the distance you get the first glimpse of the water-jet fountain in the bay of the city of Geneva. About 600 meters later you arrive at a T-crossing. The signpost directs to the left, but 150 meters to the right is the catholic St. Rita Church of Bellevue (at km 9.9).

St. Rita Church, Bellevue (Eglise Sainte-Rita à Bellevue) **206**

Chemin de la Chênaie 147, 1293 Bellevue

St. Rita

The catholic church was built in a modern style in 1962-63. The church is located in a protestant stronghold and was built to serve the Catholics of Bellevue, who had to go to another town for services until that time. Because of the small size of the congregation, the parish had difficulties to finance the construction of the church. As land was a significant part of the cost, its donation by Mrs. Rita Wells was important to realize the building plans of the church. Features like stained-glass windows, organ, and baptismal font were installed during the 10 years after its construction was completed, because of the limited budget.

The interior is almost as austere as a protestant church (save from the two small side-altars left and right of the entrance). Two features immediately catch your eye: the triangular and sloping shape of the building (the pyramidal A-shapes) and the side-walls under the sloping shape of the roof, mostly consisting of the colorful stained-glass windows. The wide stained-glass windows reflect the sunlight in a multitude of bright colors, giving the interior a unique vibrant appearance.

From the church walk back to the signposted route nr. 4 and continue for 200 meters (*Route de Collex*). On the right you pass by the campus of the Webster University. Shortly before the train station of Bellevue the route turns right and crosses the University's entrance driveway to a tarmac footpath next to the railway.

A board in an arched metal frame commemorates the Way of St. James (*Chemin de Saint-Jacques-de-Compostelle*). Against the background of a scallop it states 7.3 km to the St. Peter Cathedral of Geneva and 1'887 km to Santiago de Compostela. Next you pass by the footpath entrance to Richemont (a luxury goods company that sells jewelry and watches of brands like Cartier, Piaget, and Montblanc). Its revolving glass entrance door is heavily protected. Just like Genthod, the town Bellevue is like the Beverly Hills of Geneva.

In the mean time you are on a narrow patch of territory between France and Lake Geneva. The border to France is less than 2.5 km to the west; you might receive signals on your mobile phone from French mobile networks.

For 1.6 km the route is directly next to the railway tracks in a southern direction. You pass by the small train station of Les Tuileries, an electricity ground station, and cross over Highway A1, after which you enter the town Chambésy. Shortly before its train station the route forks to the right, away from the tracks. From here you need to ascend the only hill of stage 19. The following 1.2 km the road gradually ascends to 452 meters.

The route follows the *Chemin de Chambésy* and passes by a roofed fountain (with date 1821) with two taps: one with potable water, the other non-potable. Keep following the road signs to Pregny as the road changes into the *Route de Pregny* up the hill and passes by stately houses and mansions with park-like gardens. Chambésy qualifies as the Beverly Hills of Geneva too. At km 12.8 you arrive at the catholic St. Petronilla Church of Pregny-Chambésy.

St. Petronilla Church, Pregny-Chambésy (Eglise Sainte-Pétronille) 207

Route de Pregny 39, 1292 Pregny-Chambésy

St. Petronilla

The catholic church was built in a neo-Gothic style in 1862-63, replacing an old chapel that stood at the cemetery of Pregny. The old chapel, dedicated to St. Petronilla, was first mentioned in 1481. In 1536 the City of Pregny (and thus its chapel) accepted the Reformation and converted to Protestantism. However, nearly 150 years later the City and chapel converted back to Catholicism (1685).

The newly built church could only serve the catholic parish around Pregny-Chambésy for 13 years, until 1876. Between 1876 and 1897 it became victim of the 'Kulturkampf', which caused the church to be closed; the parishioners attended services in the mayor's barn instead. The church was allowed to open its doors for catholic worship again in 1897, after a year of renovation (20 years of non-use had dilapidated the building). More renovations were undertaken during the 20th and 21st centuries.

The beautiful stained-glass windows date from 1963.

From the church continue on the *Route de Pregny* in a southward direction. After 150 meters you pass by the Chateau of Tournay behind high walls on your right.

Nothing is known of the early history of the **Chateau of Tournay**. A fortified castle was probably first built in the 12th or 13th century. In the 14th century the lands, presumably with the castle, changed ownership to the House of Savoy and were subsequently owned by different families. The Bernese occupied the castle during the annexation of these territories in 1536.

When the Bernese troops withdrew in 1567, they gave back the Castle to the de Brosses family, who were supported by the House of Savoy. For many years the Savoy used the fortified castle as a basis to launch attacks against the City-Republic of Geneva (only 3 km to the south), which was a small independent protestant 'island' surrounded by the catholic lands of Savoy. In a counter attack Genevan troops burned down and plundered the castle in 1590.

Eleven years later, in 1601, the de Brosses family rebuilt it as a chateau, without repairing the former fortifications. Some of these former fortifications, such as a dry moat, thick walls with small windows, and the bulky square tower, can still be seen.

The chateau changed ownership many times during the 18th to 20th centuries; in 1758 Voltaire (French philosopher, author, and critic of the Catholic Church, advocating the separation of Church and State) bought a life-long lease of the chateau, but he never lived there (his theater performances there were boycotted by the Calvinist Authorities of Geneva). The chateau was renovated several times during the 20th century, determining its present appearance. It is still privately owned and not accessible.

Continuing on the *Route de Pregny*, on your left you pass by the iron-gated western entrance to a park that houses the Chateau of Rothschild.

73 Auguste Saladin built the first mansion on this site in 1822-25. The Saladin family (bankers from Geneva) already owned the nearby Chateau of Crans (about 16 km north; see point of interest nr. 68).

Genevan banker Adolphe de Rothschild bought the mansion in 1857, demolished it, and built his **Chateau of Rothschild** in a Louis XVI style in 1858-59. Maurice de Rothschild hosted meetings of the League of Nations at this chateau in 1920-39.

The League of Nations was established in Geneva in 1920, after WWI, as the first intergovernmental organization with the purpose of keeping world peace, by addressing international disputes between countries. The League of Nations was dissolved in 1939, after it had failed to prevent the outbreak of WWII. Its successor organization was the United Nations, established in 1945.

The estate is still in family ownership today. It is private property and cannot be accessed. It is so secluded behind the trees and its long driveway, that you cannot see the chateau from the street.

Pregny qualifies as the Beverly Hills of Geneva too. A little later you pass by the entrance to the outer buildings and the old stables (behind a stone wall) of the Rothschild estate. You are at the highest point of the day at 452 meters. About 200 meters later you see a large building on your right, with the modern fortifications of high iron gates, cameras, concrete barricades, and guards at its access gate. It houses the United States Mission to the United Nations. On your left you pass by the parking of the Chateau of Penthes. The route turns left into the *Chemin de l'Impératrice*, where you arrive at the entrance of the chateau and its park.

74 The **Chateau of Penthes** was first built as a fortified mansion around 1358. Over the centuries it changed ownership many times, until it was rebuilt as a chateau by the Penthes family (who gave the chateau its name) in 1761. Changes of ownership continued and Maurice Sarasin (from the Genevan banker family) renovated the building in 1870. Its most famous owners were Josephine Bonaparte, first wife of Napoleon I, and his daughter, the mother of Napoleon III.

In 1972 Canton Geneva bought the estate, which houses the Foundation for the History of the Swiss Abroad since 1978. The Canton established a research institute and museum of the Swiss activities and achievements abroad. They organize events, exhibitions, and temporary and permanent expositions, and run a restaurant. Many of the rooms have 18th and 19th century baroque interiors.

The museum is only open to the public in the afternoons (13:30-17:30), Wednesday to Sunday; a ticket costs CHF 10. Next to the restaurant is a giant hourglass. The chateau lies in one of the most beautiful parks of Geneva with good views over Lake Geneva and the Savoy Alps.

On the southern side of the park the route trails down the hill until converging with the *Chemin de l'Impératrice*. On your left you pass by an estate that houses the embassy of Italy. Between walls of the neighboring estates, the narrow tarmac road descends the hill and after passing underneath the railway tracks arrives at the northern entrance of the Botanical Gardens of the City of Geneva.

75 These **Botanical Gardens** were established after a smaller garden moved out of the center of Geneva in 1904. The conservatory that manages the gardens looks back on a 175-year history and leads many national and international botanical research programs. Nowadays the gardens have more than 16'000 different species of plants and trees, and include a winter garden; it is the largest and most beautiful and exotic garden along the Swiss Way of St. James. Entry to the Botanical Gardens is free.

The signposted route nr. 4 continues downhill on the *Chemin de l'Impératrice* until reaching road nr. 1, here called the *Rue de Lausanne*. The route turns right and follows the *Rue de Lausanne* to the southern entrance of the Botanical Garden (400 meters). The *Rue de Lausanne* is an extremely busy road, where you will be inhaling exhaust fumes from the cars, buses, and trucks that drive there and queue in front of traffic lights. Instead of walking around the Botanical Gardens and along this busy road, it is healthier and much more interesting and relaxing to walk from its northern gate through the garden to its southern gate (where you are back on the signposted route).

From the southern gate of the Botanical Gardens continue south along the *Rue de Lausanne* on a narrow pavement next to the road for 500 meters. You pass by the long building of the World Trade Organization (WTO).

Geneva is home to nearly a 100 **International Organizations**, such as the WTO, WHO (World Health Organization), ICRC (International Committee of the Red Cross), and CERN (European Organization for Nuclear Research). There are specific reasons for these organizations to have chosen Geneva as their domicile. Switzerland was always neutral and independent during the world wars and never participated in any military or political alliances (Switzerland is not a member of the European Union), but has been mediating in international affairs for more than 500 years. The small country in the center of Europe does not pose a threat to any of the world's big powers.

These organizations are in Geneva and not in the German-speaking part of Switzerland, because French was the language of the elite and diplomats from the 18th until the mid 20th centuries.

In the mean time you entered the city of Geneva. You will notice that the Way of St. James signposting is the regular yellow signs with the green/blue nr. 4. The blue square signs you saw in Fribourg and Lausanne are not used here.

The route turns left and accesses a park called *Perle du Lac* (Pearl of the Lake) through an iron gate. You pass by a fountain and a restaurant while gradually descending to the level of Lake Geneva. At the lake promenade the route turns right (south). The next 1.8 km the route stays on the broad tarmac promenade next to the lake. You pass by boat piers, small ports, and get closer to the water-jet fountain.

76

The **Water-Jet Fountain** (*Jet d'Eau*) is the number one tourist attraction and most famous landmark of Geneva. It is one of the highest fountains in the world. Two submerged pumps press the lake's water through a 16 cm nozzle with a speed of 200 km/h 140 meters in the air. At any given moment there are about 7'000 liters of water in the air. The first water-jet fountain was installed a bit more south in 1886. It was an engineering solution to release excess water pressure from the hydraulic power plant. In 1891 it was moved to its present location and purely became a tourist attraction.

On the other side of the street you see several of Geneva's five-star hotels, accommodating the many international visitors to the city's international organizations. In front of you, the two towers and green steeple of the St. Peter Cathedral tower high above the city. The cathedral stands on a hill behind office buildings with advertisements for watches and insurances. The cathedral is the destination of stage 19, but instead of going there directly, the signposted route makes a detour via the train station of Geneva.

Shortly before reaching the bridge (*Pont du Mont-Blanc*) where Lake Geneva flows into the Rhone River, you see a monument on the right side of the street. It is the **Brunswick Monument**, a mausoleum for the Duke of Brunswick. The story goes that when he died in 1873, he left his fortune to the City in exchange for a monument. The mausoleum, a replica of a neo-Gothic 14th century family tomb in Verona, was built at the lakeside in 1879. The monument is at the *Quai du Mont-Blanc* with its boat piers stretching into the lake.

This is a historical place for an additional reason. **Empress Elisabeth of Austria** (better known under her nickname Sisi) was assassinated at this location in 1898. She was a frequent visitor to the Chateau of Rothschild in Pregny, and was killed at the age of 60, the day after she returned from one of her visits and embarked a steamboat at the *Quai du Mont-Blanc*.

On the *Pont du Mont-Blanc* bridge the route crosses road nr. 1 (here called the *Quai du Mont-Blanc*) and turns right into the *Rue du Mont-Blanc*. Around the corner you pass by watch shops and 200 meters later you arrive at the reformed Holy Trinity Church at km 17.5. It stands a bit out of place between the other buildings along the busy street.

Reformed Holy Trinity Church, Geneva 208

Rue du Mont Blanc 14b, 1201 Geneva

The protestant church belongs to the Church of England. Holy Trinity stands for the concept that God is one, yet represented by three Divine Persons, the Father, the Son Jesus, and the Holy Spirit. The church serves the Anglicans who live and work in Geneva. It is a bit unusual to find an Anglican Church in the middle of the French-speaking city of Geneva.

Its history dates back to 1555. During the reign of the catholic Queen Mary of England, Protestants were persecuted and many of them fled to other cities in Europe, among others Geneva. They were called Marian Exiles (exiles of Queen Mary) and from 1555 formed a small community in Geneva. The City of Geneva lend them churches to hold their services in English, but they built their own church at the present location in 1851-53.

The Anglican church has a typical protestant interior. The stained-glass windows date from 1958-81.

Next to the church is the Tourist Information Office (Rue du Mont-Blanc 18, 1201 Geneva; tel. 022 909 70 00; www.geneve.com). Visit them in case you need support with accommodation or tips for sightseeing. This may prevent that you need to return to this location after you complete stage 19 (which is in about 2 km). The route continues for another 300 meters towards the train station, where the road becomes a pedestrian area with many souvenir- and watch-shops.

At the entrance to the train station's underground shopping center, the route turns left into the *Place de Cornavin.* It is a busy street with cars, trolley buses, and trams. Across the street you arrive at the catholic Our Lady Basilica at km 17.9.

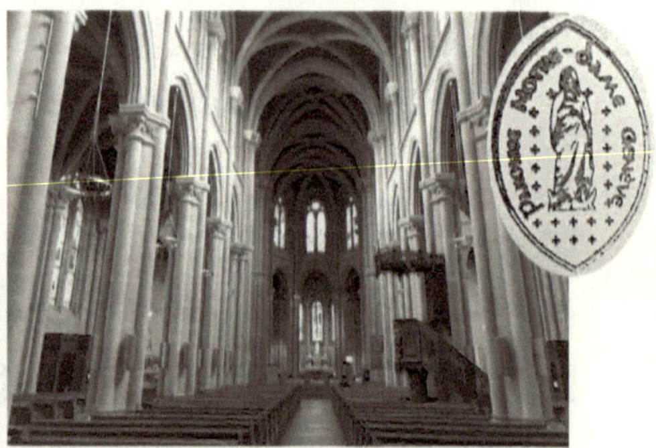

209 Our Lady Basilica, Geneva (Basilique de Notre-Dame)

- Place De Cornavin, 1201 Geneva
- Our Lady, St. Francis de Sales, Holy Family, St. Clotilde
- At the sacristy at the front-left of the nave. In case the door is open, just walk in and ask for the stamp; otherwise pull the bell left of the door or try to find the caretaker.
- The church is the main Roman-Catholic church of Geneva, after the St. Peter cathedral converted to Protestantism in 1536 (see below). Though the design and architecture of the basilica resembles other large medieval churches from the 12th and 13th centuries, it was built in 1851-58 only. Built as the first catholic church in Geneva, 322 years after the Reformation, it stands on the remains of city fortifications. It took more than three centuries for the Catholics to have their own place of worship again in Geneva, but this did not last long. Only 16 years after its consecration, the church fell victim to the 'Kulturkampf'. In 1875 the protestant Genevan government forced the church to close. This second prohibition of catholic services in Geneva lasted 37 years. The church could only be opened again in 1912, after the catholic parish bought the building from the protestant City of Geneva. After having been closed for 37 years, the building was in poor condition; restoration work lasted until 1925. Significant renovations were undertaken in 1978-86 and 2012-14.

The church received the designation of minor Basilica from Pope Pius XII in 1954 (after the parish petitioned for this designation based on the claim of it being the first church officially dedicated to the Immaculate Conception as proclaimed by Pope Pius IX in 1854).

The basilica has five side-chapels: chapel of St. Francis de Sales – Geneva's Bishop in the 17th century; chapel of the Holy Family – decorated with frescos of bees; chapel of the Virgin Mary; chapel of the Sacred Heart – partly decorated with phoenix-bird motives; and chapel of St. Clotilde – patroness Saint of people in exile.

Special features of the basilica are: a white marble statue representing the Virgin Mary from the personal library of the Pope at the Vatican, donated by Pope Pius IX in 1859; the crown on the statue, made from jewelry donated by local parishioners in 1937; the many stained-glass windows dating from 1857-75 and 1912; the colored vaulted ceilings; the four-paneled (vertical) painting that tells the story of the life of Mary and Jesus in twenty frames, dating from 2012; a torch from the St. Clare Convent dating from before the Reformation; and a carved dark-wooden panel with a relief representing the Virgin Mary from the St. Peter Cathedral, damaged by an axe during the Reformation in 1536.

Brochures in several languages explain the interior of the basilica.

From the basilica the signposted route nr. 4 crosses road nr. 1 (here called the *Rue de Chantepoulet*). The route goes straight into the *Rue de Cornavin*, which makes a left curve after 200 meters. Instead of making the left curve, make a small detour to the St. Gervase church. At the left turn, take the street on the right (*Rue des Corps Saints*) and in 200 meters you arrive at the reformed St. Gervase Church (km 18.3).

210 Reformed St. Gervase Church, Geneva (Temple de Saint-Gervais)

Rue des Terreaux-du-Temple 12, 1201 Geneva

St. Gervase, St. John the Baptist, St. Francis of Assisi, Four Evangelists, St. Christopher

A first catholic cemetery church was built on this site in the 5th century. Excavations revealed that this first church was built on even older remains of Neolithic human settlements dating as far back as 4000 BC. The 5th century deceased were buried in the crypt under the chancel, but also under the nave and annexes. Until the 15th century the church and its surrounding plots were the central burial grounds for the Christians of the city of Geneva. This first church was replaced by a Romanesque church, dedicated to St. Gervase, in 1153. A fire destroyed much of the Romanesque church in 1345. In 1430-46 the church was significantly expanded and reconstructed in a Gothic style. Side chapels were built, new choir stalls were placed, and the frescos were painted.

At the time of the Reformation in 1535, the parish converted to Protestantism. All catholic icons such as altars, paintings, and statues were removed, and the walls were whitewashed covering all frescos. Regular restorations were undertaken from the 18th to 20th centuries, in which the 15th century appearance of the Gothic church was restored as much as possible. The church is protestant, but maintained its Saint's name; an indication that its origin lies far before the Reformation.

The chancel is elevated by six steps; underneath lies the crypt. The chancel is empty, except for a small organ and the choir stalls. The main and large organ is located on the metal gallery above the entrance. Notice how the metal frame is nearly invisible, as to maintain the medieval appearance of the interior.

The restored interior of the church has many special features dating back to the Gothic church that was built in 1430-46. The nave and two side-chapels each have their wall tabernacle where the Host for the daily services was kept.

The eight high choir stalls (1445) came to the St. Gervase church from a Genevan Franciscan monastery that was secularized as a result of the Reformation in 1536. The carvings of the walnut stalls represent St. John the Baptist, St. Francis of Assisi, and angels.

The small chapel on the right side of the chancel is called the All-Saints chapel (1440). Notice that this chapel is in the base of the bell tower. The partly recovered frescos depict a tall Virgin Mary (adorned by four angels in the sky and on the lower side the population including King and Pope) and on the opposite arched wall three (of the Four) Evangelists around a table writing their scriptures in a medieval scene.

If you peek behind the tall choir stalls you will also see remnants of red-colored frescos (1430) and an original Gothic wall tabernacle. The partial mural on the

first pillar of the chancel depicts a tall St. Christopher (only his legs were uncovered from the whitewash) from around 1478.

The large chapel on the left side of the chancel is called the Escalade chapel (1478). Escalade is a military term used for climbing fortified city walls using ladders. In 1602 the city of Geneva successfully fended off attacks from the troops of the Duke of Savoy, who had tried to take the city by using ladders to get over the walls. Genevans who died in this attack were buried in the cemetery around the church. When urbanization forced the closure of this cemetery in 1895, their remains were brought to the side-chapel, which was named Escalade since then. The black memorial with this date commemorates that event. The vaulted ceiling of the Escalade side-chapel is a unique example of Gothic architecture. Notice how the top of the central pillar extends in four directions, leading to four vaulted ceilings around it.

The stained-glass window of the chancel dates from 1944, the ones in the Escalade side-chapel from 1953.

The church has limited opening times: Tuesday to Saturday, 14:00-17:00.

The foundations of the predecessor churches, the first traces of human occupation in Geneva dating from 4000 BC, and the crypt underneath the chancel can be visited as part of an archaeological site. This site is accessible by advance appointment with Geneva's Cantonal Service of Archaeology (Service Cantonal d'Archéologie – SCA; tel. 022 327 94 40; sca@etat.ge.ch). However, since the St. Peter Cathedral has a much larger public Archaeological Museum with a similar exposition, a visit to that museum is an easier way to see the old history of Geneva.

From the church turn back to the signposted route nr 4 by following the *Rue du Temple* to the Rhone River and walking towards the bridge on the left. The route crosses the bridge that connects a small island in the middle of the river.

This island is called the **Rhone Island** and is a natural island linking the two river banks. The island contains banks, restaurants, and a watch museum. You can see the water-jet fountain from this location.

North of this island is another smaller island. It is called the **Rousseau Island** (*L'Île Rousseau*). It was named after the philosopher and author Jean-Jacques Rousseau, who was born in the City-Republic of Geneva in 1712. There is a statue of him on the small island.

The second bridge connecting the Rhone Island to the old city is used as Geneva's main transportation hub for buses and trams. It is called **Place Bel-Air** and is so wide that you do not even realize being on a bridge.

Already from the time of the Romans, more than 2'000 years ago, the bridges over the Rhone Island were of strategic importance for the trade and travel routes from the south (Italy) to the north (Germany). A plaque indicates that Julius Caesar already had such a bridge destroyed in 58 BC, to block the road over the Rhone River during his military advances against the Helvetian armies.

Across the Place Bel-Air, on the side of the old city, you see a Medieval Clock Tower.

77

The **medieval Clock Tower** is the only remains of a 13th century fortified castle from the Bishopric Kingdom of Geneva. A fortified castle protected the access to the bridge and the old city of Geneva. The castle was destroyed in 1677, leaving only the gate tower. When you walk through Geneva you may be wondering why you do not see any fortifications like in other medieval towns along the Swiss Way of St. James (e.g. Fribourg). Similar to many other cities (e.g. Lausanne and Nyon), the fortifications in Geneva were demolished to make room for the urbanization and growth of the population in 1850-80.

Continue straight to follow the cobbled *Rue de la Cité* pedestrian street along shops, restaurants, and supermarkets. The route ascends to the old part of the city that was built on a hill. After 300 meters you arrive at a right side-street called *Rue de la Boulangerie.* Although the signposted route nr. 4 continues straight, it is worthwhile to make a small detour to the St. Germain church. At the end of the *Rue de la Boulangerie* (50 meters) turn left into the *Rue des Granges* and you arrive at the Christ-Catholic St. Germain Church at km 19.0. The church is in narrow streets, squashed between other buildings.

St. Germain Church, Geneva (Eglise Saint-Germain de Genève) 211

Rue de Granges 11, 1204 Geneva

St. Germain, Four Evangelists

The Christ-Catholic church is on the site of several predecessor churches. A first small church dated back to the 4th century. A Romanesque St. Germain church was first mentioned in 12th century. In 1334 a fire destroyed this Romanesque church, together with half of the old city. This church was rebuilt more than 100 years later. The 15th century building you see nowadays dates from that period. The St. Germain church was the first church in which the Genevan Reformation was preached in 1535.

After the Reformation was accepted by the local population, the catholic church was closed and all catholic statues, paintings, altars, and other icons were destroyed. The building subsequently housed a butcher shop, corn warehouse, armory, and cannon casting workshop. It was not in use as a church for 250 years.

In the 18th century the church was renovated and restored. During the periods that the protestant St. Peter cathedral was closed for renovations in the 18th century, the St. Germain church was used as a temporary place for protestant services. After Napoleon's troops occupied Geneva (1798), the church was allowed to hold catholic services. From 1803 until 1857 it was the only church in Geneva used for catholic services (until the Our Lady Basilica was built in 1857). It was not until 1873 that the church was fully available to the catholic parish.

The 'Kulturkampf' forced the church to be closed from 1875 until 1907. In 1907 it was purchased by the Christ-Catholic parish of Geneva. Because of a fire in the bell tower a few years earlier and poor condition resulting from lack of maintenance, the church had to be renovated for two years before it could open its doors in 1908. The main renovations of the interior and exterior that determined it present appearance were undertaken in 1959-66.

The church has several special features. Notice the wall tabernacle in the chancel and the 13 stained-glass windows all around the church. These windows were made in 1968-69, and mostly use blue colors, with some red and yellow, in vertical lines. They depict scenes from Jesus' life, the Four Evangelists, and the patron Saint Germain. The latter window mostly used red and is in the middle side-chapel.

Each of the three side-chapels has their own interior decorations. The middle side-chapel has paintings that were donated by Napoleon Bonaparte to the City of Geneva (1779).

When you walk to the eastern side of the church, notice the sundial on the outer wall above the fountain. It has a special scene depicting death riding a donkey, representing the vanity of earthly life, dating from 1908.

Nowadays the church is well-known for the summer concerts organized on Sundays and Mondays. The doors to the church are generally locked outside the hours of services and concerts (the nearby parish office might be able to provide access in case the doors are locked).

From the church continue on the *Rue des Granges*, after 50 meters turn left, continue straight, and you are back on the signposted route nr. 4. Follow the cobbled *Rue du Puits Saint-Pierre* for 100 meters.

On your left you pass by five 18th century cannons in front of three mosaics. It is called the **Old Arsenal**. The cannons were used to defend Geneva against invading troops until the beginning of the 19th century. The mosaics depict scenes from Geneva's history: Julius Caesar arriving in 58 BC; medieval fairs; and French Huguenots arriving in 1685.

When you turn right into the *Rue Otto Barblan*, you arrive at the square in front of the reformed St. Peter Cathedral at km 19.3. The protestant church used to be the catholic St. Peter Cathedral of the Bishopric Kingdom of Geneva, until the

Reformation in 1536. Nowadays it is one of the main tourist attractions of the city, attracting around 400'000 visitors a year.

Reformed St. Peter Cathedral, Geneva (Cathédrale Saint-Pierre) 212

Cour de Saint-Pierre, 1204 Geneva

St. Peter

At the tourist shop inside the cathedral (left of the chancel)

The former cathedral is on the site of predecessor churches that already existed in the 4th century. The cathedral was initially built between 1150 and 1250. Bishop of Geneva Arducius de Faucigny initiated the construction of the present building in 1150, which took 100 years to complete. The building you see today was rebuilt, changed, expanded, and renovated many times over the last 850 years, under the influence of wars, many fires, expansion desires of the Bishop-Kings, and the Reformation.

You can clearly identify the different architectural styles of: the Gothic galleried nave with massive pillars and the chancel, mostly dating from the 13th century; the chapel of the Maccabees, built on the right side of the entrance as an exterior extension in 1400-05; the southern white bell tower, constructed in 1510-30; the Roman portico with six giant Corinthian columns, looking out of place against the Gothic architecture, which were simply placed in front of the existing Gothic entrance facade (which was unstable) in 1752-56; the northern bell tower, reconstructed in the 19th century; the green copper spire on the roof in the middle of the transept, added in 1895, replacing a tower that burned down in the 15th century; and the stained-glass windows, dating from the renovation work in the 19th century (the originals being in the Museum of Art and History – *Musée d'Art et d'Histoire*).

From the 6th century until the Reformation in 1535 the church kept relics of St. Peter, which is why the cathedral and its predecessor churches were named after this Saint. These relics made it a medieval pilgrimage destination. During the Reformation in 1535 these relics were removed and destroyed. But the Reformation had a much bigger impact on the interior of the cathedral. It was stripped of all religious icons, decorations, statues, tapestries, paintings, frescos, colorings, winged altar pieces, organs, and so forth. The interior became as naked as you experience it today. The cathedral converted to Protestantism in 1535.

Because the cathedral was the largest building in Geneva (64 meters long), it was used for official town meetings and ceremonies for centuries, and nowadays also for concerts. Currently protestant services are held only once a week, every Sunday at 10:00; the former cathedral is turned into a tourist attraction.

The tourist shop inside the cathedral (left of the chancel) offers a tour around the building and information in several languages.

The items and areas of interest are sequentially numbered: pulpit (1); Calvin's chair (2); bell towers (3); Portugal chapel, where the princess of Portugal and her daughter are buried (4); chapel of the Holy Spirit (5); chancel (6); Rohan chapel, housing the mausoleum of the Duke of Rohan, a leader of the French Huguenots (7); 15th century choir stalls (8); commemorative plaques (9, 10); organ, from 1965 (11); Maccabees chapel (12); neoclassical portico (13). Outside the cathedral: Archaeological Museum (14); and International Museum of the Reformation (15).

You can climb the southern tower with 157 steps and go through the spire to the platform of the northern tower, providing great views over Geneva and the lake with its water-jet fountain. You can buy the ticket at the tourist counter (a combined ticket (CHF 18) for the archaeological museum, bell towers, and International Museum of the Reformation probably makes sense). Following numbers 1 to 15 may take two to three hours.

213 **Reformed Maccabees Chapel, Geneva** (Chapelle des Macchabées)

Place du Bourg-de-Four 24, 1204 Geneva

The chapel was built in a flamboyant style to house the tomb of Jean de Brogny, Cardinal under Pope Clement VII, and his family members in 1400-05. The name

Maccabees originates from followers of the Jewish leader Judas Maccabaeus, who established a Jewish Kingdom and expanded the boundaries of Judea in the 2nd and 1st centuries BC.

After the Reformation the chapel was divided into two floors, first used for salt storage, and as lecture halls for the College from 1559.

Restoration to a neo-Gothic style was undertaken in the 19th century. The vaulted ceiling was repainted with celestial chorus themes to the layout of the original frescos. Not only the frescos deserve admiration: the high stained-glass windows reflect the sunlight in beautiful colors.

This is one of the most exquisitely decorated chapels along the Swiss Way of St. James.

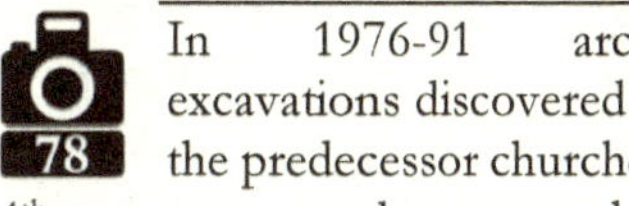

78 In 1976-91 archaeological excavations discovered remains of the predecessor churches from the 4th century, and even older Celtic foundations and artefacts from the 3rd century BC. This archaeological site was developed into an underground museum beneath the cathedral, exhibiting the findings on 3'000 square meters. The entrance to the **Cathedral Archaeological Museum** is right of the Roman portico, behind an iron fence, down the steps. The ticket price is CHF 8; or CHF 18 for a combined ticket for the archaeological museum, bell towers, and International Museum of the Reformation (entrance to the cathedral is free).

79 The **International Museum of the Reformation** exhibits the history of the religious Reformation movement. You can see books, manuscripts, paintings, and other objects from the 16th century. The museum is located at the cathedral square; open 10:00-17:00; closed on Mondays.

The Reformation had a particularly big impact on Geneva and the St. Peter cathedral because of **Jean Calvin** (a French law and theology student and author). Next to Martin Luther (a German monk) he was a main driver of the Reformation. He personally implemented the reforms in Geneva and at the cathedral in 1536-38 and 1541-64. To the interior of the cathedral his reformative activities may have been devastating, but to the people of Geneva it brought a lot of positive change. Jean Calvin caused a strong development of book printing in Geneva (he wrote many books), making Geneva the European center for books in several languages. He created a public college, boosting the intellectual reputation of the city, and established compulsory education. His reformative ideas promoted banking (loans with interest were not disallowed anymore), laying the foundations for Geneva's rise in the global banking industry. At that time the City-Republic of Geneva was a small protestant island within catholic Europe and one of the few locations to which Europeans could turn for loans. Geneva became a refuge for Protestants, attracting wealth and intellect. Calvin established hospices to take care of the poor and stimulated medical research. He proclaimed men and women were equal and allowed divorce. At the same time, however, there was no choice for the local population other than becoming protestant (Calvinist). Deviations were not tolerated and severely punished.

The city of Geneva was built on the foundations of a long and strong religious history. From the 4th century the **Bishopric Kingdom of Geneva** ruled the city (similar to the Bishopric Kingdom of Lausanne). Over the centuries the Bishops erected large churches and a castle, and ruled the city's and region's trade and commerce. A thousand years ago, Geneva was the Bishop's stronghold and their buildings dominated the town. The Bishops came from the ruling families of the region (e.g. Grandson, Savoy) and used their connections to bring wealth, power, and prestige to Geneva. By 1275 the Bishopric Kingdom encompassed extensive lands and 387 parishes in the region. They built Geneva into a city with a castle and fortifications to protect their interests. Their Kingdom ended as a result of the Reformation in 1535. The City of Geneva converted to Protestantism and formed a defensive alliance with the Bernese. The Bishops of Geneva were exiled and continued their activities from Annecy, France (about 45 km south of Geneva) until 1793. From Annecy the Bishops led the Counter-Reformation and efforts to re-catholicize the southern Cantons of the Swiss Confederation. Upon the French Revolution and Napoleon's expansion in 1793, the Bishopric in Annecy was closed. From 1801 it was re-established in Chambéry, France (about 30 km south of Annecy). Between 1798 and 1813 Geneva was part of a French province. In 1815 Geneva joined the Swiss Confederation, after which the Pope removed Geneva from the authority of the Bishop of Chambéry (France) and transferred it to the Bishop of Lausanne, who had his seat in Fribourg, in 1821. This is how the Bishopric combination of Fribourg, Lausanne, and Geneva came about.

During the middle ages the Bishopric Kingdom attracted many **Monasteries**. A church from the 5th century, dedicated to St. Victor, was changed into a Cluniac monastery around the year 1000. The Benedictine monastery St. John dated back to the 6th century. In 1263 the Dominican Order established a large monastery. In 1266 the Franciscan Order founded a monastery. In 1476 the Clare Order built a convent. The Augustinian Order settled in Geneva in 1480. All monasteries ended up being closed and secularized during the Reformation. The Cluniac, Dominican, Benedictine, and Augustinian monasteries were built outside the city walls and were all demolished in 1534, to prevent them from falling into the hands of the House of Savoy (that was beleaguering the city). The Clare convent buildings were turned into a general hospital. The Franciscan Order's buildings were used for different purposes. The remains of the Benedictine monastery buildings were used for fortifying the city walls. That is why you do not see any remains of medieval monasteries as you walk through the city.

The City of Geneva changed from a Bishopric Kingdom to a **City-State/Republic** after the Reformation in 1536. The City-Republic lasted for 262 years until 1798, when the French occupied Switzerland. From 1798 until 1813 Geneva was a municipality of a French province, and went through crisis and poverty. In 1813 Geneva re-established itself as a City-Republic and in 1815 rejoined the Swiss Confederation as the 22nd Canton, which significantly improved its fortunes. After the establishment of the Swiss Confederation in 1848, the development of Geneva sped forward. The medieval fortifications and towers (except for the clock tower) were demolished to make room for the growing urbanization and a construction boom. New churches (Our Lady, Holy Trinity), new Universities and schools, new bridges, new museums, and new districts were built within three decades (1846-76). Nowadays the city of Geneva has around 200'000 inhabitants, compared to around 495'000 for the Canton as a whole.

From the ending point

The reformed St. Peter Cathedral is the ending point of stage 19, directly on the signposted route nr. 4.

In case you are a day-hiker, you need to go to the Geneva train station (*Cornavin*). From the church to the train station is about 1.2 km, which you can cover on foot, by bus, or tram.

In case you are a thru-hiker and spend the night in Geneva, there are many accommodation possibilities, of which many expensive five-star hotels (you passed by them along the way). It is not easy to find low-priced accommodation. There is no pilgrim inn, but the City Hostel Geneva (Rue Ferrier 2, 1202 Geneva; tel. 022 901 15 00; info@cityhostel.ch; www.cityhostel.ch) and the Home St. Pierre (Cour de Saint-Pierre 4, 1204 Geneva; tel. 022 310 37 07; info@homestpierre.ch; www.homestpierre.ch) offer comparable prices. The Home St. Pierre is at the square opposite the cathedral. The City Hostel is about 500 meters north of the train station. Check out www.jakobsweg.ch or www.viajacobi4.ch for the accommodation possibilities in Geneva. Similar to Lausanne, when you spend a night at a hotel you will receive a free public transportation card. The Tourist Information Office (Rue du Mont-Blanc 18, 1201 Geneva; tel. 022 909 70 00; www.geneve.com) can also assist with finding the appropriate accommodation. The information center is next to the Holy Trinity church, on the road leading to/from the train station.

The next Stage

Stage 20 guides you from the upper city of Geneva to the French border, where the Swiss Way of St. James ends (and the pilgrimage continues on French routes). Read the next chapter to find out what that entails.

Stage 20: Geneva to French Border 8 km

The Way to France

Route stats

	Distance in km	*Time in hrs:min*
Signposted route nr. 4	8.2	1:40
Churches/chapels	0.2	0:50
Points of interest		
Rest/lunch		
Stage 20	8.4	2:30

In case you hike this stage as a daytrip, you need to add 1.2 km in Geneva from the train station to the starting point. From the French border you need to walk back 600 meters to the nearest bus stop, from where a bus and tram can take you back to the Geneva train station.

Ascent/descent/total	+143/ -66 / 209 altitude meters
Lowest/highest altitude	377 / 485 meters
Pathway/condition	easy / easy
Churches/chapels	Geneva, Carouge (2), Compesières
Monasteries	Monastery of St. John Community Geneva, Former Commandry of the Knights of St. John Compesières
Points of interest	none

Route summary

The last and short stage 20 continues in protestant **Canton Geneva**.

Stage 20 guides you from the upper city of Geneva to the French border, where the Swiss Way of St. James ends (and the pilgrimage continues on French routes).

Does it make sense to hike this final stage of the Swiss Way of St. James as a separate daytrip? No, it does not. With transportation from the French border back to Geneva, stage 20 will take less than 4 hours. The thru-hiking pilgrims who only hike the Swiss Way of St. James may end their pilgrimage in Geneva. In this case stage 20 can be considered an add-on, if time is available and you are spending the night in Geneva anyway. For thru-hiking pilgrims on their way to Santiago de Compostela, it is of course necessary to hike stage 20 and continue in France.

The first 500 meters descend from the upper city of Geneva, after which the route is flat for 3 km. From km 3.5 the route gradually ascends to a highest level of 485 meters at the end of the stage. It takes 5 out of the 8 km to get out of the city and its southern agglomeration Carouge. The short stage 20 is mostly an urban pilgrimage. The last 3 km are on tarmac roads along agricultural fields and several small villages. The route leads south, straight to the Swiss-French border.

Getting to the starting point

Today's starting point in Geneva is at the St. Peter Cathedral, directly on the signposted route nr. 4. In case you hike stage 20 as a daytrip, you need to walk 1.2 km from the Geneva train station to the cathedral.

Route Map and Profile

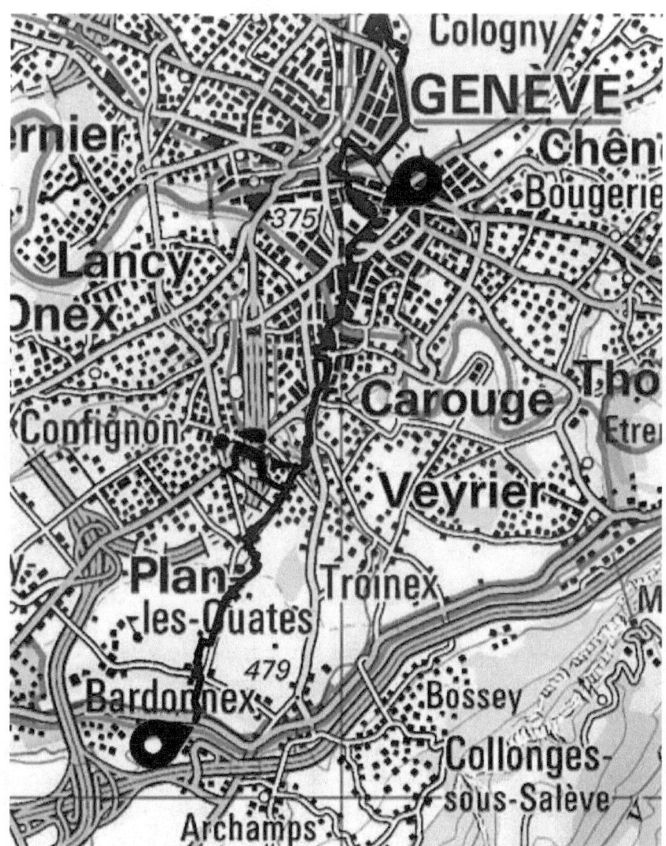

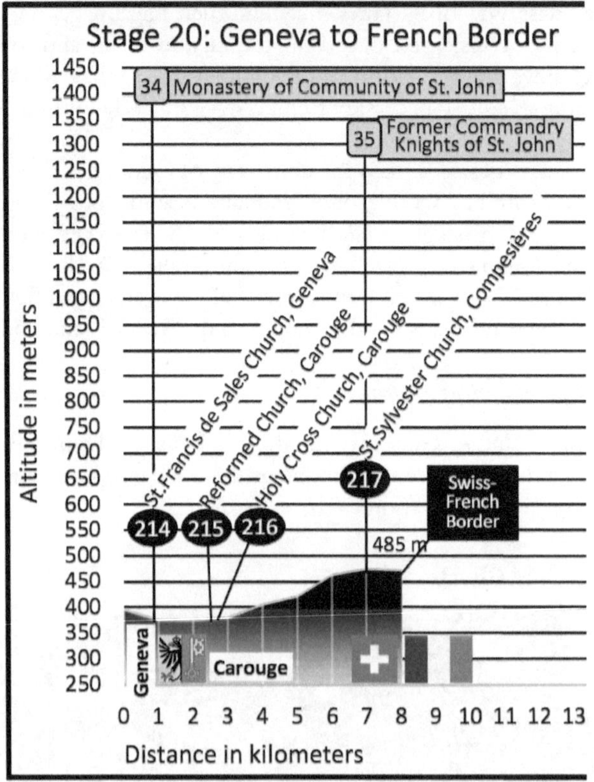

Hiking the Route

From the southern side of the St. Peter cathedral follow the Way of St. James signpost down the steps and through the small streets down the hill away from the upper city. After 200 meters you arrive at the *Rue Saint-Léger*, which is followed for 400 meters. You pass by the eastern entrance of the Bastions Park that houses the University of Geneva, but the route does not enter the park. The route crosses the broad *Boulevard des Philosophes* and goes straight into the *Rue Leschot*. After 60 meters turn left into the *Rue des Voisins* and 200 meters later you arrive at the catholic St. Francis de Sales Church (at km 0.9).

St. Francis de Sales Church, Geneva (Eglise St. François de Sales) 214

Rue des Voisins 23, 1205 Geneva

St. Francis de Sales

The catholic church was built near the site of an old chapel that was dedicated to St. Francis de Sales. The chapel was built in 1870, but had become too small for the growing population and increasing number of Catholics in the protestant city of Geneva. The present church in a neo-Gothic style was built in 1902-04.

The exterior stands in scaffolding for a major renovation project until November 2019. A second phase of interior renovations is planned from 2020 onwards, during which time the interior may not be accessible.

Except for the bright lamps at the ceiling, the church is relatively dark (particularly the side-naves); the planned renovation intends to improve the lighting. The interior is austere, without large and shiny altars. Except for a large cross and communion table, the chancel is empty.

The most interesting features of the church are its stained-glass windows, in particular the rose window. From the middle of the nave look back to the entrance facade and high above you see the rose window. After the Cathedral of Lausanne, this rose window is probably the second-most beautiful along the Swiss Way of St. James. It does not have the biblical scenes as the one in the Cathedral of Lausanne, but the flowers and their colors create a special arrangement. After renovations in the 1960s, this window was mostly covered by a large organ. Present-day renovations included removing the organ and preparing for renovating the gallery and back windows. After completion of the renovations in 2020, these windows should be visible again and let in an array of colored light.

Monastery of St. John Community, Geneva (Prieuré Saint-Jean) 34

Rue des Voisins 23, 1205 Geneva

Community of St. John

Seven brothers of the priory of the St. John Community have been managing the St. Francis de Sales parish and its church since 1986. They were the first monastic Order that settled in the protestant city of Geneva after the Reformation (1536), with the apostolic purpose to maintain and expand Catholicism.

From the church the route continues on the *Rue des Voisins* and turns right and left to the *Rue de Carouge*. This is a busy street with tram tracks in the middle. Walking through the southern districts of Geneva is quite different from its northern agglomerations. Whereas the northern agglomerations look like Beverly Hills, these southern city districts resemble the typical urban city environment. Seven-story apartment and office blocks with shops on the ground floor are packed close together. Cars and motor cycles are parked on the sides of the street and nature is nowhere to be found. After 600 meters you arrive at the bridge over the Arve River.

The **Arve River** has a length of about 100 km and springs in the glaciers of the Chamonix/Mont Blanc (France) region. It flows through France for around 94 km and the last 6 km through Switzerland. In Geneva the river flows into the Rhone River. Across the bridge you enter a southern suburb of Geneva called Carouge.

Carouge has a special history. The catholic Kingdom of Sardinia (predecessor of the Italian Kingdom and part of the House of Savoy) owned these lands south of the Arve River in the 18th century. The river was the border between the City-Republic of Geneva and the Kingdom of Sardinia. The King of Sardinia wanted to build a city around a large church, at the most northern border of his Kingdom, to counter the protestant City-Republic of Geneva (north of the Arve River). Thus, a catholic church was built in 1777-80. However, the Kingdom and the House of Savoy were conquered by Napoleon in 1792, and the King had to abandon further plans for this northern city (which became part of France, together with Geneva, in 1798). The French ceded Carouge to Canton Geneva in 1816, after which the town converted to Protestantism. Subsequently, the protestants wanted to have their own church in Carouge (which only had the catholic church), and built one in 1818-22. This explains a protestant church (see below) and a catholic church (see below) standing only 150 meters apart in Carouge.

After the bridge the route turns diagonally left into the *Rue du Pont Neuf* and takes the first street on the left (*Rue Saint-Joseph*). After about 200 meters you arrive at a long rectangular square. On your right, in about 100 meters distance, you see the protestant church of Carouge. The signposted route continues straight, but it is worthwhile to make a short detour to visit the two churches. You arrive at the reformed Church of Carouge at km 2.5.

Reformed Church, Carouge (Temple de Carouge) 215

Place du temple 13, 1227 Carouge

The protestant church was built in 1818-22, after the Republic of Geneva received these lands in 1816. The church has a neoclassical portico with four columns, similar to the one at the reformed St. Peter cathedral in Geneva. It is a typical example of a hall church.

In 1821 two side galleries were added, as the number of seats in the nave were limited. These side galleries were removed again in 1939. It is clear that the gallery at the back of the church, which contains the organ, was installed at a later stage. Notice how its woodwork interrupts the wall frescos and covers part of the stained-glass windows.

In 1910 the City of Courage transferred ownership of the church to the protestant parish, which painted the interior white. Under leadership of the then pastor Ernest Christen, the interior underwent a complete transformation in 1918-25 and 1936. The last renovations were undertaken in 1998-93, determining its present-day appearance.

From the outside the building looks colorless and dull. But its interior will surprise any visitor. The most beautiful and elaborate frescos cover the walls and ceiling. This is certainly the most glamorously decorated protestant church along the Swiss Way of St. James; very unlike the doctrine of Protestantism that was formulated by Jean Calvin in the 1530s.

Aside from these decorations, the church has a typical protestant interior limited to a pulpit (center stage in the chancel), organ, and pews for the parishioners. In this colorful setting, the usual altars, statues, and paintings of the catholic churches are not missed. Eye-catching are the frescos, stained-glass, mosaic, and wood carvings. These all date from the renovations at the beginning of the 20th century.

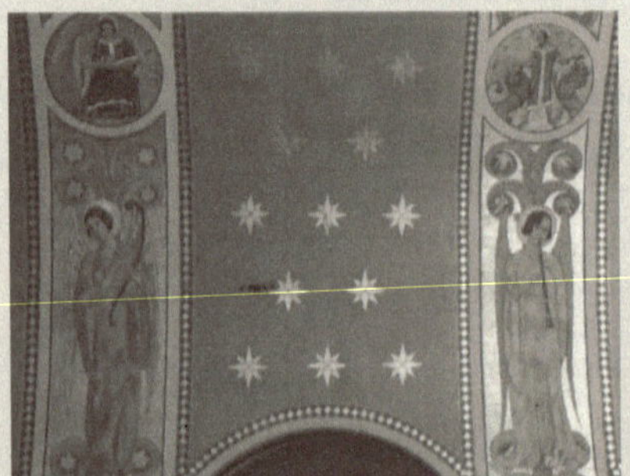

The frescos were painted by Erich Hermès in 1921-29 (name of the artist and date of 1922 on the bottom left-side of the chancel fresco). The fresco covering the chancel wall is an artistic depiction of the Christmas manger (nativity) scene. The faces of the figures were painted to reflect the faces of actual people from the parish (of those who had contributed to the transformation of the interior in the 1920s).

Perhaps even more impressive are the 16 angels in the four gold-colored borders along the arched ceiling. Their Art-Deco style of the 1920s is equally unique, not seen anywhere else along the Swiss Way of St. James. Four medallions depict the apostles, the other seven medallions prophets. Gold-colored stars on the ceiling reflect the light as in a night sky.

The stained-glass windows (1924) are densely colored and add to the kaleidoscope of colors of the interior. They depict scenes from The Bible that were designed by Hermès and made by Charles Wasem.

The gold-colored mosaic squares (1924) in the semicircular recess behind the pulpit reflect the light in an intense way. It is easy to imagine the preacher's silhouette on the elevated pulpit, which from the perspective of the parishioners sitting on the pews must look like being surrounded by a golden aura.

The pulpit, side doors, communion table, and even the support columns of the gallery all have elaborate wood carvings. Pastor Ernest Christen made these artful wood carvings himself in 1918-25. Have a closer look at these carvings. They are highly detailed and display many different scenes and symbols from The Bible.

Sit down and take in these unique icons of protestant religious art. To protect this artful interior, though, the doors of the church are generally locked. You can only access the church during services or by appointment with the parish office.

From the protestant church turn south along the *Rue Jacques Dalphin* and after 150 meters you arrive at the catholic Holy Cross Church (at km 2.7).

Holy Cross Church, Carouge (Eglise Sainte-Croix) **216**

Place du Marché 15, 1227 Carouge

St. James the Greater, St. James the Lesser, Twelve Apostles, Mary-Lourdes

The catholic church was built by the King of Sardinia in 1777-80. After Carouge was annexed by Napoleon in 1792, the church was used as a warehouse and only handed over to the catholic parish seven years later, in 1803. Carouge was ceded by the French to Canton Geneva in 1816. Subsequently the church was remodeled (entrance moved to the market square) in 1824-26, and an organ was installed in 1830.

In 1873 the protestant Authorities of Geneva confiscated the church during the 'Kulturkampf' and only handed it over to the catholic parish 48 years later (1921). For 48 years the Catholics had to hold their services in a room of the local brewery. The many years of neglect required extensive restorations and alterations in 1922-26.

The church was named after the Glorious Cross, in dedication to the high-altar of the St. Peter cathedral in Geneva from before the Reformation. A replica made by a Genevan artist is kept at the church (not visible to the public).

Special is the story of the bell tower. Two bell towers were planned, but only one was built. This one was destroyed during the French Revolution in 1796. A new tower was built too high and cracked under the pressure of its 36 bells. It was replaced by a decorative bell tower and subsequently restored to fit all 36 bells again. The carillon of the Holy Cross church contains the second-most bells of any church in Switzerland.

Notice the high ceilings of the transept and chancel. They are semicircular, just like the canopy at the high-altar. Neither the ceilings nor the walls have been colored. The grey plaster is a stark contrast to the elaborate decorations seen at the protestant church of Carouge.

Special features of the church are: the Lourdes side-chapel with a Mary-Lourdes statue in a small cave and its stained-glass window (right of the entrance); and the two rosette stained-glass windows in the transept. The famous artist Alexandre Cingria made these stained-glass windows in 1924.

The nine nearly life-size statues of apostles (called the 'nine Apostles of Courage') include the statues representing St. James the Greater and St. James the Lesser in the right-side transept. This is one of the few locations along the Swiss Way of St. James where the two Jameses are presented together like this.

From the church walk back to the signposted route nr. 4 by following the market (*Place du Marché*) in an eastern direction (100 meters). At the street with the tram tracks (*Rue du Marché*) you are back on the signposted route.

Turn right to follow the tram tracks and continue on the road that converges with the *Rue Ancienne*, until you arrive at a large roundabout (*le Rondeau de Carouge*). The route passes by the roundabout on its eastern side and crosses the *Route de Drize*.

On your right you see the white IBIS hotel and a large parking of city buses and trams. From this location the route starts ascending. For 600 meters the route follows the *Route de Drize* up the hill. You walk through an area with university, college, and school buildings. On your right you pass by the modern building of the College of Drize (named after the river that flows nearby).

About 100 meters after the roundabout the route forks to the right and slightly descends through a small patch of forest to cross the Drize River. At this location you see a first sign directing to the border (*frontière*). On a tarmac road the route ascends out of the river valley and you pass by a white building with a green banner reading *Ferme de la Chapelle*. It may sound like it is a chapel, but it is not. It is an art gallery.

The route follows the *Route de Saconnex-d'Arve* south for 1.1 km, along residential areas with villas behind high hedges, and passes through several agricultural fields on a tarmac road. The views open up and to the left you see the grey cliffs and forested sides of the Mont Salève, with an elevation of around 1'200 meters. The mountain range is parallel to the Way of St. James, from north to south. You are now close to Highway A1 and can hear the traffic on your right.

In a village the route turns left and zigzags on a narrow footpath between hedges and a small patch of forest, after which you arrive at the *Chemin de l'Abérieu*. You walk along a steadily ascending road past agricultural fields and through another small village (Saconnex-d'Arve-Dessus) with a concrete road cross. On a tarmac footpath next to the road you pass by several plastic-covered greenhouses.

From a distance you can already see the former Commandry and Church, looking rough and austere in light brown/grey plaster. They seem to stand lost in the landscape of the agricultural fields. After a right turn you arrive at the former

Commandry of the Knights of St. John and catholic St. Sylvester Church (at km 7.3).

35 Former Commandry of the Knights of St. John, Compesières (La Commanderie l'Ordre des Hospitaliers de Saint-Jean de Jérusalem)

Route de Cugny 99, 1257 Compesières

Order of the Knights of St. John

The former Commandry of the Knights of St. John was built after the Bishop of Geneva donated the St. Sylvester Church (see below) in 1270. The present fortified commandry was built in the first half of 15th century, and housed the regional commander of the Knights of St. John as well as a hospital.

After the Reformation the commandry was closed and secularized. It was occupied by protestant Bernese troops and the Bernese Sheriff in 1536-67.

In 1567 the Bernese ceded the area to the catholic House of Savoy, and the Order received back its monastery. The fortified commandry was completely renovated in 1705-20. The last commander left and the commandry was abandoned after 500 years, when the French troops of Napoleon conquered the lands of Savoy in 1792.

The commandry and its hospital were closed and put to a different use. In the subsequent centuries they housed a factory, a school, municipal offices, and parish offices. Since 1822 it is owned by the municipality Compesières. Around 1900 the hospital building and the fortified walls, that had surrounded the commandry, hospital, and church since 1617, were demolished. The building was renovated in 1954-55 and 1971, when some of its medieval appearance was restored.

The second floor houses a small museum dedicated to the Order of the Knights of St. John, with a Knight's hall, its history, and some costumes and attires. The museum is only open by appointment (tel. 079 202 55 64; michele@zanetta.org).

St. Sylvester Church, Compesières (Eglise de St-Sylvestre) 217

Route de Cugny 99, 1257 Compesières

St. Sylvester

On a shelf dedicated to the Way of St. James (*Chemin de Saint-Jacques de Compostelle*) left of the entrance

The catholic church was first mentioned in official documents in 1270, when it was donated by the Bishop of Geneva to the Order of the Knights of St. John. The history of the church is closely linked to that of the commandry. The church, dedicated to St. Sylvester, was destroyed during the Bernese occupation in 1536-67. After Savoy troops reconquered the area, the church was rebuilt by the Order of the Knights of St. John and remained catholic.

The church was renovated together with the fortified commandry in 1705-20 (the altar dates from this time). After the Order of the Knights of St. John was forced to leave the commandry in 1792, the church became dilapidated. It was reconstructed in 1834-35. In the 19th and 20th centuries several renovations were undertaken, closely linked to those of the commandry.

Pleasant organ music plays automatically upon entering the church. Its interior is austere, with only a few decorations and statues. Special is the ceiling of the nave. Similar to the church in Crans-près-Céligny (see church nr. 200, stage 18) the ceiling looks like a memory game: it has 165 panels painted with themes of The Bible, the coat-of-arms of the commanders of the Order of the Knights of St. John, and generic fillers (in green color). They date from the renovations in 1953-54.

The St. Sylvester church is the last church along the Way of St. James through Switzerland. From the church cross the street and follow a narrow tarmac footpath between agricultural fields, past two soccer fields, and plastic-covered greenhouses. In the village Charrot the route turns left and right. At this right turn (at km 7.8) you find a grey box with the green/blue number 4 sticker, several scallops, and a note with the words Information and *Tampon* (French for stamp).

In the box you find: the last pilgrim stamp, which is the same as in the St. Sylvester church of Compesières; and a flyer with a high-level route map for the continuation of the Way of St. James in France.

The last 600 meters south on the *Chemin de la Chécande* are between fields and curve left down the hill along a wall and the last Swiss vineyards of the route. Then, at km 8.4 you arrive at the Swiss-French border crossing. This crossing is only 3 km east of Swiss-French border town Perly, where road nr. 1 ends. Road nr. 1 started at the German-Swiss border in Konstanz/Kreuzlingen and now ends close to the end of the Swiss Way of St. James too. The **Swiss-French border crossing** is unlike anything you would expect.

There are no custom officials, security booths, or fences with barbed wire. Nobody will wave you goodbye from Switzerland or welcome you to France. Like many of the trails through Switzerland, you are on an isolated trail alone in nature. The border is just a low swiveling gate, in front of a small bridge over the Rau stream (which is the official border). The last green/blue nr. 4 sign is fixed to a pole, directing beyond the gate. A small board of the Swiss Way of St. James says goodbye. Still 1'865 km to go to Santiago de Compostela.

From the ending point

The gate at the Swiss-French border marks the end of the Way of St. James through Switzerland.

In case you are a thru-hiker and continue your pilgrimage into France, Bon Camino!

In case you want to go back to the Geneva train station, public transportation can take you there in less than 40 minutes. Walk back the same 600 meters to the village Charrot. You find the bus stop close to the location where the route turns right, back towards Compesières. At the bus stop on the *Route de Foliaz* take bus number 46 in the direction of *Courage GE, Stade de Genève*, departing every 50 minutes. At *Grand-Lancy, Bachat-de-Pesay* (11 minutes, 9th stop) change to bus D or tram 12, departing every 15 minutes to *Geneva Bel-Air* (18 minutes). From the Place Bel-Air it is an 800-meter walk to the train station (or continue on another tram).

In case you flew from your home country to Zurich airport for pilgrimaging on the Way of St. James through Switzerland, you will need to go back to the airport. You could organize your return flight from either Geneva airport or Zurich airport. From Geneva train station *Cornavin* a direct train goes to *Genève-Aéroport* five times an hour (8 minutes; CHF 4). A train departs from the Geneva train station to *Zurich Flughafen* twice an hour (3 hours; CHF 92).

Is there a next Stage in Switzerland?

Which route did you hike on your pilgrimage through Switzerland? Did you start in Konstanz or Rorschach? Did you go via Rapperswil or Siebnen? Did you hike via Alpine Lakes (Interlaken) or Luzern/Bern? Did you follow the trails via Romont or Payerne?

In case you are a one-time pilgrim on the Swiss Camino, you have finished.

In case you are planning to return to some of the routes, up to 12 additional stages can be hiked (depending on your first route through Switzerland). See the chapter Hiking Routes, pages 46 to 54 of the General Introduction in Volume I. That chapter explains the composition of the Swiss Way of St. James routes and will enable you to identify the additional stages you can hike. You probably have many more 1'000-year-old churches, chapels, monasteries, and castles to explore along the Way of St. James through Switzerland. Your next day-hike or thru-hike awaits!

APPENDICES

Appendix 1: List of Churches

Appendix 1 lists all churches and chapels along the Way of St. James in South-West Switzerland, with references to the locations, stages, and page numbers. The numbering continues from Volume II.
The descriptions of their history and special features are included in the chapters of the respective hiking stages.

Churches from Fribourg to Geneva/French Border, via Romont

Nr.	Name	City	Stage	Page
158	Ursuline Convent Church	Fribourg	14	33
159	Reformed Church	Fribourg	14	35
160	St. Peter Church	Fribourg	14	35
161	St. Joseph Chapel	Fribourg	14	37
162	St. Peter and Paul Church	Villars-sur-Glâne	14	38
163	St. Apollonia Chapel	Villars-sur-Glâne	14	40
164	Farm Chapel	Les Muéses	14	41
165	Sacred Heart Chapel	Posieux	14	42
166	Our Lady of the Assumption Church	Ecuvillens	14	44
167	Our Lady Chapel	Posat	14	45
168	St. Maurice Church	Autigny	14	47
169	St. John the Baptist Chapel	Chavannes-sous-Orsonnens	14	48
170	Cistercian Convent Church	Romont	14	50
171	Capuchin Monastery Church	Romont	14	52
172	Reformed Chapel	Romont	14	54
173	Our Lady of the Assumption Church	Romont	14	55
174	St. Maurice Church	Billens	15	65
175	St. Bernard Chapel	Hennens	15	65
176	Reformed Church	Lovatens	15	67
177	Reformed St. Peter Church	Curtilles	15	69
178	Reformed St. Stephen Church	Moudon	15	71
179	St. Amadeus Church	Moudon	15	72
180	Reformed Church	Syens	16	122
181	Reformed Chapel	Vucherens	16	123
182	Reformed Church	Montpreveyres	16	125
183	Reformed Chapel	Vers-chez-les-Blanc	16	128
184	Reformed Church	Les Croisettes	16	129
185	Reformed Our Lady Cathedral	Lausanne	16	134
186	Reformed St. Francis Church	Lausanne	17	146
187	Reformed Church	Lausanne	17	147
188	Reformed St. Lazarus Chapel	Lausanne	17	149
189	Reformed Cluniac Monastery Church	St-Sulpice	17	151
190	Reformed Church	Morges	17	154
191	Reformed Church	Saint-Prex	17	157

Nr.	Name	City	Stage	Page
192	Reformed Chapel	Buchillon	17	160
193	Reformed Our Lady Church	Perroy	17	163
194	St. Joseph Church	Rolle	17	166
195	Reformed Church	Rolle	17	166
196	Reformed Church	Bursinel	18	174
197	Reformed Church	Prangins	18	178
198	St. Colombière Church	Nyon	18	181
199	Reformed Our Lady Church	Nyon	18	182
200	Reformed Church	Crans-près-Céligny	18	186
201	Reformed Church	Céligny	18	188
202	Ecumenical Chapel	Bossey	18	191
203	Reformed Church	Commugny	18	193
204	Reformed Dominican Monastery Church	Coppet	18	195
205	Reformed Church	Genthod	19	204
206	St. Rita Church	Bellevue	19	205
207	St. Petronilla Church	Pregny-Chambésy	19	207
208	Reformed Holy Trinity Church	Geneva	19	213
209	Our Lady Basilica	Geneva	19	214
210	Reformed St. Gervase Church	Geneva	19	216
211	St. Germain Church	Geneva	19	219
212	Reformed St. Peter Cathedral	Geneva	19	221
213	Reformed Maccabees Chapel	Geneva	19	222
214	St. Francis de Sales Church	Geneva	20	229
215	Reformed Church	Carouge	20	231
216	Holy Cross Church	Carouge	20	233
217	St. Sylvester Church	Compesières	20	237

Churches from Villars-sur-Glâne to Lucens, via Payerne

Nr.	Name	City	Stage	Page
P-1	St. James Church	Noréaz	P1	84
P-2	Immaculate Conception Church	Montagny	P1	87
P-3	Our Lady Church	Tours	P1	91
P-4	Reformed Church	Corcelles-près-Payerne	P1	92
P-5	Reformed Church	Payerne	P1	94
P-6	Reformed Our Lady Church	Payerne	P1	95
P-7	Reformed Cluniac Monastery Church	Payerne	P1	96
P-8	Immaculate Our Lady Church	Payerne	P2	103
P-9	Reformed Our Lady Church	Granges-près-Marnand	P2	105
P-10	St. John Church	Granges-près-Marnand	P2	106
P-11	Reformed Church	Henniez	P2	107
P-12	Reformed St. Agnes Chapel	Lucens	P2	111
P-13	Our Lady of Immaculate Conception Church	Lucens	P2	112

Appendix 2: Biography of Saints

Appendix 2 lists, in alphabetical order, all the names of saints represented along the Way of St. James in South-West Switzerland, with references to the church numbers.

A short biography of these saints, in alphabetical order, is provided on the next pages. Their biography should be read in the context of the background of saints and Roman catacomb relics, as described in the chapter Religious Context of the General Introduction to the Swiss Camino in Volume I.

Saints from Fribourg to Geneva/French Border (via Romont and Payerne)

Name	Church nr.
St. Agnes	P-12
St. Amadeus	179
St. Andrew	169
St. Anthony of Padua	171
St. Apollonia	163
St. Barbara	164
St. Bernard	175
St. Christopher	210
St. Clotilde	209
St. Colombière	198
St. Donatus	171
Four Evangelists	160, P-2, 204, 210, 211
St. Francis de Sales	209, 215
St. Francis of Assisi	171, 186, 210
St. Germain	211
St. Gervase	210
Holy Family	209
St. James the Greater	168, P-1, 185, 189, 217
St. James the Lesser	169, 217
St. John the Baptist	169, 210
St. John the Evangelist	P-10
St. Joseph	161, 194
St. Lazarus	188
(Mary-) Lourdes	217
St. Marius	P-6, 185
St. Mary	164, 166, 167, 168, 173, P-2, P-3, P-6, P-7, P-8, P-9, P-13, 185, 193, 199, 209
St. Maurice	168, 174
St. Nicholas of Flüe	160, 165

Name	Church nr.
St. Nicholas (of Myra)	P-4, 189
Our Lady	*See St. Mary*
St. Paul	162
St. Peter	160, 162, 164, 177, 212
St. Petronilla	207
St. Prothasius	191
St. Rita	206
St. Stephen	178
St. Sulpicius	189
St. Sylvester	176, 218
St. Thérèse of Lisieux	160
Twelve Apostles	185, 217
St. Ursula	158

Biography of Saints

St. Agnes
St. Agnes (of Rome) was a young Christian girl, who refused her suitors. Out of revenge a suitor reported her Christianity to the Roman Authorities. She was beheaded for not renouncing her Christian faith at the age of 13 in 304. She became the patroness Saint of chastity and virgins.

St. Amadeus
St. Amadeus (of Lausanne) was born into a noble family in Grenoble (France), but renounced his family's wealth to become a monk. He was both Abbot of the Cistercian Monastery of Hautecombe (France) and Bishop of Lausanne in 1144-59. St. Amadeus became known for his eight sermons on the Virgin Mary. His tomb and relics were discovered in the Cathedral of Lausanne in 1911. The worshipping of him as a Saint was confirmed by Popes, although he was never canonized as such.

St. Andrew
St. Andrew was one of the Twelve Apostles and the brother of St. Peter. As his brother, St. Andrew was a fisherman before becoming a follower of Jesus. According to legend, he traveled to eastern European countries such as Turkey, Ukraine, and Russia to preach and convert pagans to Christianity. He was said to have established the Bishopric of Byzantium (Constantinople or Istanbul) and to have been martyred in Greece. From the middle ages he was said to have been crucified (tied with ropes) to an X-shaped cross, now known as the St. Andrew's Cross. St. Andrew became the patron Saint of many countries and cities, of which several have the X-shaped cross in their flag (e.g. Scotland).

St. Anthony of Padua
St. Anthony of Padua was a Portuguese friar (from Lisbon) in the Franciscan Order, well known for his teaching and preaching. He died from an illness in Padua, Italy in 1231. He became the patron Saint of lost souls, lost people, and lost things. A novice stole his psalm book, which was returned to him after he prayed for it to be found.

St. Apollonia

St. Apollonia was a martyr who lived in Alexandria, Egypt. During an uprising against Christians she was captured and tortured; all her teeth were pulled. She refused to renounce her Christian faith and upon the threat of getting burned alive, she went into the fire voluntarily and burned to death (249). She became the patroness Saint of dentists and was invoked against tooth problems.

St. Barbara

St. Barbara's legends first appeared in the 7th century. These told that she was imprisoned in a tower by her father, who wanted to keep her safe until the right husband was found. When her father found out she had converted to Christianity, he wanted to kill her. Her prayers opened a hole in the tower and she could flee. She was found, captured, and tortured, but refused to renounce her faith. Each morning all inflicted wounds had miraculously healed. Torches were used to burn her, but the flames could not harm her. She was beheaded by her father, who was subsequently struck by lightning and burned to death. She was one of the Fourteen Holy Helpers and became the patroness Saint of artillerymen, miners, and geologists. Because of the fictional person, her feast day was removed from the Roman calendar in 1969.

St. Bernard

St. Bernard (of Menthon) was a priest born in Annecy, France, around 1020. He became archdeacon of the Cathedral in the northern Italian town Aosta, at the southern foothills of the Swiss Alps. Many pilgrims who crossed the Alps from the Swiss Canton Valais on their way to Rome or Jerusalem halted at his Cathedral in Aosta. To provide better care for the safety and health of travelers and pilgrims, he founded a hospice and a canon regular monastery at the St. Bernard Pass in the Swiss Alps in 1050. It was one of the highest situated European monasteries at 2'469 meters. From the 17th century St. Bernard dogs were used for rescuing travelers in winter. Both the mountain pass and the dogs were named after him. He died in 1081 and was canonized in 1681. He became the patron Saint of the Swiss Alps and mountaineers.

St. Christopher

St. Christopher probably lived in the 3rd century. Nothing is known of his life or death, and some historians doubt he really existed. His broad popularity as a Saint originated from legends created in the 6th century. By the 9th century his legends spread through Europe and he became a popular Saint of travelers and children. This despite the fact that he was never recognized by the Church, nor canonized as a Saint. He was one of the Fourteen Holy Helpers. The name Christopher was derived from 'Christ-bearer', linked to the following legend.

Christopher was a tall and strong man, born in Arabia. He wanted to serve the most fearless King. After he saw that the King was afraid of the devil, he went to search for the devil. He met the head of a bandit gang, who called himself the devil. He started serving him, but soon found out that this bandit was afraid of Christ. Christopher continued to look for Christ, who supposedly was the most fearless person. A hermit advised him to serve Christ by carrying people across a dangerous river, where many had died in the currents. After doing so for a while, a young boy asked him to be carried across. While Christopher was crossing the river, the water level rose and the boy's weight increased to become almost impossible to carry. He asked the boy why he was so heavy. The child responded that he was Christ and carried the weight of the world. Christopher converted to Catholicism and subsequently converted many pagans. He was beheaded upon his refusal to make offerings to pagan Gods.

St. Clotilde

St. Clotilde was the wife of Frankish King Clovis I. She was brought up as a Christian and was the main influence on her husband's conversion to Christianity and his baptism by Bishop Remigius of Reims in 496. After her husband's death she became a nun at the Abbey of St. Martin in Tours in 511. She had several churches and monasteries built, and died in Tours in 545. She became the patroness Saint of parents and widows.

St. Colombière

St. Claude de la Colombière was a French Jesuit priest who lived in 1641-82. In 1675 Colombière became counselor of a Convent of the Visitation Sisters. One of the nuns, Margaret Mary Alacoque, shared her revelations of Christ, where He had promoted devotion to his Sacred Heart. Colombière became one of the main contributors to the establishment of the Sacred Heart of Jesus devotion. He was canonized in 1992.

St. Donatus

St. Donatus (of Arezzo) was a Bishop of Arezzo, Italy. He was beheaded for refusing to denounce his faith in 362 (though there is no historical account of his martyring).

Four Evangelists

The Four Evangelists were Matthew, Mark, Luke and John, accredited with writing the four Gospel accounts of the New Testament. Matthew (a former tax collector) and John (a former fisherman) were two of the Twelve Apostles, whereas Mark was a travel companion and interpreter of St. Peter, and Luke was a former physician. Matthew was often symbolized as a winged man, Mark as a winged lion, Luke as a winged ox, and John as an eagle. The four Gospels, probably written in 66-110, gave an account of the life of Jesus.

St. Francis de Sales

St. Francis de Sales (pronounce in French) was a Bishop of Geneva in 1602-22, and an important contributor to the Counter-Reformation. Because Geneva was under the control of Calvinists, he resided in Annecy, France (about 45 km south of Geneva). He became the patron Saint of authors (he used books to convert Protestants to Catholicism) and the deaf (he developed a sign language to convert a deaf man).

St. Francis of Assisi

St. Francis of Assisi was an Italian friar, who lived in 1182-1226. He became one of the most well-known religious figures and was canonized in 1228. He became the patron Saint of animals; he prayed to birds and persuaded a wolf not to attack a village. He was the first one to arrange a live nativity (birth) scene (nowadays known as the Christmas manger) in 1223. St. Francis established the Franciscan Order in 1209.

St. Germain

St. Germain (of Paris) was a Bishop of Paris and known for his almsgiving to the poor. He died in 576.

St. Gervase

St. Gervase lived in Milan, Italy, in the 2nd century. St. Gervase was often named together with St. Protase, who was his twin brother. St. Gervase was beaten to death for not renouncing his faith (his twin brother was beheaded at the same time). St. Gervase became the patron Saint of haymakers and was invoked for discovering thieves.

Holy Family

The Holy Family consisted of Joseph, Mary, and Jesus.

St. James the Greater

St. James (the Greater or the Elder) was one of the Twelve Apostles. He was called the Greater (or Elder) to distinguish from James the Lesser, who was also one of the Twelve Apostles and the first Bishop of Jerusalem. St. James the Greater was either taller or older than the other James. King Herod had James (the Greater) beheaded by the sword in Jerusalem in the year 44; he was considered the first apostle who died for his faith in Christ. He became the patron Saint of Spain and pilgrims.

The legend that the remains of St. James were kept in Spain (Santiago de Compostela) arose around 900. According to this legend, St. James was a missionary in Iberia and after his execution in Jerusalem, his remains were miraculously shipped from Jerusalem to Santiago de Compostela. His remains were allegedly discovered in Spain in the 9th century (although he had died in the 1st century). In the 9th century the Spanish hermit Pelagius was said to have had a revelation of the location of the tomb of St. James. The then bishop of the region identified the tomb, the Spanish King Alfonso II had a church built for the relics in Santiago de Compostela, and Pope Leo XIII officially recognized this legend in 1884. Several versions of the legend were told: some said that St. James was an apostle in Spain before going back to Jerusalem (this version surfaced in the 9th century); others said he was never in Spain. It is, however, likely that his remains were spread over several locations in Europe, amongst others Santiago de Compostela.

St. James the Lesser

St. James the Lesser (or Minor, or Younger) was called like that to distinguish him from St. James the Greater (see above). St. James the Lesser was one of the Twelve Apostles and the first Bishop of Jerusalem. He was martyred for his faith in the year 62.

St. John the Baptist

St. John the Baptist was considered a prophet, as he announced the coming of Jesus. He was born around the same time as Jesus: a pregnant Mary visited his pregnant mother Elisabeth, known from the scene of the Mary Visitation. St. John baptized Jesus when He was around 30 years of age. King Herod had St. John beheaded around 28-36, after St. John had criticized the King for divorcing his wife and taking the wife of his brother.

St. John the Evangelist

St. John the Evangelist was one of the Twelve Apostles, also called John the Apostle. He was the younger brother of St. James the Greater. He died of old age around the year 100 and was the only Apostle who was not martyred.

St. Joseph

St. Joseph was married to Mary and was Jesus' foster father. He became the patron Saint of fathers and carpenters (he raised Jesus and was a carpenter).

St. Lazarus

St. Lazarus (of Bethany) was resurrected to life by Jesus four days after his death. He became the patron Saint of the ill, particularly lepers, and hospitals.

(Mary-) Lourdes

Mary-Lourdes, or Our Lady of Lourdes, is a title of the Virgin Mary at the location of Lourdes. Lourdes (France) is the site where the Virgin Mary was reported to have appeared 18 times in 1858. The Virgin Mary appeared to a local 14-year-old girl called Bernadette Soubirous, who was canonized in 1933 (Saint Bernadette of Lourdes). The spring water of the Lourdes cave is said to have healing powers and the Catholic Church has officially recognized several dozens of miraculous healings. Every year millions of pilgrims visit the Lourdes cave and drink the spring water.

St. Marius

St. Marius (of Avenches) transferred the diocese from Avenches (55 km north of Lausanne, 16 km northwest of Fribourg) to Lausanne after becoming Bishop in Avenches in 574. St. Marius died in Lausanne in 594 and was canonized in 1605.

St. Mary

St. Mary was the mother of Jesus and known under many different names, such as Virgin Mary, Our Lady, Mother of God, Madonna, and Queen of Heaven. She was the daughter of St. Joachim and St. Anne, and was born in Nazareth around 18 BC. According to tradition, Jesus was conceived through the Holy Spirit, while she remained a virgin. She was married to Joseph. Besides the adoration of Jesus, the adoration of Mary became the most widespread in Christianity.

St. Maurice

St. Maurice was an Egyptian commander of the Theban Legion of the Roman Empire in the 3rd century. According to legend, the Theban Legion was sent to Switzerland to clear the Great St. Bernhard Pass from rebelling Swiss Christians. St. Maurice and his soldiers were ordered to slay fellow Christians, but they refused. As punishment Roman Emperor Maximinus had Maurice and his soldiers executed. The Abbey of St. Maurice in Canton Valais was dedicated to the martyrs of the Theban Legion (and still keeps their relics), as it was believed that the executions took place at that location. The Swiss alpine ski resort St. Moritz was named after him. He became the patron Saint of soldiers.

Other soldiers from the Theban Legion, who became martyrs together with St. Maurice, were St. Victor, St. Felix and Regula, and St. Innocence.

St. Nicholas of Flüe

St. Nicholas of Flüe (also called Brother Klaus, *Bruder Klaus*, or *Niklaus von Flüe*) was born in 1417 and served in the Swiss Confederate Army of Unterwalden until the age of 37. He subsequently served as a judge and counselor for the Canton. After a vision he retreated from his wife Dorothee and 10 children, and became a hermit in a gorge close to their house. He lived an ascetic life, allegedly living of Eucharist for 20 years. He was sought after for his wisdom and counsel, by pilgrims and Authorities. Many pilgrims visited him in his cell to ask for advice. In 1481 he had a decisive consulting role that prevented a civil war, which would likely have caused a split of the Swiss Confederation. He died in 1487 and was canonized in 1947. He became the patron Saint of Switzerland and the Swiss Guard at the Vatican. He is Switzerland's most well-known medieval hermit, mystic, and counselor.

St. Nicholas (of Myra)

St. Nicholas (of Myra) was a Bishop of Myra (Turkey) in the Roman Empire. He died in 342. Though not much is known of his historical person, there are many legends about him. The most famous legends are: secret gift-giving, such as giving three purses of money as dowry for three neighboring virgin girls (so that they could get married), or secretly leaving coins in shoes; staving off a storm and waves that threatened to sink the ship he was on; and reviving three children that had been killed by a butcher, their flesh intended to be sold as ham during a time of famine. These legends made him the medieval patron Saint of children, sailors, and fishermen.

The legend of the secret gift-giving has survived nearly 1'700 years, though nowadays it is called Santa Claus (a popularization of the name Saint Nicholas). Santa Claus has its origins in Dutch traditions, where on 5th/6th December, the commemorative day of St. Nicholas' death, Sinterklaas (or Sint Nikolaas; Dutch derived from Saint Nicholas) would leave small presents in the shoes of children. When the Dutch established New Amsterdam (nowadays named New York) in 1625, they continued this tradition. Under the American commercialization of Sint Nikolaas in the 19th century, he was renamed Santa Claus and the timing of the gift-giving shifted to 24th/25th of December.

Our Lady

Our Lady, see St. Mary. In German *Unser Liebe Frau*, in French *Notre Dame.*

St. Paul

St. Paul was also known as St. Paul the Apostle, though he was not one of the Twelve Apostles. He lived in the first century (5-65). According to legend, he was persecuting followers of Jesus, but was converted to Christianity when a resurrected Jesus appeared to him while he was on the road to Damascus. He started preaching the word of God and traveled extensively through the Roman Empire, where he established churches. According to legend he was decapitated in Rome by order of Emperor Nero. He became the patron Saint of missionaries and authors.

St. Peter

St. Peter (originally named Simon) was one of the Twelve Apostles and the brother of St. Andrew. He was a fisherman before becoming a follower of Jesus. He was the first Pope of Rome and was crucified by Emperor Nero around the year 66. He became the patron Saint of fishermen and clergy. The St. Peter's Basilica in the Vatican was built on the site of the grave of St. Peter. This basilica became one of the most well-known churches of Christianity, after which many other churches chose St. Peter as their patron Saint.

St. Petronilla
St. Petronilla lived in 1st century Rome and was a close follower of St. Peter the Apostle. According to legend, she was so beautiful that St. Peter had to lock her up to save her from pagan men, who were pursuing to marry her. St. Peter asked God to give her a fever that caused facial paralysis. St. Peter only cured her after she showed perfect dedication to God. She was invoked against fever.

St. Prothasius
St. Prothasius was a Bishop of Lausanne, who died near the city of Saint-Prex around 652.

St. Rita
St. Rita (of Cascia, Italy) was forced into an arranged marriage when she was 12 years of age. After 18 years of marriage to an abusive husband, he was killed in a vendetta by another family. Rita joined the Augustinian Order and became a nun. She died in 1457 and was canonized in 1900. She became the patroness Saint of abused wives and widows.

St. Stephen
St. Stephen was a deacon (a member of clergy responsible for charity) in the early Church in Jerusalem. He was considered the first martyr of Christianity. In the year 34 he was stoned to death after he denounced the Jewish Authorities, who accused him of blasphemy. He became the patron Saint of masons.

St. Sulpicius
St. Sulpicius (the Pious) was a Bishop of Bourges (France) in 624-46. He devoted himself to charity and caring for the poor.

St. Sylvester
St. Sylvester was a Pope in the 4th century and died on 31 December 335. The celebration of the last day of the year, New Year's Eve, was named after him; it is called Saint Sylvester's Day (or *Silvester* in the Germanic countries).

St. Thérèse of Lisieux
St. Thérèse of Lisieux was a nun (from the age of 15) in the Carmelite Convent of Lisieux, France. She died in 1897 (age 24), after many years of suffering from tuberculosis, and was canonized in 1925. After her death she became well-known for her spiritual writings and memoires, offering simple and practical religious viewpoints from a suffering young girl. This gave her the nickname 'The little Flower (of Jesus)'. She became the patroness Saint of florists and gardeners.

Twelve Apostles
The Twelve Apostles were 12 men chosen by Jesus to be sent out on apostolic missions. Initially they were sent out in pairs. These 12 men were: St. Peter (Simon) and his brother St. Andrew, St. James the Greater and his brother St. John the

Evangelist, St. Bartholomew, St. James the Lesser, St. Judas, St. Matthew, St. Philip, St. Simon the Zealot, St. Thaddaeus, and St. Thomas.

St. Ursula

St. Ursula most likely lived in the 4th century. Not much is certain of her story. According to legend, she was a Christian of British nobility who went on a European pilgrimage before (or to avoid) marrying a pagan Lord. She was accompanied by a few maids. In Cologne (Germany) besieging Huns killed them in 383.

In the 9th/10th century a fabulous legend around St. Ursula was created, which told that she had been accompanied by 11'000 virgin maids, who had been killed together with her in Cologne. Because of the unreliability of this story, her feast day was removed from the Roman Calendar in 1969. St. Ursula became the patroness Saint of female students upon the foundation of the Order of Ursulines (1535), which was dedicated to the education of girls.

Appendix 3: History of Monastic Orders

Appendix 3 lists all monasteries and convents along the Way of St. James in South-West Switzerland, with references to the locations, stages, and page numbers. The numbering continues from Volume II.
The descriptions of their history and special features are included in the chapters of the respective hiking stages.

A short history of these monastic Orders, in alphabetical order, is provided on the next pages. Their history should be read in the context of the medieval monastic world, as described in the chapter Religious Context of the General Introduction to the Swiss Camino in Volume I.

Monasteries from Fribourg to Geneva/French Border, via Romont

Nr.	Name	Location	Stage	Page
23	Ursuline Convent	Fribourg	14	33
24	Former Norbertine Convent	Posat	14	46
25	Cistercian Convent of the Daughters of God	Romont	14	51
26	Former Capuchin Monastery	Romont	14	53
27	Former Great St. Bernard Monastery	Montpreveyres	16	124
28	Former Carmelite Monastery	Jorat Forest	16	127
29	Former Franciscan Monastery	Lausanne	17	146
30	Former Cluniac Monastery	St-Sulpice	17	152
31	Former Benedictine Monastery	Perroy	17	162
32	Former Augustinian Monastery	Nyon	18	183
33	Former Dominican Monastery	Coppet	18	195
34	Monastery of St. John Community	Geneva	20	229
35	Former Commandry of the Knights of St. John	Compesières	20	236

Monasteries from Villars-sur-Glâne to Lucens, via Payerne

Nr.	Name	Location	Stage	Page
P-1	Former Cluniac Monastery	Payerne	P1	98

History of Monastic Orders

Augustinian Order

The Augustinian Order follows the Rule of St. Augustine of Hippo. He was a Roman north-African Bishop, from a region in modern-day Algeria, who lived in 354-430. During his early life he spent considerable time teaching philosophy and theology in Tunisia and Italy (Rome, Milan), after he converted to Christianity in 368. Between 400 and 423 he wrote several documents, which together made up a rule-book outlining key aspects of a Christian religious life. His rules focused on chastity, poverty, obedience, and caring for the ill. In effect his rules established the first standards for Western monasteries.

Inspired by his Rule, many monasteries were established in northern Africa and southern Europe during the following century. In the 6th century the Order and their monasteries were in decline, and basically ceased to exist. St. Benedict established his Rule in 529, borrowing from the Rule of St. Augustine. The Rule of St. Benedict was better adjusted to the times of the mid first-millennium and became the new standard for Christian monastic life. As the first Augustinian Order ceased to exist, the new Benedictine Order flourished from the 6th to the 12th century. By the 12th century the Rule of St. Benedict had become outdated, as a result of intellectual and economical changes in society, increasing urbanization, and shifting power and wealth. This led to a revival of the Rule of St. Augustine, which refocused monastic life on the original ascetic and austere rules.

The old Rule found high acceptance and spread over monasteries in western Europe. New Orders such as the Premonstratensians (Norbertines) and Dominicans applied the Rule. The revived Order of St. Augustine was formally established by joining several local hermit Orders in the Tuscany region of Italy in 1244. This gave them the official name of the Order of Hermits of Saint Augustine. In order to adapt to the changed society, Pope Alexander IV enhanced the original Rule of St. Augustine with the mendicant purpose of bringing Catholicism to the people in the cities. From 1256 the mendicant Augustinian Order established monasteries in developing cities for preaching to and converting of the population, and helping the poor.

Nowadays the Order maintains no presence in Switzerland.

Benedictine Order

The Benedictine Order, also called the Order of Saint Benedict, was founded by Benedict of Nursia in Italy in 529. The Order revolved around prayer and physical labor ('Ora et Labora') under the Rule of St. Benedict. Each Benedictine abbey was independent and governed by their own abbot. A supervising abbot was often appointed by local noblemen, with the assignment to control and protect a monastery's assets. The monasteries were autonomous; there was no mother house that set a policy or appointed the abbots. Monks had to vow to stay within the same community and be obedient to the abbot and the Rule of St. Benedict. This gave the abbot full control over the monks: he set the rules for silence, reading, prayer, meals, sleep, and work. They would spend most of their time in prayer (eight times a day), several hours reading, and working the fields (to be self-sufficient). Application of these foundational rules resulted in tight communities of monks, who stayed in one location their whole (monastic) life. This resulted in stability and productivity; they amassed significant wealth in assets (donations of lands and income by noblemen) and knowledge (from studying and copying handwritten books). Monks were often the few people (apart from noblemen) who could read and write. This enabled them to collect and contain knowledge, often resulting in extensive libraries (for example the libraries of the Abbeys of St. Gallen and Einsiedeln). These monasteries created the first universities that collected and transferred knowledge (though within their Order, not to the public in general).

The Benedictine monasteries flourished and dominated the western monastic landscape until the 12th century. They are considered the foundation of western monastic life. They became wealthy through extensive ownership of lands, towns, and income. The medieval Christian doctrine focused on heaven and hell, in which the monasteries and their churches played a central role. Donations were considered a good way to attain salvation for a person's soul. It was the monastery as a community or institution that received the donations, not the individual monks. So long as the community continued to exist through succession of abbots, the monastery would keep accumulating wealth. After several centuries, these Benedictine monasteries had amassed so much wealth (lands, rights, and knowledge) that they often became the center of power of large territories. Their increasing wealth, knowledge, and land ownership resulted in increasing resistance from monarchs, noblemen, and state governors who saw their own territories and rule undermined.

During the 11th and 12th centuries society was changing and the population increasingly concentrated in towns. This set in the decline of the Benedictine monasteries. The application of the Rule of St. Benedict (already 600 years old) often resulted in inflexibility and isolation from the developing society and cities around them. They became complacent as a result of the wealth they had accumulated over the many centuries, and focused more on earthly than spiritual matters. Other Orders arose, such as the Franciscans and Augustinians, which were better adapted to the changing society, the development of cities, and were based on a vow of poverty (instead of amassing wealth) and care for the ill and poor (instead of staying within their own monastery). The Benedictines stayed in their monasteries, which became isolated from society and cities that developed in new areas and territories, while the new Orders participated in supporting the needy.

Nowadays the Order maintains eight monasteries and 12 convents in Switzerland (of which two and one respectively along the Swiss Way of St. James).

Capuchin Order
The Order of Friars Minor Capuchin is a branch of the Franciscan Order. The Capuchin Order was established by Matteo de Bascio, who sought a stricter reinterpretation of the Rule of St. Francis of Assisi, in Italy in 1525. This entailed a simpler life of austerity and poverty, and preaching to and caring for the poor. The Capuchin Order was a mendicant Order, established during the Counter-Reformation. Since they were a beggar-order, they had to be close to the population. Pastoral care and caring for the elderly, ill, and poor required them to be in the towns. The male members of the Order were called friars instead of monks. They dressed in a brown long pointy hooded habit that was tied around the waste with a white cord with three

knots, and wore sandals on their feet. Customarily they had a long untrimmed beard. Their name was derived from the hoods, which were called capuchins (in Italian). The Italian coffee cappuccino was named after the shade of brown of their habit.

Nowadays the Order maintains 11 monasteries and 12 convents (of the Capuchin Order of Poor Clares) in Switzerland (of which three and one respectively along the Swiss Way of St. James).

Carmelite Order

The Carmelite Order (Order of the Brothers of the Blessed Virgin Mary of Mount Carmel) is a mendicant monastic Order that was named after Mount Carmel (Israel), where hermits settled around 1190. The Order had a strong devotion to the Virgin Mary and the prophet Elias, and focused on contemplation (prayer, community, and service). From 1210/1247 they followed the Rule of St. Albert, which was created specifically for them, to adjust their way of life after returning from the Israeli desert to Europe. They remained relatively small compared to the other monastic Orders.

Nowadays the Order maintains three convents in Switzerland (none along the Swiss Way of St. James).

Cistercian Order

The Order of Cistercians is a branch of the Benedictine Order that followed a stricter interpretation of the Rule of St. Benedict. The Order split off from the Cluniac Order in 1098, when Robert of Molesme established a first monastery in the city of Citeaux, eastern France. The name Cistercians was derived from the name of this city. The Cistercians separated themselves from the Cluniac Order, which had deviated too much from the original Rule and focused too much on wealth and earthly matters. The Cistercians sought to live by the Rule of St. Benedict, as it was originally written in the 6th century. The main distinction was austerity, self-sufficiency, and their return to physical labor, mostly in agricultural fields. They initiated many of the medieval agricultural innovations, such as the use of technology and equipment for land development. They flourished until the 13th century, and were the main European influential monastic order in those days. During the following centuries their influence waned. They were replaced by mendicant Orders (beggar orders who settled in the urban areas to evangelize and help the poor) in many regions.

A reformation of the Cistercian Order developed and the so-called **Trappists** (named after the Trappe Abbey in France) split off in the 17th century. They again sought a stricter interpretation of the Rule of St. Benedict. The Trappists were secluded from the world around them. They became an enclosed Order, focusing on prayer and labor, with limited interaction with lay people.

Nowadays the Cistercian Order maintains two monasteries and seven convents in Switzerland (of which one convent along the Swiss Way of St. James).

Cluniac Order

The Cluniac Order was established by the Duke of Aquitaine in Cluny, France, as an offshoot of the Benedictine Order in 910. The name Cluniac was derived from the French town called Cluny (150 km west of Geneva) that housed the first and mother

Abbey. The Order sought a reformation of the 6th century Rule of St. Benedict, which had become out of date. The Order and its monasteries were independent, i.e. freed from oversight by lay noblemen and outside the control of the bishops. The Order applied a stricter interpretation of the Rule of St. Benedict, focusing on the traditional monastic life such as liturgy, prayers, copying of manuscripts, and caring for the poor and pilgrims, instead of on physical labor. As the Order became more popular their possessions grew through donations of lands, rights, and goods by nobility. They became the strongest western monastic reform movement of their time, and had many hundreds of subsidiaries during their peak (950-1130). Typical for the Cluniac Order, they had a strong hierarchy and centralization of decisions, where the mother Abbey of Cluny controlled many aspects of their subsidiary monasteries (e.g. the appointment of priors).

Their churches had very specific architecture with Romanesque features: massive walls; few and tiny windows; the bell tower on top of the crossing of the transept; the clear footprint of a Latin cross; three, five, or more apses to the east (of which the chancel in the middle was the largest); and Lombard bands (decorative blind arcades) on the outer walls of the apses.

By 1100 the Cluniac Order was at its peak and had amassed significant wealth, which changed their focus and positioning to earthly matters. Just like the Benedictine Order had become complacent after several centuries of success, so had the Cluniac Order. The Order's decline set in at the beginning of the 12th century. Their network had become too large to be effectively controlled from the center. Poor leadership and decadence as a result of its important position and wealth led to its downfall. The large organization could not adapt to the changing times, as the Benedictine Order could not either.

The Order was dissolved at the time of the French Revolution in the 1790s.

Community of St. John
The Community of St. John (original name in French: *Famille Saint-Jean*) was established by Dominican friar Marie-Dominique Philippe (a Theology professor at the Catholic University of Fribourg) in France in 1975. The monks have an apostolic mission, with the focus on local parishes and helping people in need. They derive their spiritual guidance from St. John the Evangelist.

Nowadays the Community maintains one monastery in Switzerland (which is along the Swiss Way of St. James).

Dominican Order
The Dominican Order, also called the Order of the Preachers, was established by the Spaniard St. Dominic of Guzman in 1216. He recruited priests, brothers, and nuns to preach the true teachings of Christianity. They were not bound by the usual monastic rules of being assigned to one location for life. With their apostolic missions they went out in the world, following the example of the Twelve Apostles. Their focus on preaching, studying, prayer, and meditation made them a leading force of theological intellect during the middle ages. As mendicant Order the Dominicans preached to the poor in a language they understood (instead of the difficult Latin or liturgical words).

Nowadays the Order maintains three monasteries and 11 convents in Switzerland (of which two convents along the Swiss Way of St. James).

Franciscan Order

The Franciscan Order was established by St. Francis of Assisi in 1209. He was an Italian catholic friar, deacon, and preacher. The Rule of St. Francis required its members to live in austerity and poverty, in the image of Jesus' life, while preaching Christianity as He had done. This brought them close to the poor and weak members of society. As a mendicant Order they were also called a beggar or barefoot Order, as a reflection of their vow to poverty. In French the Franciscan friars are called ***Cordeliers***, referring to the white rope (*corde*) with three knots, with which they tie their brown habit around their waste.

Nowadays the Order maintains three monasteries and two convents in Switzerland (of which one monastery along the Swiss Way of St. James).

Great St. Bernard Order

The Order of Great St. Bernard was established by St. Bernard (of Menthon) in 1050. To provide better care for the safety and health of travelers and pilgrims, he founded a hospice and canon regular monastery at the Great St. Bernard Pass in the Swiss Alps. Many pilgrims crossing the Alps from the Swiss Canton Valais on their way to Rome or Jerusalem halted at this hospice and monastery. It was one of the highest situated European monasteries at 2'469 meters. The Order of Great St. Bernard followed the Rule of St. Augustine. From the 17th century St. Bernard dogs were used for rescuing travelers in winter. Both the mountain pass and the dogs were named after the founder of the Order.

Nowadays the Order maintains three hospices in Switzerland (none along the Swiss Way of St. James).

Knights of St. John Order

The 'Order of Knights of the Hospital of Saint John of Jerusalem' is better known as the Maltese Order or the Hospitaller Order. The Order was established at the time of the Crusades in Jerusalem around 1048. Their task was to build a hospital to care for the ill and wounded pilgrims, and secure their safety at the times of military battles for the Holy Land. It was a military organization made up of Knights of noble background with Christian faith. After Islamic troops conquered Jerusalem, they relocated their base to Cyprus (1291), Rhodes (1310), and finally Malta (1530). This last location gave them their name under which they became more popularly known. The Order was seriously weakened by the Reformation that swept over Europe from the 1520s, and the conquests by Napoleon around 1798. They had to give up many of their commandries, and the Order was disrupted when Napoleon conquered the Island of Malta.

Between 1180 and 1456 the Order of the Knights of St. John maintained 20 commandries in Switzerland, which were situated at strategic locations enabling care for the ill and pilgrims. The Swiss Reformation had a devastating impact on the commandries, causing the closure of many of them between 1523 and 1536. The remaining commandries were closed or secularized from 1798, after Napoleon conquered Switzerland.

Nowadays the Order maintains one commandry in Switzerland (which is not along the Swiss Way of St. James).

Minim Order

The Minim Order was established as a branch of the Franciscan Order by St. Francis of Paola in 1435. The mendicant Minim Order derived its name from their minimum living conditions, which were based on poverty, hermitage, and vegan food.

Nowadays the Order maintains no presence in Switzerland.

Norbertine Order

The Order of St. Norbert, also called the Premonstratensians, are from the Order of Canons Regular of Prémontré, France, founded by St. Norbert of Xanten in 1120. The town Prémontré lies about 140 km northeast of Paris. As canon regular they were not monks, but still followed the Rule of St. Augustine. They went preaching in the towns that surrounded their monasteries and made their income from physical labor, such as farming, brewing, and printing. They played an important missionary role in central Europe (Germany, Poland, Czech, Austria). Like many of the other Orders, they were suppressed during the Reformation and the French Revolution. They were almost non-existent after Napoleon's conquests around 1798.

Nowadays the Order maintains one convent in Switzerland (which is not along the Swiss Way of St. James).

Ursuline Order

The Order of St. Ursula started as the Ursuline Group, established in Brescia, Italy, by Angela Merici in 1535. The Group was named after Saint Ursula and was dedicated to the education of young girls. Angela Merici had written a number of rules before her death in 1540. Pope Gregory XIII approved these rules (on the initiative of Charles Borromeo, archbishop of Milan) in 1572. As a result, the Group became an enclosed monastic Order for religious women, placed under the Rule of St. Augustine. The Order of St. Ursula established convents with churches and schools for the education of young girls. They founded catholic women's colleges and high schools all over the world. They can be regarded the counterpart of the Jesuits (which Order focused on the higher-level education of boys and was established around the same time).

Nowadays the Order maintains 3 convents in Switzerland (of which one along the Swiss Way of St. James).

Appendix 4: List of Points of Interest

Appendix 4 lists all points of interest along the Way of St. James in South-West Switzerland, with references to the locations, stages, and page numbers. The numbering continues from Volume II.
The descriptions of their history and special features are included in the chapters of the respective hiking stages.

Points of Interest from Fribourg to Geneva/French Border, via Romont

Nr.	Name	Location	Stage	Page
44	St. James Cross	Fribourg	14	37
45	Healing Spring	Posat	14	46
46	Castle of Romont	Romont	14	56
47	Stained-Glass Museum	Romont	14	58
48	Medieval City Fortifications	Romont	14	59
49	Former Castle of Billens	Billens	15	65
50	Former Castle of Bishopric Kingdom of Lausanne	Curtilles	15	69
51	Historic Upper City	Moudon	15	73
52	Former Castle of Bishopric Kingdom of Lausanne	Lausanne	16	133
53	Former Castle of Bishopric Kingdom of Lausanne	Lausanne	16	139
54	Olympic Museum	Lausanne	16	140
55	Stairs of the Market	Lausanne	17	145
56	Roman Archaeological Site	Lausanne	17	149
57	Castle of Morges	Morges	17	155
58	Medieval City of Saint-Prex	Saint-Prex	17	158
59	Former Castle of Bishopric Kingdom of Lausanne	Saint-Prex	17	159
60	Castle of Rolle	Rolle	17	164
61	Harpe Island	Rolle	17	165
62	Chateau of Bursinel	Bursinel	18	173
63	Chateau of Dully	Dully	18	174
64	Toblerone Trail	Gland	18	176
65	Chateau of Prangins	Prangins	18	177
66	Castle of Nyon	Nyon	18	180
67	Roman Archaeological Site and Museum	Nyon	18	181
68	Chateau of Crans	Crans-près-Céligny	18	185
69	Chateau of Cèligny	Céligny	18	189
70	Chateau of Bossey	Bossey	18	190
71	Chateau of Coppet	Coppet	18	194

Nr.	Name	Location	Stage	Page
72	Chateau of Tournay	Pregny-Chambésy	19	208
73	Chateau of Rothschild	Pregny-Chambésy	19	209
74	Chateau of Penthes	Pregny-Chambésy	19	209
75	Botanical Gardens	Geneva	19	210
76	Water-Jet Fountain	Geneva	19	212
77	Medieval Clock Tower	Geneva	19	218
78	Cathedral Archaeological Museum	Geneva	19	223
79	International Museum of the Reformation	Geneva	19	223

Points of Interest from Villars-sur-Glâne to Lucens, via Payerne

Nr.	Name	Location	Stage	Page
P-1	Site of Neolithic Pile Houses	Noréaz	P1	84
P-2	Site of Roman Aqueduct	Montagny	P1	86
P-3	Ruins Castle of Montagny	Montagny	P1	88
P-4	Medieval City Fortifications	Payerne	P1	95
P-5	Cluniac Monastery Church Museum	Payerne	P1	99
P-6	Henniez Mineral Springs	Henniez	P2	107
P-7	Former Castle of Bishopric Kingdom of Lausanne	Lucens	P2	110
P-8	Sherlock Holmes Museum	Lucens	P2	110

Bibliography and Copyrights

Icons

Hiking Icon, Church Icon, Castle Icon, Camera Icon, Angel Icon, Antique Building Icon, Skeleton Icon, Rubber Stamp Icon, Shell Icon, all made by Freepik from www.flaticon.com, 2019

Monastery Icon and Pin Icon made by Smashicons from www.flaticon.com, 2019

Pray Icon made by FJStudio from www.flaticon.com

Flags of Cantons from Swiss Cantonal Authorities, 2019

Photos

Page 54: Christinet, Isabelle. Paroisse évangélique réformée de la Glane – Romont. Photo de l'intérieur de la chapelle Le bon Berger à Romont, 2019

Page 67: Jouhet, Jean-Claude. Commune de Lovatens. Photo de l'intérieur de la Eglise de Lovatens, 2019

Page 105: Droz, Anne-Marie. Photo de Intérieur du Temple de Granges-près-Marnand, 2019

Page 128: Baatard, Francois. Paroisse Les Croisettes. Photo de l'intérieur de la chapelle de Vers-chez-les-Blanc, 2019

Page 147: Savaux, Geneviève. Paroisse du Sud-ouest lausannois. Photo de l'intérieur de la Eglise de Sévelin, 2019

Page 148: Righetti, Roselyne. Pasteur de Paroisse Saint-Jean Lausanne. Photo de l'intérieur de la chapelle de la Maladière, 2018

Page 188: Sublet, Andrée. Paroisse de Terre Sainte-Céligny. Photo de l'intérieur de la Eglise de Celigny, 2019

Geographical Maps

Pages 18, 21, 31, 62, 79, 101, 119, 143, 170, 179, 200, 227, and cover: Geographical Maps from Swiss Federal Office of Topography, 2019

Biographies of Saints

Catholic Online, 2018, www.catholic.org

Commission on Tourism, Leisure and Pastoral Care for Pilgrims, 2018, www.chkath.ch

Schäfer, Joachim. Ökumenisches Heiligenlexikon, 2018, www.heiligenlexikon.de

Historical Information (in geographical order of the chapters/stages)

Stage 14: Fribourg to Romont

Fribourg Tourisme, 2018, https://www.fribourgtourisme.ch/en/P8354/church-and-convent-of-the-ursulines

Sœurs de Ste-Ursule, 2019, http://fribourg.ste-ursule.org/a-propos/

Morel, Marcel. Fribourg, Le couvent et le pensionnat des Ursulines, in notrehistoise.ch, 2019, https://www.notrehistoire.ch/medias/51438

Fribourg Tourisme, 2018, https://www.fribourgtourisme.ch/en/P5448/guided-tour-of-st-peter-church

Paroisse Saint-Pierre, Fribourg, 2015, Information brochures at the Church St-Pierre, Fribourg

Les Amis du Chemin de Saint-Jacques, Association Helvétique, Historique de la Croix Saint-Jacques, Villars-sur-Glane, 2018

Commune de Villars-sur-Glâne, 2018, https://www.villars-sur-glane.ch/la-commune/historique#tab4

Commune de Villars-sur-Glâne, 2018, https://www.villars-sur-glane.ch/la-commune/paroisse/leglise-paroissiale-saints-pierre-et-paul

Andrey, Georges. Villars-sur- Glâne, in: Dictionnaire Historique de la Suisse (DHS) 2014, URL: http://www.hls-dhs- dss.ch/textes/f/F981.php

Gumy, Serge. Chapelles Fribourgeoises, Editions La Sarine, Fribourg, 2003, p. 85-86

Rolle, Marianne. Posieux, in: Dictionnaire Historique de la Suisse (DHS) 2010, URL: http://www.hls-dhs-dss.ch/textes/f/F973.php

Commune de Hauterive, 2019, https://hauterivefr.ch/histoire.html

Rolle, Marianne. Ecuvillens, in: Dictionnaire Historique de la Suisse (DHS) 2015, URL: http://www.hls-dhs-dss.ch/textes/f/F946.php

Chavaillaz, Gilles. La Paroisse de Notre-Dame de l'Assomption d'Ecuvillens, 1994

Rolle, Marianne. Posat, in: Dictionnaire Historique de la Suisse (DHS) 2016, URL: http://www.hls-dhs-dss.ch/textes/f/F972.php

Wirz Restauratoren, 2019, http://www.nussli-restauratoren.ch/referenz/chapelle-de-la-sainte-vierge-de-posat-fribourg/

Catholic Online, Catholic.org, reprinted with permission of Catholic Online, 2018, https://www.catholic.org/prayers/mystery.php,

Bovet, Pascal. A la source de Posat, in L'essentiel, 14.10.2017, https://lelien.lessentiel-mag.ch/blog/a-la-source-de-posat/

Chèvre, G. et Curé-Doyen de Porrentruy. Les Principaux Sanctuaires de Marie dans La Suisse Catholique, 1898, http://www.abbaye-saint-benoit.ch/

The Order of Prémontré, 2018, http://www.premontre.org/chapter/cat/welcome/who-are-the-premonstratensians/

Unité Pastorale Notre-Dame de la Brillaz, 2019, Paroisse d'Autigny, https://upndlabrillaz.ch/eglises-et-chapelles

Galliker, Michel. Abbaye1500, 2014, http://www.abbaye1500.ch/index.php/lieux-dedies/lieux-dedies-suisse/eglise-saint-maurice-autigny

Rolle, Marianne. Autigny, in: Dictionnaire Historique de la Suisse (DHS) 2009, URL: http://www.hls-dhs-dss.ch/textes/f/F933.php

Unité Pastorale de la Glâne, 2019, Paroisse Orsonnens, http://www.upglane.ch/paroisses/orsonnens

Maradan, Evelyne. Chavannes-sous-Orsonnens, in: Dictionnaire Historique de la Suisse (DHS) 2003, URL: http://www.hls-dhs-dss.ch/textes/f/F854.php

Abbaye Cistercienne de la Fille-Dieu, 2019, http://www.fille-dieu.ch/histoire-de-labbaye

Office du Tourisme de Romont et sa Region, Romont, 2018, https://www.romontregion.ch/fr/P5859/eglise-des-capucins

Office du Tourisme de Romont et sa Region, Brochure Romont Historical Tour, 2018, https://static.mycity.travel/manage/uploads/7/42/61576/1/brochure-balade-historique-2018-pdf.pdf

Office du Tourisme de Romont et sa Region, Romont, 2018, https://www.romontregion.ch/fr/P12789/chapelle-reformee

Unité Pastorale de la Glâne, Paroisse Romont, 2018, http://www.upglane.ch/paroisses/romont

Office du Tourisme de Romont et sa Region, Romont, 2018, https://www.romontregion.ch/en/P5828/collegiale-notre-dame-de-l-assomption

Defferrard, Florian. Romont (FR), in: Dictionnaire Historique de la Suisse (DHS) 2012, URL: http://www.hls-dhs-dss.ch/textes/f/F876.php

Commune de Romont, 2019, http://www.romont.ch/fr/presentation/histoire/

Office du Tourisme de Romont et sa Region, Romont, 2018, https://www.romontregion.ch/fr/P12660/chateau-de-romont

The Swiss Castles, 2018, http://www.swisscastles.ch/Fribourg/romontd.html

Vitromusée Romont, 2018, http://www.vitromusee.ch

Stage 15: Romont to Moudon

Unité Pastorale de la Glâne, Paroisse Billens, 2018, http://www.upglane.ch/paroisses/billens

Rolle, Marianne. Billens, in: Dictionnaire Historique de la Suisse (DHS) 2004, http://www.hls-dhs-dss.ch/textes/f/F847.php

Maradan, Evelyne. Hennens, in: Dictionnaire Historique de la Suisse (DHS) 2009, http://www.hls-dhs-dss.ch/textes/f/F861.php

Bouquet, Jean-Jacques. Lovatens, in: Dictionnaire Historique de la Suisse (DHS) 2008, http://www.hls-dhs-dss.ch/textes/f/F2474.php

Fontannaz, Monique and Brigitte Pradervand. Le district de la Broye-Vully I, Les Monuments d'art et d'histoire de la Suisse, Canton Vaud. Societé d'histoire de l'art en Suisse SHAS, Bern 2015. p. 304-306

Favez, Valérie. Curtilles, in: Dictionnaire Historique de la Suisse (DHS) 2004, http://www.hls-dhs-dss.ch/textes/f/F2469.php

Commune de Curtilles, 2018, http://www.curtilles.ch/index.php/le-village/histoire-du-village/l-eglise

Commune de Curtilles, 2018, information brochure and plate at the church

Fontannaz, Monique and Brigitte Pradervand. Le district de la Broye-Vully I, Les Monuments d'art et d'histoire de la Suisse, Canton Vaud. Societé d'histoire de l'art en Suisse SHAS, Bern 2015. p. 279-285

Eglise Evangélique Réformée du Canton de Vaud, l'Association Cumpanis, 2018, http://www.stetienne-moudon.ch

Pastoral Unit St-Pierre Les Roches, 2014, http://www.upierroches.ch/paroisse%20Moudon.htm

Feller-Vest, Veronika. Amadeus, in: Dictionnaire Historique de la Suisse (DHS) 2001, http://www.hls-dhs-dss.ch/textes/f/F10210.php

Fontannaz, Monique. Moudon, in: Dictionnaire Historique de la Suisse (DHS) 2010, http://www.hls-dhs-dss.ch/textes/f/F2478.php

Tourist Information Office Moudon, 2018, www.moudon-tourisme.ch.

Commune de Moudon, 2018, http://www.moudon.ch/fr/22/moudon-en-bref

Stage P1: Villars-sur-Glâne to Payerne

Rolle, Marianne. Noréaz, in: Historisches Lexikon der Schweiz, (HLS) 2009, URL: http://www.hls-dhs-dss.ch/textes/d/D967.php

Commune de Noréaz, 2018, http://www.noreaz.ch/index.php/decouvrir/histoire

Barras, Jean-Marie. Histoire et histoires de Noréaz, 2001, https://www.nervo.ch/wp-content/uploads/2017/03/Histoire_et_histoires_de_Noreaz.pdf, p. 72-73

UP Notre-Dame de Tours, 2018, https://upnotredamedetours.ch/2017/10/26/paroisse-de-montagny-tours/

Jäggi, Stefan. Montagny (FR, Herrschaft), in: Historisches Lexikon der Schweiz, (HLS) 2008, URL: http://www.hls-dhs-dss.ch/textes/d/D8141.php

The Swiss Castles, 2018, http://www.swisscastles.ch/Fribourg/montagnyd.html

Commune de Montagny, 2017, http://montagny-fr.ch/chateau-de-montagny/

Rolle, Marianne. Tours, in: Dictionnaire Historique de la Suisse (DHS), 2012, URL: http://www.hls-dhs-dss.ch/textes/f/D7998.php

Commune de Montagny, 2017, http://montagny-fr.ch/lenclave-de-tours/

Barras, Jean-Marie. 2018, https://www.nervo.ch/wp-content/uploads/2017/03/3_Eglises_et_oeuvres_d_art.pdf, p. 7-11

Deutschsprachige Kirchgemeinde Broyetal, 2018, https://www.kirchgemeinde-broyetal.ch

Brand, Christian. Eine kurze Zusammenfassung der Geschichte der deutschsprachigen Kirchgemeinden im Kanton Waadt. Pfarrkollegium deutschsprachiger Pfarrer in der Westschweiz, 2016. S. 9, 23

Marion, Gilbert. Payerne (commune), in: Dictionnaire Historique de la Suisse (DHS), 2010, URL: http://www.hls-dhs-dss.ch/textes/f/F2584.php

Hausmann, Germain. Payerne (abbaye), in: Dictionnaire Historique de la Suisse (DHS), 2016, URL: http://www.hls-dhs-dss.ch/textes/f/F11866.php

Commune de Payerne, 2018, http://www.abbatiale-payerne.ch/abbatiale/historique/

Payerne Tourisme, www.estavayer-payerne.ch, 2014, Self-guided QR-code tour: Payerne – Connecting earth and sky. https://static.mycity.travel/manage/uploads/7/38/28183/6b0f3c0d9dee2d476dfa9a84d9e96e67e2074da2.pdf

Stage P2: Payerne to Lucens

Paroisse Catholique Payerne, 125 ans Paroisse Catholique Payerne. Payerne: 2014

Favez, Valérie. Granges-près-Marnand, in: Dictionnaire Historique de la Suisse (DHS), 2017, URL: http://www.hls-dhs-dss.ch/textes/f/F2580.php

Fontannaz, Monique and Brigitte Pradervand. Le district de la Broye-Vully I, Les Monuments d'art et d'histoire de la Suisse, Canton Vaud. Societé d'histoire de l'art en Suisse SHAS, Bern 2015. p. 388-396

Canton Vaud, Section monuments et sites, information table at the Eglise de Granges-Marnand, 2006

Fontannaz, Monique and Brigitte Pradervand. Le district de la Broye-Vully I, Les Monuments d'art et d'histoire de la Suisse, Canton Vaud. Societé d'histoire de l'art en Suisse SHAS, Bern 2015. p. 396

Favez, Valérie. Henniez, in: Dictionnaire Historique de la Suisse (DHS), 2007, URL: http://www.hls-dhs-dss.ch/textes/f/F2581.php

Nestlé, 2018, https://www.henniez.ch/histoire/

Pahud, Alexandre. Lucens, in: Dictionnaire Historique de la Suisse (DHS), 2017, URL: http://www.hls-dhs-dss.ch/textes/f/F2475.php

Chateau de Lucens, 2018, https://chateaudelucens.ch/en/history/

The Swiss Castles, 2018, http://www.swisscastles.ch/Vaud/chateau/Lucens.html

Commune de Lucens, 2018, http://www.lucens.ch/N604/histoire.html

Commune de Lucens, 2018, http://www.lucens.ch/sherlockholmes

Fontannaz, Monique and Brigitte Pradervand. Le district de la Broye-Vully I, Les Monuments d'art et d'histoire de la Suisse, Canton Vaud. Societé d'histoire de l'art en Suisse SHAS, Bern 2015. p. 172-181

Paroisse St Pierre Les Roches, 2018, https://www.cath-vd.ch/cvd_parish/lucens/

Fontannaz, Monique and Brigitte Pradervand. Le district de la Broye-Vully I, Les Monuments d'art et d'histoire de la Suisse, Canton Vaud. Societé d'histoire de l'art en Suisse SHAS, Bern 2015. p. 197

Stage 16: Moudon to Lausanne

Commune de Syens, 2018, https://www.syens.ch/index.php/decouvrir

Meystre-Schaeren, Nicole. Syens, in: Dictionnaire Historique de la Suisse (DHS) 2012, http://www.hls-dhs-dss.ch/textes/f/F2488.php

Fontannaz, Monique and Brigitte Pradervand. Le district de la Broye-Vully I, Les Monuments d'art et d'histoire de la Suisse, Canton Vaud. Societé d'histoire de l'art en Suisse SHAS, Bern 2015. p. 94-96

Commune de Vucherens, 2019, http://vucherens.ch/vie-locale/a-voir-a-faire/

Abetel, Emmanuel. Vucherens, in: Dictionnaire Historique de la Suisse (DHS) 2013, http://www.hls-dhs-dss.ch/textes/f/F2492.php

Fontannaz, Monique and Brigitte Pradervand. Le district de la Broye-Vully I, Les Monuments d'art et d'histoire de la Suisse, Canton Vaud. Societé d'histoire de l'art en Suisse SHAS, Bern 2015. p. 105-106
Commune de Montpreveyres, 2018, https://www.montpreveyres.ch/site/a-propos-du-village/presentation-et-histoire/
Bouquet, Jean-Jacques. Montpreveyres, in: Dictionnaire Historique de la Suisse (DHS) 2008, http://www.hls-dhs-dss.ch/textes/f/F2561.php
Dubois, Olivier. Jorat, in: Dictionnaire Historique de la Suisse (DHS) 2007, http://www.hls-dhs-dss.ch/textes/f/F12240.php
Chaudet, Valentine. DIRH-DGMR et DFIRE-SIPAL-Division Patrimone, Information table in Jorat forests, 2017
Commune de Lausanne, 2018, http://www.lausanne.ch/lausanne-officielle/administration/enfance-jeunesse-et-quartiers/secretariat-general-ejq/cultes-et-temples/paroisses-et-lieux-de-cultes/extrasArea/00/links/00/linkBinary/eglises-lieux-de-cultes.pdf, p. 20
Canton Vaud, Section monuments et sites, Information table at the church Les Croisettes, 2016
Commune de Lausanne, 2018, http://www.lausanne.ch/lausanne-officielle/administration/enfance-jeunesse-et-quartiers/secretariat-general-ejq/cultes-et-temples/paroisses-et-lieux-de-cultes/extrasArea/00/links/00/linkBinary/eglises-lieux-de-cultes.pdf, p. 10-11
Béboux, François. Les Croisettes, in: Dictionnaire Historique de la Suisse (DHS) 2004, http://www.hls-dhs-dss.ch/textes/f/F8449.php
Ville de Lausanne, 2018, http://www.lausanne.ch/thematiques/nature-parcs-et-domaines/espaces-verts/parcs-et-promenades/les-sites-de-loisirs/site-de-sauvabelin.html
Ville de Lausanne, 2018, https://www.lausanne.ch/portrait/culture/architecture-et-monuments/capitale-d-un-nouveau-canton/campagne-de-l-hermitage.html
Ville de Lausanne, 2018, https://www.lausanne.ch/portrait/culture/architecture-et-monuments/lausanne-medievale/chateau-st-maire.html
The Swiss Castles, 2018, http://www.swisscastles.ch/Vaud/chateau/stmaire_d.html
Cathédral de Lausanne, 2011, http://www.patrimoine.vd.ch/cathedrale-de-lausanne
Cathédral de Lausanne, 2018, Information Brochures at the Cathedral of Lausanne
Ville de Lausanne, 2018, https://www.lausanne.ch/portrait/culture/architecture-et-monuments/lausanne-medievale/cathedrale-de-lausanne.html
Commune de Lausanne, 2018, http://www.lausanne.ch/lausanne-officielle/administration/enfance-jeunesse-et-quartiers/secretariat-general-ejq/cultes-et-temples/paroisses-et-lieux-de-cultes/extrasArea/00/links/00/linkBinary/eglises-lieux-de-cultes.pdf, p. 7
Andenmatten, Bernard. Otto I von Grandson, in: Dictionnaire Historique de la Suisse (DHS) 2008, http://www.hls-dhs-dss.ch/textes/f/F17791.php
Sacred destinations, 2005-18, http://www.sacred-destinations.com/switzerland/lausanne-cathedral
Coutaz, Gilbert and Anne Radeff. Lausanne (Commune), in: Dictionnaire Historique de la Suisse (DHS) 2014, http://www.hls-dhs-dss.ch/textes/f/F2408.php
Coutaz, Gilbert. Lausanne (diocese), in: Dictionnaire Historique de la Suisse (DHS) 2013, http://www.hls-dhs-dss.ch/textes/f/F11400.php
Morerod, Jean-Daniel. Lausanne (évêché), in: Dictionnaire Historique de la Suisse (DHS) 2008, http://www.hls-dhs-dss.ch/textes/f/F8559.php
The Swiss Castles, 2018, http://www.swisscastles.ch/Vaud/chateau/ouchy_d.html
Ville de Lausanne, 2018, https://www.lausanne.ch/portrait/culture/architecture-et-monuments/lausanne-1900/chateau-d-ouchy.html
Ville de Lausanne, 2018, http://www.lausanne.ch/thematiques/culture-et-patrimoine/culture-a-vivre/musees/adresses-musees/musee-olympique.html
The Olympic Museum, 2018, www.olympic.org/

Stage 17: Lausanne to Rolle

Ville de Lausanne, 2018, https://www.lausanne.ch/portrait/culture/architecture-et-monuments/ancien-regime/escaliers-du-marche.html
Ville de Lausanne, 2018, https://www.lausanne.ch/portrait/culture/architecture-et-monuments/lausanne-medievale/eglise-saint-francois.html
Ville de Lausanne, http://www.lausanne.ch/lausanne-officielle/administration/enfance-jeunesse-et-quartiers/secretariat-general-ejq/cultes-et-temples/paroisses-et-lieux-de-cultes/extrasArea/00/links/00/linkBinary/eglises-lieux-de-cultes.pdf, p. 24-25
Ville de Lausanne, 2018, http://www.lausanne.ch/lausanne-officielle/administration/culture-et-developpement-urbain/secretariat-municipal/lieux-de-reception-et-exposition/casino-de-montbenon.html

Commune de Lausanne, 2018, http://www.lausanne.ch/lausanne-officielle/administration/enfance-jeunesse-et-quartiers/secretariat-general-ejq/cultes-et-temples/paroisses-et-lieux-de-cultes/extrasArea/00/links/00/linkBinary/eglises-lieux-de-cultes.pdf, p. 40
Ville de Lausanne, 2018, http://www.lausanne.ch/lausanne-officielle/administration/securite-et-economie/service-economie/deces-inhumations-incinerations/inhumations/cimetiere-bois-de-vaux.html
Commune de Lausanne, 2018, http://www.lausanne.ch/lausanne-officielle/administration/enfance-jeunesse-et-quartiers/secretariat-general-ejq/cultes-et-temples/paroisses-et-lieux-de-cultes/extrasArea/00/links/00/linkBinary/eglises-lieux-de-cultes.pdf, p. 14
Nicollier, Marie. Vestige du parc à lépreux à la Maladière, 27.06.2018, en 24 heures, https://www.24heures.ch/vaud-regions/signe-Lausanne/Vestige-du-parc-a-lepreux-a-la-Maladiere/story/16350179
Chapelle de la Maladière, Lausanne, Information plate at the chapel, 2018
Ville de Lausanne, 2018, http://www.lausanne.ch/en/thematiques/culture-et-patrimoine/culture-a-vivre/musees/adresses-musees/musee-romain-de-vidy.html
Musée Roman Lausanne-Vidy, Information table at the archaeological site, 2018
Paroisse d'Ecublens – Saint-Sulpice, 2018, http://ecublenssaintsulpice.eerv.ch/eglise-de-saint-sulpice/114/2014/09/eglise_st-sulpice-fr.pdf
Paroisse d'Ecublens – Saint-Sulpice, 2018, http://ecublenssaintsulpice.eerv.ch/eglise-de-saint-sulpice/2014/12/notes_margot.pdf
Béboux, François. Saint-Sulpice (VD), in: Dictionnaire Historique de la Suisse (DHS) 2011, URL: http://www.hls-dhs-dss.ch/textes/f/F2453.php
Morges, Reformed Church, Information table at the church, 2016
Bissegger, Paul. Morges (Commune), in: Dictionnaire Historique de la Suisse (DHS) 2012, URL: http://www.hls-dhs-dss.ch/textes/f/F2447.php
Chateau Morges, 2018, http://www.chateau-morges.ch/le-chateau/histoire/
The Swiss Castles, 2018, http://www.swisscastles.ch/Vaud/morges/default.htm
Santschi, Catherine. Saint-Prex, in: Dictionnaire Historique de la Suisse (DHS) 2011, URL: http://www.hls-dhs-dss.ch/textes/f/F2451.php
Commune de Saint-Prex, 2018, www.saint-prex.ch/fr/viesociale/paroisses
Commune Saint-Prex, 2018, http://www.saint-prex.ch/fr/decouvrir/histoire/
Commune Saint-Prex, 2018, Information sign at the historical city and the church
Stöckli, Werner. Information table at the Reformed Church of Saint-Prex, 2019
Zoell, Jean-Paul. Information brochure at the Reformed Church of Saint-Prex, 2019
The Swiss Castles, 2018, http://www.swisscastles.ch/Vaud/chateau/stprex_d.html
Rickenbacher, Anne. La Chapelle de Buchillon. Buchillon, 2003
Canton Vaud, Section des Monuments historique, Information table at the Perroy church, 1987
Commune Perroy, 2018, http://www.perroy.ch/accueil/histoire/
Hausmann, Germain. Perroy, in: Dictionnaire Historique de la Suisse (DHS) 2010, URL: http://www.hls-dhs-dss.ch/textes/f/F2605.php
Hausmann, Germain. Rolle, in: Dictionnaire Historique de la Suisse (DHS) 2010, URL: http://www.hls-dhs-dss.ch/textes/f/F2606.php
Commune Rolle, 2018, Information table at Chateau de Rolle
Association des Amis du Chateau de Rolle, 2019, http://chateauderolle.ch/wordpress/histoir/
Commune Rolle, 2018, Information table at Ile de la Harpe
Commune Rolle, 2018, http://www.tourisme-rolle.ch/net/Net_Otr.asp?NoOFS=8102&Sty=&NumStr=50.10
Canton Vaud, Section des Monuments historique, Information table at the Rolle church, 2001

Stage 18: Rolle to Coppet
Swiss Castles, 2018, http://www.swisscastles.ch/Vaud/chateau/bursinel_d.html
Schürch, Madeleine. 15.04.2014, Le chateau des chevaliers de la Cuiller est à vendre, in 24heures, https://www.24heures.ch/vaud-regions/la-cote/chteau-chevaliers-cuiller-vendre/story/21261060
Ebinger, Raphael. 15.04.2015, Le Chateau de Bursinel a de nouveaux proprietaries, in 24heures, https://www.24heures.ch/vaud- regions/la-cote/chteau-bursinel-nouveaux-proprietaires/story/12283072
Vodoz, François. Bursinel, in: Dictionnaire Historique de la Suisse (DHS) 2003, http://www.hls-dhs-dss.ch/textes/f/F2597.php
Baudère, Reymond. De l'ancienne à la nouvelle église, p. 44-53 en l'histoire de village Bursinel de 1731 à 1850.
Swiss Castles, 2018, http://www.swisscastles.ch/Vaud/chateau/dully_d.html
Switzerland Tourism, 2018, https://www.myswitzerland.com/en-ch/toblerone-trail-from-the-jura-to-lake-geneva-in-unspoilt-countryside.html

Swiss Castles, 2018, http://www.swisscastles.ch/Vaud/prangins.htm
Chateau de Prangins, 2018, https://www.nationalmuseum.ch/e/prangins
Christe, François. Prangins, in: Dictionnaire Historique de la Suisse (DHS) 2013, http://www.hls-dhs-dss.ch/textes/f/F2517.php
Dunant, Cristiane (November 1986), Nicole Staremberg (July 2009). Le Temple de Prangins. 2009
Ville de Nyon, 2019, https://www.nyon.ch/fr/ville/nyon-une-ville-d-histoire-0-4115
Chateau de Nyon, 2019, www.chateaudenyon.ch
Swiss Castles, 2019, http://www.swisscastles.ch/Vaud/chateau/Nyon.html
Abetel, Emmanuel. Nyon (Commune), in: Dictionnaire Historique de la Suisse (DHS) 2015, http://www.hls-dhs-dss.ch/textes/f/F2516.php
Glasson, B, and R. Joris. Chronique de léglise de La Colombière 1837-1977. Nyon: Paroisse de Nyon, 1977
Roman Museum of Nyon, 2019, https://www.mrn.ch
Nyon Région Tourisme, 2019, https://www.lacote-tourisme.ch/en/P25163/roman-columns-in-nyon
Bazzanella, Sylvie. Le temple de Nyon, 26/01/2017, on NotreHistoire.ch, https://www.notrehistoire.ch/medias/101947
Nyon Région Tourisme, 2019, https://www.lacote-tourisme.ch/en/P6661/nyon-temple
Swiss Castles, 2018, http://www.swisscastles.ch/Vaud/chateau/crans.html
Chateau de Crans, 2018, www.chateau-de-crans.ch
Pradervand, Brigitte. Le décor de l'église de Crans-près-Céligny (information table at the church), 2014
Hausmann, Germain. Crans-près-Céligny, in: Dictionnaire Historique de la Suisse (DHS) 2004, http://www.hls-dhs-dss.ch/textes/f/F2505.php
Santschi, Catherine. Céligny, in: Dictionnaire Historique de la Suisse (DHS) 2005, http://www.hls-dhs-dss.ch/textes/f/F2892.php
Commune de Celigny, 2018, http://www.celigny.ch/la-commune-en-bref
Bujard, Jacques. Le temple de Céligny, 2018
Swiss Castles, 2018, http://www.swisscastles.ch/Geneve/celigny/
Swiss Castles, 2018, http://www.swisscastles.ch/Geneve/bossey/
World Council of Churches, 2018, www.institute.oikoumene.org
Chateau de Bossey, 2018, www.chateaudebossey.ch
Commune de Commugny, 2018, Présentation, http://www.commugny.ch/net/Net_commugny.asp?NoOFS=5711&Sty=&NumStr=10
Commune de Commugny, 2018, Information table at the church of Commugny.
Henny, Christophe. Commugny, in: Dictionnaire Historique de la Suisse (DHS) 2005, http://www.hls-dhs-dss.ch/textes/f/F2503.php
Swiss Castles, 2018, http://www.swisscastles.ch/Vaud/Coppet/cohistoire.html
Fondation Othenin d'Haussonville, 2016, https://www.chateaudecoppet.com
Gilbert, Marion. Coppet, in: Dictionnaire Historique de la Suisse (DHS) 2004, http://www.hls-dhs-dss.ch/textes/f/F2504.php
Paroisse de Terre Sainte-Céligny, 2018, http://terresainte.eerv.ch/temple-coppet/
Information leaflet 'The church of Coppet' at the church of Coppet, 2019
Commune de Coppet, 2018, http://www.coppet.ch/fr/portrait/histoire/

Stage 19: Coppet to Geneva

Paroisse des 5 Communes, 2018, https://templedegenthod.ch/lhistoire_/un-peu-dhistoire/
Piguet, Martine. Genthod, in: Dictionnaire Historique de la Suisse (DHS) 2006, http://www.hls-dhs-dss.ch/textes/f/F2904.php
Paroisse Catholique Saint-Loup – Sainte-Rita, 2019, www.ecr-ge.ch
Commune de Bellevue, 2018, http://www.mairie-bellevue.ch/fr/portrait/histoire/welcome.php?action=showinfo&info_id=6616
Piguet, Martine. Bellevue, in: Dictionnaire Historique de la Suisse (DHS) 2018, http://www.hls-dhs-dss.ch/textes/f/D2888.php
Commune de Pregny-Chambésy, 2018, http://www.pregny-chambesy.ch/fr/portrait/histoire
Commune de Pregny-Chambésy, 2018, Information leaflet at the St. Petronilla church
Torrione-Vouilloz, Dominique. Pregny-Chambésy, in: Dictionnaire Historique de la Suisse (DHS) 2010, http://www.hls-dhs-dss.ch/textes/f/F2916.php
Bischof, Franz Xavier. Kulturkampf, in: Dictionnaire Historique de la Suisse (DHS) 2018, http://www.hls-dhs-dss.ch/textes/f/D17244.php
Swiss Castles, 2018, http://www.swisscastles.ch/Geneve/tournay_d.html
Burgy, François. Tournay, in: Dictionnaire Historique de la Suisse (DHS) 2012, http://www.hls-dhs-dss.ch/textes/f/F7754.php
The Rothschild Archive, 2018, https://family.rothschildarchive.org/estates/51-chateau-de-pregny

Fondation pour l'histoire des Suisses dans le Monde, 2018, www.penthes.ch
Geneva info, 2018, http://www.geneva.info/botanical-gardens/
Federal Department of Foreign Affairs, 2018, https://houseofswitzerland.org/swissstories/history/story-geneva-s-jet-d-eau
Switzerland Tourism, 2018, https://www.myswitzerland.com/en-ch/brunswick-monument-geneve.html
Europeana Newspapers, 10 September 2015, The assassination of Empress Elisabeth of Austria, http://www.europeana-newspapers.eu/assassination-sisi/
Holy Trinity Geneva, 2018, https://holytrinitygeneva.org/welcome/our-church/
Werlé, Christine. agence Apic, 14.05.2013, https://www.cath.ch/newsf/notre-dame-de-geneve-la-basilique-qui-touche-le-coeur-des-croyants/
Eglise Catholique Romaine-Genève, 2018, https://ecr-ge.ch/notre-dame/notre-paroisse/histoire-basilique/
Paroisse de Saint-Gervais-Pâquis, 2018, http://saint-gervais-paquis.epg.ch/temple-saint-gervais/
Espace Saint-Gervais, 2019, http://saint-gervais-paquis.epg.ch/temple-saint-gervais/
Schätti, Nicolas, Jean Terrier, Diego Innocenzi. The Church of St. Gervais 6000 years of history. Geneva: Espace Saint-Gervais et Paroisse de Saint-Gervais-Paquis, 2019
Schweizer, Andréas. Imprimerie des Arts écomusée Saint-Gervais, 15.10.2003, http://www.imprimeriedesarts.ch/spip/spip.php?article8
Geneva info, 2018, http://www.geneva.info/rousseau-island/
Switzerland Tourism, 2018, https://www.myswitzerland.com/en-ch/pont-et-tour-d-e-l-ile.html
Eglise Catholique-Chretienne de la Suisse, 2018, http://www.catholique-chretien.ch/geneve.php
Paroisse de Saint-Pierre-Fusterie, 2018, http://www.saintpierre-geneve.ch
Fondation des Clefs de St-Pierre, 2018, https://www.cathedrale-geneve.ch
Site archéologique de la Cathédrale Saint-Pierre de Genève, 2018, www.site-archeologique.ch
Musée international de la Réforme, 2019, https://www.musee-reforme.ch/en/the-museum/
Mottu-Weber, Liliane. Genève (commune), in: Dictionnaire Historique de la Suisse (DHS) 2018, http://www.hls-dhs-dss.ch/textes/f/D2903.php
Santschi, Catherine. Genève (diocese, eveché), in: Dictionnaire Historique de la Suisse (DHS) 2007, http://www.hls-dhs-dss.ch/textes/f/F11399.php

Stage 20: Geneva to Border
Paroisse Saint François de Sales, 2018, http://www.stfrancois-ge.ch
Zumkeller, Dominique. Carouge, in: Dictionnaire Historique de la Suisse (DHS) 2011, http://www.hls-dhs-dss.ch/textes/f/F2890.php
Paroisse de Carouge, 2018, http://carouge.epg.ch/le-temple/
Dreyfus, Fernand. Le Temple de Carouge, Présentation d'un lieu historique, artistique et spiritual. Genève: Labor et Fides, 1999
Paroisses Sainte-Croix & Sainte-Claire, 2018, http://upca.ch/index.php/sainte-croix/32-depuis-1777
Swiss Castles, 2018, http://www.swisscastles.ch/Geneve/compesieres_d.html
Le musée de l'Ordre de Malta, 2018, http://www.smommuseum.ch/version2/
Brunier, Isabelle. Compesière (commandarie), in: Dictionnaire Historique de la Suisse (DHS) 2003, http://www.hls-dhs-dss.ch/textes/f/F11142.php

www.ingramcontent.com/pod-product-compliance
Lightning Source LLC
LaVergne TN
LVHW091037080826
845145LV00002B/534

* 9 7 8 3 9 0 6 8 6 1 3 8 8 *